I SHARE MY HEART WITH AFRICA

A JOURNEY LIKE NO OTHER

Denise Carnihan

DENISE CARNIHAN

I SHARE MY HEART WITH AFRICA
© Denise Carnihan 2015

National Library of Australia Cataloguing-in-Publication entry (pbk)

Author:	Carnihan, Denise, author.
Title:	I share my heart with Africa : a journey like no other / Denise Carnihan
ISBN:	978-0-473-31724-9 (paperback)
Subjects:	Carnihan, Denise. Education, Primary--Kenya. Community development--Kenya.
Dewey Number:	372.96762

Published by Denise Carnihan and InHouse Publishing
www.inhousepublishing.com.au

Printed using Envirocare paper.

Most of the names and places are true and correct, however there are a couple of people and places that need to remain anonymous for various reasons, and therefore I have changed their identity in the book.

"It gets under your skin and into your soul. It changes you. This is Africa."

For you, Mum
xxx

CONTENTS

PART THREE: UNBROKEN SPIRIT

Foreword

Living in the small coastal town of Mossel Bay, on the southern part of the Cape Province in South Africa, my life was taking a big turnaround, when my parents found a letter in their mail box sent to them by Denise. This letter set me on a trail of discovery and inner searching for who I was. Nothing in life happens by accident, or by luck. Meeting Denise and her husband Chris showed me that our lives were, and are, well-planned, and it was just a matter of time before the right things aligned. In this case, purpose was just waiting to be discovered. Meeting Denise led me to a deep conviction for a need to come to peace with my past as a coloured man growing up in apartheid South Africa. It was very difficult for me to think outside the box of my upbringing and perception of life in South Africa, but her love and acceptance towards me and my family caused me to walk over that bridge of uncertainty.

I believe that many of those whom you will read about in this book have experienced this feeling of discovering their worth and value, because that's what Denise is all about. She makes you feel as if she would cross the highest mountain, and sail the deepest sea, and walk right into your heart just to make you feel special.

I cannot imagine not having her in my life, and may reading this book bring you closer to the heart of this remarkable woman, full of life and love. The energy and passion to do good to others influenced many of us in Africa. I am grateful and glad to be a part of this woman's life—she has impacted my own.

Greetings from South Africa
Edgar Anthony Hermanus
Mossel Bay
South Africa.

PART ONE

FAMILY CONNECTION

Chapter One

A frica fascinated me. As a young girl in the 1960s I remember very clearly my Aunty Totty, as she was affectionately known, and Uncle Leo, leaving for a trip to South Africa. They travelled overseas a lot, to all sorts of exotic places. Mum, Dad, my brothers and I loved to hear of their travel adventures and couldn't wait for them to arrive home so we could go and visit. They always seemed to be going to such amazing places. When they headed off for three months travelling in Africa though, it seemed to be that much more exciting. Wow, Africa! Back then there was no such thing as social media, so apart from the occasional postcard, we had to wait till they returned home to hear of their adventures. It was always exciting because they bought us loads of cool presents. My aunty and uncle had no children of their own so we were the closest and next best thing. They would set up a white sheet in their living room and we would sit and watch a slide show of their latest travels.

I can still to this day remember going in to their home in Newtown, Wellington when they arrived back to New Zealand from Africa. It was a Sunday afternoon. It was always a Sunday afternoon that we visited. My gift was a colourful beaded bag and a similar beaded necklace; I loved them both. For me, this trip somehow seemed different to their others. Watching the slideshow and seeing the people, their culture, their dancing, singing, and where and how they lived really fascinated me. I dreamed that one day I too would visit this enchanting, magical, mystical place that was Africa.

Fast forward many years to when I was eighteen years old. I met my husband Chris in 1978 in a pub in Wellington, we fell in love, and in 1981 we got married. As was the normal thing to do back then, we busily set about saving hard for a deposit on a house, but three weeks before the wedding we had a sudden and spontaneous change of plans. Blow this! We decided that instead of buying a house, we would travel—indefinitely. With a sudden flurry, we were not only organising our upcoming wedding, but arranging our trip; booking tickets, quitting jobs, sorting out all our travel necessities, and arranging for our accumulated stash of furniture and household wares to be stored away.

The wedding was a magical day and everything we had wished for. Afterwards we went for a week honeymooning at a friend's beach house at Waitarere Beach just north of Wellington, then we spent a couple of nights at a friend's flat before leaving New Zealand on our great overseas adventure, or 'OE' as we Kiwis call it. Back then, this was a fairly new, trendy thing to do for young New Zealanders, but has since become a large part of our culture.

First stop was Brisbane, Australia, where we planned on spending just a few months making as much money as we could to enable us to travel for a longer period of time. We had no plans to work once we left Australia. Everything went accordingly and after about eight months we did what most other young Kiwis do and headed for London, where we met other Kiwi friends, and took up residence dossing on the floor of an overcrowded flat in Hammersmith.

We immediately started travelling extensively; firstly through the UK, then back to the flat, and then off again through Europe, using the flat as a base to leave all our gear at. At that time the idea of going to Africa, while still a great desire of mine, seemed a little far-fetched. As much as I liked to think we had the courage, we were still relatively inexperienced travellers and it seemed a little too scary for us at the time. The small taste of Africa that we did manage was a couple of weeks touring Morocco in the north of the continent on an organised camping trip. We absolutely loved it because everything was taken care of—we didn't have to worry about a thing. I started to feel more confident as a traveller and so the idea of Africa started to seem possible. However, by this stage we were rapidly running out of money and I was starting to feel homesick, so we decided to head back home to New Zealand.

We realised there was still a big wide world to be discovered, so with my heart set on Africa we loosely planned to return to New Zealand, sort out the homesickness, get jobs, save hard again, and go back overseas. Africa was still firmly in my sights.

As unsettled as we were in those early days back in New Zealand, once we had secured good jobs and set up home in a cosy little flat, things became comfy and before long, those plans of heading back overseas changed.

Our thoughts turned to saving hard to buy our own home. After eighteen months, we bought a section of land, a year later we built a house, and all was well. Not too long after we moved into our gorgeous home we started thinking about babies.

Our firstborn Craig arrived in 1987, followed two-and-a-half years later by his baby sister Hayley. Many fabulous years passed raising our two kids and we thrived on being a tight-knit family of four. We were in a completely new and exciting phase of our lives revolving around children and friends and families. Other than small occasional trips to Australia and Bali, extensive travel was nowhere on our horizon.

Just before I turned forty, I discovered the reason for my unusual connection to Africa. Little did I know at that point just how much it would change the direction of my life.

Craig was by now in Year 8 at Pukerua Bay School. He came home from school this day and announced that he had a project to work on. It was on family roots. He wanted to focus his project on Nana's father (my grandfather). I phoned mum and explained about Craig's project and we arranged to go to my parent's house

7

the following Sunday for lunch so that Craig could discuss his project with Nana, and hear her story.

I was also interested to hear stories about my grandfather, because on reflection, I couldn't remember very much ever being said about him. He had died before my brothers and I were born so he didn't really feature in our lives. Come to think of it, I don't even remember seeing photos of him either.

Craig asked questions and mum embarked on a very brief story of how her father had been born and raised in South Africa. He was coloured, with an African mother and an English father. She didn't have much information to share other than that he was born and raised in the South African Western Cape provincial town of Mossel Bay; and that he had joined the Merchant Navy as a young teen, ending up in New Zealand a few years later. That was really all she could tell us. I was completely shocked. African? Are you serious? It seemed to be some sort of joke. I promptly started asking more.

I couldn't wait to get home and phone my two older brothers Graeme and Murray—I felt quite sure they would have known this and had kept it from me. I was really annoyed with them; after all it was my heritage too. I felt hurt that this secret had been kept so well-hidden and couldn't understand why. However, they didn't know either, and all they could do was laugh. They didn't believe it for a second that our grandfather was half-African and half-English.

It was quite bizarre that while we didn't know, our many cousins had known all their lives, and more astonishingly, after being told to keep it quiet, they actually did. Even as kids, not a word was spoken, which was surprising in itself. It was very strange finding out stuff about my own family at the age of forty. For me personally, however, something struck a chord and in an odd sort of way, it all started to make some sort of sense.

I asked mum on several occasions why she didn't ever tell us about her African roots, and all she seemed to say was that growing up in the 1930s and 40s in a mixed-race family was quite difficult, and a continual struggle even in New Zealand during that era. She said the family were constantly moving houses and schools because of bullying and harassment to her and her siblings, and for whatever reason she simply decided it would remain a 'skeleton in the closet'. Little did we know at that time however, just how much Mum's views were about to change completely.

After that Sunday sitting around Mum and Dad's dining room table, my grandfather wasn't really talked about again. Craig produced his project on the little information that he was able to extract from Mum and Mum's younger sister Aunty Dawne, who had the most information on their father's roots of all members of the family, and that was more or less the end of it. Mum had made it clear that the subject was now closed.

However, for me a nagging intrigue developed and I was constantly thinking about the family that I knew nothing about. I wanted to know much more and I became increasingly frustrated that I couldn't talk to Mum about it. Aunty Dawne was my only key to finding out more and we would often have secret little chats. It still wasn't enough. Eventually I decided to set out and do my own research.

I quickly became engrossed in researching my grandfather's life and it became almost an obsession. Over the next couple of years I spent countless hours searching internet genealogy websites, war records, and shipping records, looking for even the tiniest snippet of information that could be added to my collection of data on the family. Frustratingly I learnt very early on that extracting information from South African historical records was extremely difficult and many times my searches were fruitless. Over and over again I was told by archivists that most of the records of South

Africa at the turn of the 20th century were destroyed. However, in spite of all the knockbacks and brick walls, little by little I was able to piece together information to a point where the story of my grandfather's life was emerging.

Chapter Two

I learnt that my grandfather was the result of a relationship between a young African housemaid and the son of the family she worked for. This young couple went on to get married, and had another child, a daughter Lorena, sometime later. This was at the turn of the century in South Africa; a time when growing up as a 'half-cast' was not really acceptable.

And so the story goes—when my grandfather was fourteen years old, he was given a sum of money by his parents and sent off to join the Merchant Navy. This took him away from his somewhat unpredictable life in South Africa. A few years were spent sailing back and forth between South Africa and England before New Zealand was included in the Navy run. It was here that he left the ship at the age of eighteen.

At nineteen, he met and fell in love with a young Frances Burns (my grandmother). They married, settled in Wellington and had five children; one of them my mother, Doreen Shirley Wakefield. In spite of the racial problems mum and her siblings experienced as children, they lived a very happy family life. Sadly, my grandfather died here in New Zealand at the young age of fifty-four—well before my brothers and I were born. We never had the privilege of meeting him.

Time went on, and I didn't feel I was making enough headway gathering information about the family in South Africa. My dream was to find living relatives. That was my ultimate goal. However it was consuming too much of my life and I made the decision to put a temporary halt on my search efforts. I decided to content myself with the small amount of information I had found, and intended carrying out the search at a later date.

A couple of years went by and our daughter Hayley, aged seventeen, met a coloured South African boy Jonathan with whom she had a two-year relationship. His father, Gregory Fortuin, was the Mandela-appointed South African Consul to New Zealand. The day he met Hayley for the first time, was in their home. Hayley, on looking at all the beautiful African artwork and crafts in the house, announced that she too was African. Hayley was blonde, with pale skin. Gregory thought it was highly amusing, and the first time we met he asked me about it. I briefly explained what I knew, and he was immediately interested in the story; particularly as he too was 'coloured' and could understand only too well the issues my mother had struggled with all her life.

In time, Gregory was to become a major influence in changing my mum's outlook on her South African roots, to the point where she would embrace it with pride. For the moment though, after explaining how much time, effort, and frustration I had endured trying to trace the family to the present day, Gregory set out on his own investigations to find further information on my family.

One day, several months after our first chat about my African family, Gregory arrived at our house and handed me a piece of paper with the names and addresses of two relatives of mine living in Mossel Bay, South Africa. He said I must write a letter to each of them. I couldn't believe it, and with great excitement I immediately sat and typed out two identical letters outlining my story with as much information as I had, and included my email address. Nervously I popped them in the post box. No sooner had I done that, I realised that in my haste I had typed the wrong email address—one that had long been cancelled. I was so annoyed but there was nothing I could do, I could hardly turn around and type out another letter explaining my stupid mistake—that would have made me look ridiculous.

Four months later and with any thoughts of receiving a reply almost forgotten, I received a letter from Mossel Bay. It was from the son of one of the recipients of my letter, written on behalf of his ill father. Edgar wrote apologising for the lengthy delay in replying, and how he had tried several times to email me, but the emails kept bouncing back to his inbox. He spoke of the family's reaction to receiving my letter, initially unsure if this was a hoax or whether it was actually genuine. A lot of discussion had taken place in his family since receiving my letter, and with very vague knowledge that there was family over here in this part of the world, Edgar and his dad decided they should send a reply.

The day I received his letter was the beginning of a crazy rapid journey of connection and discovery for Edgar and me. From a distance we bonded immediately, and emailed constantly. We promptly sent photos to each other, which created a great source of amusement on both sides of the world. Edgar and his side of the family were coloured; I was and my side of the family were white. And yet, we were all part of the same family.

We had connected in such an extraordinary way and we both agreed that there was something very unique and completely inexplicable about it. We had never spoken on the phone, our communication was all by email at that stage, and yet we felt we had always been a part of each other's lives. It was a very mysterious feeling that even though our paths had only recently crossed, our connection felt so complete.

Emails soon turned into texts, and before long Edgar and I knew so much about each other and our respective families. Corresponding by email and text was no longer enough and I desperately wanted to meet him and other members of my family. Eighteen months later, both Craig and Hayley had left home and were embarking on their own lives, and Chris and I were suddenly on our own again. The time was perfect to start planning our trip to Africa in 2009.

I was beside myself with excitement; we were finally going to Africa—and more importantly, meeting my family. It seemed surreal.

I casually mentioned to Chris that as we were going such a long way to South Africa, perhaps we should extend our travel and explore a little further afield. He agreed and we decided to take three months' leave and make a good trip of it. We booked on an African overland trip starting in Cape Town, South Africa, travelling through seven countries and ending in Kenya.

Many months of planning and preparation took place. We were going to be away from home for three months so there was a lot to organise, and our checklist grew longer by the minute. The excitement between Edgar and me was euphoric with emails and texts frantically going back and forth with details of dates and plans. About two months before leaving New Zealand Edgar asked me if we would consider staying with his family which included his wife (also named Denise) and their teenage daughter Nadia. Of course, we jumped at the chance; we felt very honoured to have been asked. We had no idea that it was a very big deal for Edgar to ask us and that he feared we would say no because they live in a coloured community and there were no other white people living there. Didn't matter to us!

On 8 August 2009, we left New Zealand bound for Cape Town. Little did I know at that point that we were setting out on a journey that was going to change my life and my own family forever. The flights, via Singapore, were long and tiring, and trying to catch a few hours' sleep was difficult, but who cared—we were on our way to Africa! And more to the point, we were going to meet members of my family that until recently I didn't even know existed.

One of my first African magical moments was watching the sunrise as we approached the enormous land mass of Africa. Dawn was just breaking and we watched the sky transform from ink-black to an eclectic blend of vivid reds, oranges, and crimsons, the horizon becoming a glow of electric colour for as far as the eye could see. It was truly spectacular.

We touched down in Cape Town and I was beside myself with excitement. Finally we were in South Africa and about to start living this crazy dream I had waited and planned so long for.

We were met by the host of the backpackers' hostel we had booked into for the first night. The following morning, we would take the Greyhound bus to Mossel Bay, a six-hour journey. Our host was lovely, and as we travelled the fairly lengthy journey from the airport, through the city to the hostel, she provided a running commentary of the dos and don'ts and must-sees of Cape Town, plus pointing out interesting sights along the way.

By the time we arrived at the hostel, in spite of having just travelled for almost two days, Chris and I couldn't wait to start exploring the city. We wasted no time in checking into our room, showering, changing into cooler clothes and venturing out into colourful Cape Town to soak up the atmosphere of this vibrant city.

Cape Town was pretty, with a backdrop of Table Mountain standing majestically above the city. I had read in my travel guide prior to arriving that the walk up to the mountain summit, although not for the faint-hearted, was a must-do. As inviting as it looked, we decided that after travelling for forty hours, today was probably not a good day to be climbing mountains; we were tired and would wait until another time to tackle the mountain climb.

Very much aware that we were in a totally different environment to what we were used to, we decided instead to take a short stroll around the local vicinity of our hostel, to familiarise ourselves with the atmosphere and culture. We were both feeling a little cautious and slightly wary of walking too far—after all this was Africa, very foreign to us, and after the warnings from our host, we were a little unsure.

It was a public holiday in South Africa on the day we arrived, and as most of the shops were closed, the streets around our hostel area were relatively quiet and deserted apart from a sprinkling of people loitering about, and the large number of armed security guards sitting inside shop doorways and building foyers.

Three times we went back and forth to our hostel and each time we went out, we ventured a little further. We eventually stumbled across a lively, colourful open-air craft market just a few blocks from the hostel. In stark contrast, the area was alive with people, abuzz with the sounds of African drums, the smells of delicious food being cooked over small gas burners wafting through the air, an abundance of colourful craft stalls erected under makeshift canvas canopies with hawkers selling a vast array of handmade African jewellery, clothing, and wooden craft. Artisans were putting finishing touches to their works of art. By this time we were feeling a lot more relaxed and comfortable and spent a good few hours wandering about the market sampling the local delicacies, indulging in a few small purchases, and chatting to the hawkers.

Before we had left New Zealand and during my last contact with Edgar he instructed me to phone him when we arrived in Cape Town to let him know we had arrived safely. I had no local SIM card and set about looking for a public phone. We noticed a shop's doors were open and decided to head there to ask for directions to a phone. Inside we discovered a very large African craft market that sprawled out on three levels. I asked one of the shop assistants where I might find a public phone, explaining briefly the importance of making a phone call to Mossel Bay, and he happily directed us to an internet cafe downstairs.

By now I was beside myself with excitement, I was extremely nervous, and my stomach bounced with butterflies. I called Edgar's phone number and waited for him to answer, feeling the tears building up and the lump in my throat. A very soft voice answered.

"Hello Denise," came through on the other end of the phone.

It took me by surprise. I hadn't spoken to Edgar before now, our communication was only by email and text. After having seen photos of Edgar, I was expecting a loud, deep, powerful voice on the other end of the phone, but instead, the softly-spoken voice that greeted me was almost surprising.

"Denise, I have been waiting my whole life for you," he said.

The tears flowed, I struggled to talk, I giggled nervously, cried some more, and the conversation was full of uncontrollable laughter from both of us.

Chapter Three

I hardly slept that night.

Next morning, we were up well before dawn, packing our bags and waiting for our taxi to arrive to deliver us to the bus station for our six-hour journey to Mossel Bay. Stepping out into the very early and dark Cape Town morning from the hostel was a little unnerving for Chris and I. There were many drunken, dodgy looking people loitering around the shop doorways and alleyways, and as they seemed to be watching our every move we weren't quite sure of their intentions. This was probably made a little more exaggerated by the constant reminders from well-meaning friends who had previously visited South Africa, to keep safe.

We quickly threw our gear into the boot of the taxi, jumped into the back of the cab, and promptly locked the doors. As we pulled up outside the bus terminal, there, spilling out all over the pavement and wooden seats in front of us, were another large bunch of drunken, down-and-out looking characters.

Our taxi driver, sensing our hesitation, turned around to us and said, "You will be ok," pointing to the security guard standing outside the terminal office with a machine gun slung over his shoulder.

We decided it was a fairly accurate assumption that if we stood close by the guard while waiting for the office to open, then we might have a very good chance of staying safe.

After an hour of waiting, the office door opened and swarms of people flocked inside to buy tickets, have documents processed and luggage checked before being ushered aboard the waiting coach. We had pre-purchased our bus tickets before leaving New

Zealand but even so, completing the required paperwork was still a lengthy process, and even once the bus had departed, staff on board continued processing documents and updating charts on clipboards, double-checking tickets, allocating seats and so on. It did occur to us though that this excessive processing and the additional on-board tea- and coffee-making meant many jobs were created simply because of the long process involved with catching a bus to Mossel Bay.

Even though I was anxious, nervous, and feeling the urgency to get to Mossel Bay, the six-hour bus journey was really nice. We passed through many little towns, and the pretty rural scenery along the way reminded us very much of home, except lacking in sheep. The lush green pasture was beautiful.

After what seemed an eternity we arrived in Mossel Bay, and as the Shell petrol station, our bus stop, came into view I was once again overcome with emotion, a real mix of extreme excitement, nervousness beyond control, and an overwhelming sense of coming back to my roots.

We pulled into the forecourt of the petrol station and I couldn't get off the bus fast enough, expecting to see the familiar face of Edgar standing there waiting. I managed to conduct a quick scan of the surrounding forecourt area but saw nobody that looked vaguely familiar. Disappointment overwhelmed me. Chris, having sensed my mood, provided immediate distraction by suggesting we gather our luggage and move off the forecourt to some seats by the shop so we could wait without being in the way of motorists pumping gas.

As we did all this, I noticed out of the corner of my eye the man I had been communicating with all this time. Strolling towards us across the forecourt was a very tall, dark man with an enormous smile that lit up the entire universe. Without so much as a second thought, I dropped everything and rushed over to Edgar. We stood there, hugging and crying for what was probably an eternity. It was completely surreal. Chris, watching all this unfold, equated it to a scene from a movie, and couldn't help but notice the people who were at the petrol station and the look of shock and puzzlement on their faces. Of course—this was South Africa, Edgar was coloured, I was white.

Once we calmed down, the tears sort of stopped, briefly, Edgar started laughing as he explained how he and his wife Denise had been waiting for what seemed forever for our bus to arrive, how he had decided to sit and wait in the car and watch us from a distance for a little while. He himself had struggled with the reality of it all. Caught up in my own emotions, I had forgotten that for him also, this was a very extraordinary set of circumstances.

We gathered some composure, and after introducing our respective spouses, we piled our luggage into the tiny boot of the car, clambering in the back seat with stuff crammed in on top of us. As we drove off, I could honestly not believe all this was happening. I felt I was reading a story of someone else's life, and definitely not living my own.

Edgar, Denise, and their daughter Nadia's home was in a coloured community in Mossel Bay and it soon became very obvious, by the reactions of the locals as we drove through the neighbourhood, that we were the only white people to be seen in this area for quite some time. We weren't phased by this at all, and in fact if anything, it was intriguing to see for ourselves that this was South Africa, and yes, the colour of our skin was of interest in this community.

One of the first things we did once we had settled into our home away from home was to go and visit Edgar's father and mother. It was Edgar's father who had initially received one of the letters I had written when I first found out about our family in Mossel Bay. It was an emotional arrival, especially as Edgar's dad was Mum's generation so he was an even closer relative than what Edgar and I were. He was a very ill man when we visited, and was confined to his bed, but we still managed to share very special, long moments as we talked non-stop about the family, piecing together various parts of the jigsaw puzzle, and how through many twists of fate we had made this incredible connection.

The following ten days spent with the family went by like a dream, and in a way it felt like I had embarked on a pilgrimage. I loved my connection with Edgar, and we spent many hours together just talking through family stuff, and also what it meant for us both to have connected half-way through our lives. We had a magical, fantastic time. Edgar and his family showed us everything—historical sites where my grandfather was born and raised, where my African great-grandmother would have lived, and all the fabulous members of the extended family. We took every opportunity to find out as much as possible and where we all fitted in. Wherever we went, whoever we met, whether it be other family members or friends, we were completely overwhelmed with kindness, hospitality, and love.

When Edgar and I first made the connection, he had visited the local museum to find out if they had any further records that may be of relevance to our family. He had chatted with the curator who had been so intrigued by our story of a coloured South African and white New Zealander family connection that she had kindly offered to research the family on Edgar's behalf. During our time in Mossel Bay we visited the museum and met the curator. She was still completely fascinated by our story and took time out to show us around the museum. The enthusiasm from this lady was quite overwhelming.

Edgar and Denise took us everywhere, and showed us everything. One day two cousins—one who was the other member of the family that I wrote those very first letters to, and who incidentally threw my letter in the rubbish bin, thinking it was a hoax, and who we spent many times laughing about that with— came and collected Edgar, Chris, and me in their car and took us on a sightseeing adventure. We visited some caves high up in the mountains. The scenery was stunning and as we climbed higher and higher up into the mountain ranges we could see the coastal outline of Mossel Bay disappearing into the distance. The caves were absolutely spectacular. We also visited a wildlife sanctuary and I even had a ride on a camel, which provided a source of entertainment to the others who were constantly in fits of laughter watching me bumbling along on his hump.

In our experience the cultural coloured-white division indeed still existed in South Africa—well, at least in the smaller areas of South Africa, and indeed in Mossel Bay. We struggled with this. One day while strolling through the local shopping mall with Edgar and Denise, it was close to lunch time, and I suggested that we go into a nearby café for a bite to eat. Chris and I sensed a slight hesitation from Edgar and Denise, and when I asked if something was wrong with the café, they started laughing.

"No, but we've never eaten in here Denise—this is for white people," they said.

We questioned them on it, given that racial discrimination had been abolished in South Africa, and they said that while yes, the law states that they were free to go wherever they chose, they still usually stuck to their own. Kind of like an unspoken rule, really. We were quite shocked by this but eventually persuaded them as there didn't seem to be anywhere else to have lunch. We could definitely feel an atmosphere in the café as we entered, but ignored everybody staring as if it was completely natural to be there, which it should have been. We became acutely aware from then on that there was a division that still existed, and although we tried to ignore being constantly stared at and talked about whenever we were all out together in public, it also fascinated us that people should react in such a way.

We felt very much at home staying at Edgar and Denise's home, but always mindful that we caused a lot of attention in the community. Almost immediately after arriving at their home, word spread around the neighbourhood that there were white people staying in the area. Over the next ten days we got very used to locals peering into the house if they were out strolling, or people in cars slowing to a crawl if driving past, and sometimes even stopping, all trying to catch a glimpse of us. It didn't bother us in the slightest.

Often Chris and I would sit outside in the front yard in the sun with a cup of coffee, watching the world go by, and when people walked past we would take a few seconds to say hi and exchange greetings. The general reaction from most people was genuine surprise that we would bother to speak to them.

Sadly our memorable stay in Mossel Bay was over all too soon, and as we packed our bags I was dreading the moment when it was time to say goodbye to Edgar, Denise, Nadia, and the rest of my beautiful African family. It had been such an amazing experience, one that I would never forget as long as I lived. And the same for Edgar.

And so there we were, once again back at the Shell petrol station, waiting on the forecourt with the same gut-wrenching feeling I had experienced ten days beforehand. Only this time it was due to overwhelming sadness, and amidst the farewell tears firm promises were made to return to Mossel Bay in the very near future. After all, this was family that both sides didn't know existed until recently, and we weren't prepared to let go any time soon.

It was a very sombre trip back to Cape Town and in complete contrast to the one we had going to Mossel Bay. We had Denise accompany us on the journey as she was going to Cape Town to stay with her brother for a few days. This was one of the first times she had left Edgar and Nadia and travelled by herself, and so the two of us, probably not the best company for each other, sat miserably staring out of the window for most of the trip. I found time however to sit back and reflect on every single second of the last ten days. And whilst I was convinced it was all a dream, I was indeed very much living that dream, and so I slumped back in the bus chair and smiled so much that I thought I would burst with happiness.

I was a firm believer that people who came in and out of our lives and events we experienced and journeys our life carried us on, had a purpose. For me, the people, the feelings I carried in my heart of Africa, and the more recent chain of events, had all come together and led me to those magical ten days in Mossel Bay, South Africa.

We arrived back in Cape Town to be greeted by Jeremy and Grace, brother and sister-in-law of Gregory, our South African friend in New Zealand; the one who had played such a significant part in this whole journey. Before we left New Zealand, we had arranged to stay for five days with them. Although we had never met, they opened their hearts and home to us with their generosity and hospitality, so much so that the first morning we discovered they had given up their gorgeous sumptuous bed for us, while they had squashed into a single bed in the spare room. We were horrified, insisting we swap places, but they wouldn't hear of it.

We had a fantastic few days with Jeremy and Grace and their children and we shared many stories and many giggles. I found it to be a good distraction from Edgar who I was missing terribly. We enjoyed whirlwind sightseeing tours of Cape Town, visiting all the places of interest and the beautiful beaches skirting the city. Some of the areas reminded us very much of Wellington; particularly the waterfront with its outdoor bars, cafes, and shops. The entire time we were in the city, Table Mountain was shrouded in mist, so there wasn't much point in climbing it if we couldn't see anything once we reached the top. It was best left for another time, and I knew that would be definite, so it didn't matter.

Again, it all ended too soon and we were packing our bags once more, and saying our goodbyes to our lovely new South African friends. We had a wonderful time with them, and again promised that we would be back. It was a lovely feeling knowing we would be leaving South Africa having forged very special bonds with our beautiful family in Mossel Bay and friendship with the Fortuin family in Cape Town.

We were about to begin the next phase of our African adventure. Jeremy and Grace's son drove us to a hotel in the centre of Cape Town for the starting point of a seven-week overland camping trip. We would travel in a truck with fourteen to eighteen other like-minded people from all over the world, through seven countries, starting in South Africa and ending in Kenya.

Chapter Four

On the evening prior to our departure from Cape Town, we assembled with our fellow travelling buddies in the pre-departure hotel dining room. There we exchanged greetings and introductions all round, then sat and listened to the trip briefing by our tour leader Victor.

After the briefing, many of us decided to find a cheap place to have dinner. For the next seven weeks we would be living together 24/7, so we thought it would be a good idea to start the process of getting to know each other as soon as possible. Chris and I noticed immediately that we were by far the oldest amongst the group— but that didn't bother us, age doesn't matter to us, and the fact that we all shared the same interest in travelling through Africa was what mattered most. It didn't take very long to realise that we would easily fit in with this bunch of adventurous, cool young people from all over the world.

Early the next morning we assembled outside the hotel with our backpacks holding everything we could possibly need for the trip, and stashed them all into our designated lockers at the back of the truck. We then helped to load mountains of food into the carefully designed food lockers that were accessible from outside the truck. Next, we climbed on board what was going to basically be our home for the next seven weeks, and settled into our seats before departing on, for most of us, the adventure of a lifetime.

First we drove south to the southernmost tip of Africa, to the Cape of Good Hope, and after exploring the local area we assembled for our first official group photo. We then started our journey north towards Namibia, passing expansive acres of vineyards and beautiful farmland that again reminded us of home.

We spent the first night camping in the grounds of a remote vineyard close to the Namibian border. Sitting around the campfire on a perfect evening eating the sumptuous dinner cooked for us by the vineyard owners, while swapping stories and enjoying a few beers and glasses of wine under the most beautiful night sky I've ever seen, was a perfect start to our African overland adventure. It was pure magic. The African night sky was stunning and looked distinctly like a pot of silver glitter had been sprinkled lavishly over a blank, black-painted canvas. There was nothing quite so special as lying in our tent later that evening, peering out through the mosquito screen and gazing at the stars. They seemed so close that I was sure I could reach out and touch them. We all slept soundly that first night, out there in the fresh air, under the stars of the African sky.

The next day we continued on our way, heading to the border between South Africa and Namibia. As soon as we crossed the border, we almost instantly witnessed and experienced vast transformations in landscape and scenery. This was to become apparent with every country we visited. The contrasts in this sparsely populated country of Namibia awed us. From rolling green pastures to rugged mountain ranges to vast, barren, lifeless desert; from dense purple carpets of wild desert flowers, to the hundreds of kilometres of spectacular sand dune mountains. The extremities of the ever-changing landscape were breathtakingly beautiful. With every new day this continual change became more and more evident.

We camped on the banks of the beautiful Orange River those first nights in Namibia, and one morning after breakfast we piled into canoes for a twelve kilometre paddle down the river. It was a perfectly still, silent morning and the water was like a millpond. The trip was fantastic, and the scenery captivated us. We saw little thatched huts scattered along the riverbanks, children playing near the river's edge, and the odd wild animal making its presence heard by popping its head up amongst the grasses and letting out a low, deep grunt.

It didn't take long for the competitive spirits to emerge among us, and our lovely tranquil, leisurely paddle down the river rapidly turned into a frantic race. Chris seized every opportunity to attempt to capsize overtaking canoes, which of course started an all-out battle to the imaginary line. It was so much fun.

Later that same day we drove to Fish River Canyon, an enormous expanse of nothingness, where we enjoyed a stroll along the rim of the canyon in time to watch the sunset. It was so beautiful and I was completely enraptured by this beautiful Africa.

Our camps so far were lovely, and carefully planned out. In contrast to the beauty of the Orange River, we next pitched our tents in a tiny oasis in the middle of the barren desert, sharing the camp with jackals, snakes, and scorpions. This was our first experience of sharing space with the wildlife of Africa, and I spent the entire evening tip-toeing around the camp terrified that I would stand on a snake or scorpion. Funnily enough, when I look back, it was something I very soon got used to, and it didn't take long before I didn't even think of those creatures; I walked barefoot during the day or walked in the pitch black night with just a torch, which became very natural to me.

We witnessed another spectacular sunrise, this time from the top of the mighty Namibian sand dunes that spanned hundreds of kilometres out to the west coast of Africa. We had gotten up exceptionally early that morning, in order to drive by jeep out to the dunes. Chris had taken on the responsibility of setting his alarm clock to make sure everybody was up at the designated time of 4:00 a.m. Unfortunately for us, he was still on South African time, which was an hour ahead, so the wake-up call at 3:00 a.m. instead of 4:00 a.m. was not pleasantly received.

We had to tackle a fairly challenging climb to the top of one of the brightly coloured orange, golden, and yellow-hued enormous sand mountains, all before dawn so we could sit on the ridge and watch the sun rise over Africa. It was breathtaking and well worth the early start and effort to get to the top. We had a race down the dune to the bottom where the truck was parked—Victor our tour guide won, followed closely by Chris. It was hilarious and we were all bathed in sand.

We spent a couple of nights camped in the dunes, and spent an awesome day sand-boarding on pieces of plywood. It was so much fun, and the speeds we got up to were pretty surprising. With momentum built up, the boards could travel for miles gliding up and down over the dunes until inevitably coming to a grinding halt—in my case with my face planted heavily into the sand. Again the competitors of the group decided on time trials—not content to just enjoy the experience, they insisted on racing against the clock. Not surprisingly, Chris was again up there amongst others on the leading board.

It was time to leave the dunes and head inland across the desert. We came across an enormous boulder-rock formation that looked completely out of place in this remote, flat, lifeless land. It had very distinct similarities to Flinstones Bedrock Café. We set up camp there for the night, sheltered amongst the rocks and caves, built a bonfire, cooked dinner, and spent the evening relaxing under yet another beautiful night sky. We were in heaven.

Meanwhile we were all settling in to life on the truck and we were having fun—loads of fun. There were sixteen of us, from many countries around the world, all with different backgrounds, cultures, lifestyles, and ranging in age from mid-twenties to early-fifties (that was us), and yet we all bonded immediately.

We agreed it was the common factor of wanting the same African experiences that probably had a lot to do with it. It didn't take any time at all to adapt to life on the road. Sleeping on a four-centimetre mat on the ground inside our little two-person canvas tent became very much normal daily life, and the absence of a toilet or shower for days on end was neither here nor there. It just made it all the more of a treat when we did have those luxuries.

Before we embarked on our trip to Africa, I had absolutely no desire to ever leap out of a plane, not ever, and definitely not over the desert of Namibia in Africa. I quickly discovered though, that when living and experiencing this type of adventure holiday with other similarly minded people, it was very easy to become caught up and carried along in everything going on around you. And so it was that I found myself harnessed and wedged firmly between the legs of my designated tandem-master, kitted up in my special skydiving suit and jam-packed into a tiny plane with other crazies from our truck. As we sat watching landmarks on the ground rapidly transforming into little specks in the distance, I suddenly wondered what the hell I was doing. I was quietly relieved that before we got into the plane, I had asked if I could go first because I really didn't think I could have coped with watching someone fall straight out of the side of a plane, knowing that my turn would be coming.

As I dangled my legs over the side of the plane's open doorway, petrified, I realised at that point that there was absolutely no going back, and on my tandem-master's instructions I plunged straight out of the plane, completely forgetting all previous on-ground instructions of arching back and spreading arms as wide as can be. The fear that had been building up while in the plane was soon overtaken by the sheer and utter thrill of free-falling through the skies over Africa. I screamed and yelled at the top of my lungs, and it dawned on me that I was actually experiencing the wildest, most crazy time of my life in this incredible continent that had captured me so deeply. Watching the vast expanse of desert below

31

felt absolutely insane, but hugely exhilarating. I do remember feeling a sudden gasp of relief as the parachute flung open and whooshed us upward into the sky, a happy assurance that we were not going to plummet to the ground attached to a failed chute and that indeed I would still be around to live another day and to tell my beautiful story.

Part of the itinerary was an overnight stay with the San bushmen, a primitive Namibian tribe who lived in the bush, way off the beaten track. The drive was long and rough, much of it ploughing through sand tracks with tree branches crashing at the truck windows. At one stage we got stuck in deep, loose sand and we all had to pile out while the crew and some of the blokes dug trenches and wedged flat metal plates they hauled out of the bus under the wheels to provide traction. It was a very hot and dusty day and we were all relieved when Dan, our driver, finally managed to manoeuvre the truck out of its predicament and we could all climb back on board and get moving again.

We arrived at the tribal village and were immediately greeted by loads of happy, smiling kids who swarmed the truck. Out came one of the footballs we had on board and straight away the kids had a game of soccer underway. We all joined in, charging about the sand with a feeling of joy at having the opportunity to unleash some pent-up energy after our long drive.

After the football, which incidentally resulted in a few strained muscles and other minor ailments, we were introduced to some members of the tribe and then spent the rest of the day and evening sharing in their daily chores of gathering wood and collecting seeds and medicinal plants from the surrounding bush. They showed us how they utilised the plants for making medicine and how they built and lit fires using only sticks. These people still lived very much by their traditions, wearing very little in the way of clothing and living off the land in primitive and extremely remote conditions. Their physique was unusual—very lean-framed, with legs no thicker than my forearms (both men and women), but with thick, protruding butts. This apparently was where their fat stores were. I kept thinking how much I would long for one of those bodies.

Next morning, after a tasty, hearty breakfast, we loaded up the truck once again, bid farewell to our new friends, and hit the road. We were headed to Etosha National Park near the Namibia-Botswana border for our first real wildlife experience. Everybody on our truck had been waiting for that quintessential moment of seeing first hand wild animals in their natural habitat of Africa. It was what we had seen on every National Geographic documentary and every Animal Planet programme all over the world, all our lives.

We set up camp very close to a watering hole in the savannah of Etosha National Park. This allowed us the opportunity to get up close and personal with some of the world's finest animals. After the evening dinner and usual cleaning up process, it was time to get organised, arm ourselves with binoculars, cameras, video cameras, and any other electronic devices, and set ourselves up in prime but obscured positions at a respectable distance from the watering hole to watch for any animals who decided to pay a visit during the evening. We were not disappointed.

The spectacle we witnessed that evening was like a well-rehearsed theatre show. The watering hole was alive with activity, and as we watched groups of giraffe, zebra, elephants, warthogs, and other animals come and go at various times during the evening, drinking and frolicking in the water, it seemed completely unreal.

And then, if that wasn't enough, the best was yet to come. The grand finale of the evening's concert provided a perfect ending to a magical evening.

Imagine being plonked in the middle of thousands of squared kilometres of natural savannah in a pitch black still night, so silent you could hear a pin drop, when quite suddenly appearing through the darkness, heading for the watering hole came a large herd of elephants. Mothers with adorable little babies frantically tried to keep up. The protective mothers stood very close by with watchful eyes as the babies played and frolicked in the water. It was beautiful to watch.

After about an hour of this spectacle, there was sudden movement among the adult elephants; something was clearly not right. Mums began to close in on their babies in a tight cluster that completely encircled them all. Suddenly, a lion came striding into view, seemingly heading straight for the herd. Luckily for this bunch of mums and babies however, he simply carried on striding past and out into the darkness again. The baby elephants were safe, firmly enclosed in their mothers' clutches.

As the lion strode out of view, in what we could interpret as a final bow he let out an almighty roar that seemed to echo out all over Africa. It couldn't possibly get any better than that.

Chapter Five

From beautiful Namibia we crossed the border into Botswana, and again noticed immediately the differences in landscape and scenery from what it had been in South Africa and Namibia.

Now whenever I thought of Botswana, I daydreamed back to paradise (also known as the Okavango Delta). Laying back in a mokoro (dug-out canoe) built for two, poled along by a local tribesman, skimming the top of a myriad of tiny waterways with the silence disturbed only by the sound of the odd hippo grunting, or bird fluttering. Gliding over lily pads, water reeds, spying the occasional elephant standing on the banks eyeing us curiously and watching with nervous apprehension groups of hippos almost completely submerged in water just metres from our canoe. It was very hard to imagine there could be another place of such magnificent peace, tranquillity, and beauty anywhere in the world.

The delta was made up of over 10,000 squared kilometres of inland waterways deriving from the Okavango River, which flowed and settled in the Botswana lowlands and spread out into a water maze of enormous proportions.

Included in our trip itinerary were some nights of bush camping on tiny islets in the remote delta. The only means of transport was by mokoro. As we parked the truck up on the banks of the delta, a group of local tribal pole-men sitting in their mokoros greeted us. They were ready to transport us to our bush island destination. We loaded up the canoes with just enough supplies to last the duration of our island stay, and set off for our journey through the delta.

The islets were dotted sporadically through the delta, and generally comprised of nothing else but bush and scrub, meaning we would be completely free-camping. As soon as we had arrived at our first little hideaway and carried our gear to a suitable clearing to set up camp for the night, our tour guide Victor set about digging a long-drop toilet. This was positioned in a very well-thought-out place discreetly hidden by bush, far enough away from the campsite but close enough to be rescued if there just so happened to be any close encounters with hippo or any other wild animal whilst attending to ablutions. Chris had carried in his backpack from home, a small blow-up plastic kiwi bird and so he discreetly positioned it amongst a couple of bushes in direct view of someone squatting on the canvas throne. It didn't take long for the bird to be spotted, and he then became a regular 'pop-up', appearing in random places throughout the remainder of our trip.

After the usual hustle and bustle of erecting tents, setting up beds, organising seating arrangements and a makeshift cooking area, and helping our cook Ken with preparing and cooking dinner, we settled down for evening entertainment with our pole-men. It was a fun night of beer drinking, with a concert of national songs and dance recitals, and lots of singing around the campfire. I finally got into bed and snuggled down into my sleeping bag with the tent well zipped up. I hoped and prayed that I would sleep all night and not wake up having to pay a visit to our long-drop in the pitch black night, in the middle of Africa where animals roamed freely. Luckily for me and for Chris (because I would surely have dragged him out with me), I slept soundly.

The following morning we packed up, loaded the mokoros with everything we had taken in and leaving only footprints behind, headed off to our next little island that was situated further up the delta. This was a larger island that connected with the mainland, so after the usual setting-up camp process, a bunch of us decided to go for an exploratory walk.

We had no sooner left camp when suddenly we got the shock of our lives to see an elephant casually strolling through the bush, obviously out for his own wee stroll. Elephants were extremely dangerous animals and so we immediately instigated all the instructions we had received about dealing with African wildlife. The most important thing was not to attract attention, which meant we had to stop dead in our tracks and wait for him to move on. It seemed this elephant was in no great hurry however, and we felt stranded statue-still at his discretion for what seemed like forever. Only when he had moved on and was well out of sight did we feel safe enough to start walking again, ever so slowly and constantly looking over our shoulders, mindful that he would more than likely be roaming in the vicinity of our track. We never did see him again, but it snapped us into alert-mode for sure.

During our mokoro journey back to where we had left our truck on the mainland we spotted a hippo who suddenly popped its head out of the water not too far from where we were paddling. Next minute another one appeared … then another … then another. We counted eight in total, and they would have been no more than twenty to thirty metres away. This was a little scary to say the least, because we weren't quite sure exactly how many other hippos were close by, or exactly where else they would suddenly spring up out of the water. The thought of being heaved up into the air by a hippo emerging from under our mokoro was unnerving if I thought about it long enough, but at the same time I relished in the natural beauty of the Okavango, and I simply couldn't get enough.

We left the tranquillity of the Okavango Delta and headed to Chobe National Park where we camped out on the edge of the Chobe River. This part of our journey was going to be focused on safari, with the objective being to spot animals, and in particular of course, the elusive 'big five': lion, buffalo, leopard, elephant, and rhino. The name 'big five' was coined by game hunters who back in the day identified these animals as the most difficult to hunt with the most danger involved.

We spent the afternoon and evening relaxing at camp, catching up on emails, washing, and enjoying life outside the truck. We had an early night in preparation for our big day of game driving the following morning. At dawn our safari jeeps were waiting for us, so we all piled in and headed off for the day. Many hours were spent tracking animals with binoculars pinned to our eyes, scanning and searching every inch of grass, every acacia tree, every river, hoping to spot some of Africa's finest wildlife. We were not disappointed, spotting four of the big five in one afternoon. The evening was spent swapping safari stories, exchanging photos, and watching personal video moments.

Chapter Six

The border crossing from Botswana to Zambia was not without drama. Up until this point in our trip moving from one country to another had been fast and hassle-free, but on this occasion it was not to be.

Whereas the previous borders had been relatively quiet with minimal traffic, this border was chaotic, with long lines of trucks, cars, and people all jostling for position in the queue. There were cars trying to jump queues, trucks reversing into other vehicles, and irate drivers ranting and raving at each other with a lot of arm and hand gestures.

For nearly three hours and in 40+ degree celsius heat we waited, alternating between sheltering in the truck and under tree canopies. It was stiflingly hot. We couldn't understand what the hold-up with border personnel was all about. We had paid for our visas, we knew we were going to be allowed into Zambia, we just didn't know when or what they wanted from us. However, finally after much heated negotiation and a lot of hostile facial expressions and finger-pointing between border staff and our truck crew, we were given the all-clear to leave Botswana and enter Zambia. Thank goodness! The thought of spending further hours, or even possibly the night, at the border crossing was not something we were looking forward to at all.

Zambia was home to the mighty Victoria Falls and to the late great explorer, David Livingstone. This also marked the half-way point in our trip so the plan was to spend a few days at the camp unwinding and recharging our batteries in readiness for the second leg of our journey. Our camp was gorgeous and we had the opportunity to upgrade to a chalet or cabin if we wanted to. Chris and I decided to indulge in a little luxury and upgraded to a 'permanent tent', which resembled a cute little cabin, only in canvas, with proper beds, bedside tables, and chairs. Some of our original passengers who had joined the trip in Cape Town were leaving the trip here, while others were joining for the first time, taking in the second half of the journey.

It was a time for farewells—dinners, drinks, and sad goodbyes with people we had forged firm friendships with over the last weeks, with promises of keeping in touch and planning reunions. It was also a time to get to know our new truck-buddies who would be with the remainder of us travelling on to Kenya.

Aside from relaxing and unwinding in the camp, there was also the opportunity to partake in many of the adventure activities on offer for those of us ready to indulge in something outrageously out of our comfort zone—like bungy jumping over Victoria Falls into the Zambezi River, for instance.

Described as 'Mosi-oa-Tunya' or 'The Smoke that Thunders', Victoria Falls was a spectacular sight of awe-inspiring beauty on the Zambezi River, which flowed through Zambia and Zimbabwe. It was there that I found myself teetering on the edge of a platform protruding 111 metres above the fast-flowing Zambezi River with a rope firmly tied around both ankles (one would hope!), and where on the count of one, two, three, without any chance of changing my mind, or having any time to contemplate the possible repercussions of my actions, I plunged over the side. For me, it was terrifying! I must add that again I had no previous desire to throw myself off any bridge, anywhere, at any time, and particularly not in Africa.

This time Chris also decided to join in this crazy adrenaline-charged moment of madness, along with half-a-dozen others from our truck. As with the sky dive, I asked if I could go first but wished I hadn't because I would have learnt very quickly from others before me not to do it. On reflection we all agreed it was without a doubt the scariest thing any of us had ever done in our lives. For both Chris and I, it was a once-in-a-lifetime only. Chris maintained that his jaw was thrown out of alignment in the fall and he now had a permanent clicking in his jaw.

While we were leaping off the bridge, others took to all manner of other adrenaline-charged activities such as white-water rafting, elephant riding, and micro-lite flights over the falls, which I now wish I had done. The photos taken above the falls were spectacular.

The next day, while I chose to stay at the camp in the sun with a book, Chris and some of our others went white-water rafting on the crocodile-infested Zambezi River (although I didn't think that was widely known at that stage). They were away all day and had a fantastic but challenging experience, arriving back absolutely battered, bruised, and exhausted. The next day Chris couldn't move a single muscle, and it took a good couple of days for him to recover fully from his 'rapid' adventure.

The experiences we were privileged to have encountered up to this half-way point in our trip were confirming the wonderful spirit of Africa that I always imagined. Everything about the whole African experience thus far was burrowing deep into my soul and I couldn't get enough. Whether it be my beautiful African family, or other local people, the culture, the landscapes, the wildlife, or even the crazy adventurous activities, I was soaking it up at a great rate of knots. Sometimes there were long days of driving and most of the others on the truck used the time to catch up on sleep. Not me; I was usually up out of my seat, standing at the front of the truck, wide-eyed. I couldn't bear the thought of missing out on anything. I also realised that I was rapidly becoming fearless.

By this time the African people we had met along the way had already made a huge impact on me. Their overwhelming fight for existence, their courage, and their incredible ancient rituals, strong traditions, culture, and simple ways of living so firmly embedded in their lives to this day, absorbed me. Africa was getting under my skin.

I believed Africa had a unique way of changing some people. I didn't think you could help but be changed. You started questioning your lifestyle, your own possessions and day-to-day lives. You started thinking about what really mattered in life, what was necessary, and what wasn't. When you travelled through Africa on a truck and lived in a tent, you were out of your comfort zone; you became tough and resilient, and you made do.

One time while we were travelling in remote Namibia, one of the guys, Andy, desperately wanted a haircut. The area was very sparsely populated, so the chances of finding a barber would have been almost zero. I offered to have a go at cutting his hair, but the only scissors we had on board were a pair of curved nail scissors. After a lot of convincing, Andy finally agreed to sitting outside on a camp chair while I proceeded to lop off the overgrown locks into an 'it will do' sort of shape. I actually thought it looked pretty ok considering the tools I had to work with. Andy assured me it was ok too, but I'm not entirely sure if he was telling the truth.

We had fantastic fun on our trip, all of us getting on very well considering the age and personality differences, not to mention our confined living conditions. We became one big family very early on.

After three nights, it was time to leave Victoria Falls, and head further east through Zambia towards Malawi. By this time we were really in the thick of Africa, and we started seeing an abundance of wildlife, in particular elephants, zebras, and hippos freely wandering across dirt roads, through the bush, and even around our camp. It was an amazing experience. Our earlier excitement of catching a momentary glimpse of a zebra, giraffe, or lion hundreds of metres away paled into insignificance now; we were seeing these same animals right in front of us literally a couple of metres away.

Zambia was a cotton-producing country, so we started seeing many cotton fields and crops spanning the landscape. Roads were all dirt tracks in varying degrees of roughness and colour. Houses were little thatched straw or mud huts and they appeared to be sprinkled in clusters. The roadside was a hive of activity in what seemed to be the hub of the community, with bunches of veggie stalls set up along the roadside, people either walking, loitering, or just sitting in small groups, and much to our horror, many tiny children playing what seemed like inches away from speeding traffic.

The modes of transport in Zambia were interesting, if not highly amusing. If there were not twenty to thirty people crammed into the back of a pick-up, then they were crammed into carts and pulled along by donkeys—the Zambian taxi service.

Chapter Seven

Malawi was the next country on our itinerary. It was ranked one of the poorest countries in the world. Ironically they were also known to be the friendliest, happiest people in East Africa, and we could easily understand why they had this reputation. Everywhere we went, whether it was us passing through villages in the overland truck or strolling the streets and markets, both adults and children would come running from everywhere—out of their little huts, out of the bush, or from across the road. They would wave and cheer at us as we drove by and if we were out walking, they would rush up and grab our hands or hang off our legs.

We crossed the border from Zambia into Malawi and headed straight for the mountain region. We were going to spend the following day with local villagers, joining them for a meal, learning how they lived day-to-day in this remote area, and enjoying each others' company.

After setting up camp in the idyllic mountain hideaway, we spent the rest of the day relaxing in camp, catching up on washing, writing diaries, and generally chilling out. The following morning, after an early breakfast, we prepared for our journey to the village. Many of us piled into the tray of an open-backed ute and rocked and rolled along pot-holed dirt tracks to the village, while others chose to walk the lengthy distance of many kilometres. We arrived with extra kids crammed in the back of the ute too, although no one could actually remember stopping and picking them up; they just had a way of jumping on board and tagging along for the ride.

We were very warmly greeted by villagers of all ages. The children rushed to us and hung off our arms and legs, giggling and chatting in their mother tongue. The villagers were extremely proud of where they lived, their land, and how they utilised it.

Almost immediately upon arrival, and after exchanging warm, friendly greetings with the village chief and others of importance, we were ushered into a hut where women were busy laying tables with pristine cloths and bustling about arranging seating for us all. Other women walked in carrying huge steaming pots of food.

We were then invited to sit down and we were served a delicious meal of beautiful beef and chicken stews, vegetable dishes with beans and lentils, followed by chai tea. As soon as the meal was over we were taken on a tour of the local area, proudly led by the village chief and his entourage of local children who took great delight in pointing out various spots of interest, including flourishing plantations of crops. They would cling to our hands like they never wanted to let go. After the walk we were invited to spend the rest of the afternoon mingling with the local community while a local drum and dance group of children entertained us. Everyone got very excited and launched into hysterical laughter when we got up and attempted to copy the dance moves.

All too soon it was time to depart and so once again we said goodbye to our newfound friends. Those of us who opted out of walking the journey back to camp piled on top of each other into the back of a ute and again we rocked, rattled, and rolled our way along the deeply rutted dirt track back to camp.

We left our mountain hideaway the next morning and, for contrast, headed to Kande Beach situated on the shores of beautiful Lake Malawi. Here we enjoyed a few days of rest and relaxation. It was a long drive from the mountains and so the sight of an extremely inviting white sandy palm tree-fringed beach, with water gently lolling in and out of the shore, was very inviting. With temperatures well into the 30s (Celcius), we couldn't wait to get off the truck, into swimming attire, and into the warm waters.

It was heaven on earth. Most of us had previously been warned by our travel doctors back at home about the dangers of swimming in Lake Malawi, and that it should be avoided because of a certain type of nasty parasite, bilharzia, that lived in the waters. The temptation was simply too hard to resist.

Gorgeous days followed, with hours and hours spent lounging around on the beach and in and out of the water when it got too hot. Some of the energetic ones booked horse riding safaris, and others booked walking trips through the local village and strolled to the markets. Malawi was known as the craft capital of East Africa, particularly for intricate, hand-carved woodwork. I knew the minute I laid eyes on the beautiful work of these craftspeople that I could not resist buying some to take home. Absolutely no thought of freight issues or costs ever crossed my mind as I whiled away many hours bartering for beautiful carved chairs, small tables, lamps, bowls, figurines, and animals. I thought it would be easier to try and figure out the freight issue later.

Chris and I decided to splash out and upgrade our accommodation at Kande Beach, and booked a couple of nights in a cute little thatched wooden hut perched up on wooden stilts right on the beach. We decided we'd earned it. There was something very appealing about the hut, and even though it was very basic, consisting only of a bed encased in a mosquito net and a single chair, we were excited to be sleeping in a real bed for a change, and I must say, it felt luxurious.

We lay in our little hut at night, door wide open to create a gentle breeze, drifting off to sleep to the soft sound of tiny waves washing onto the shore, the far-away beating of drums, and people chanting and hollering in the distance. This was a special kind of magic.

Chapter Eight

Once we left beautiful Lake Malawi, we had a couple of long drives ahead as we drove towards Tanzania, the next African country on our itinerary. Tanzania lay on the east coast of the African continent, bordering the Indian Ocean. The diversity of this country was extreme and the changes were almost immediately obvious the minute we crossed the border from Malawi.

The housing was different to what we'd seen previously, it was somewhat more westernised and we were now seeing many brick houses dotted amongst the more traditional mud and thatched huts similar to those we had seen in other countries. There was an abundance of bicycles used both as a form of private transport and as taxis. They were everywhere. The landscape was different too, and was largely made up of tea plantations, potato crops, and sisal and peat plantations all spread across the countryside and contributing substantially to Tanzania's economy.

Tanzania was an interesting and colourful combination of Arab, Muslim, African, and Christian cultures, particularly evident at both the port city of Dar es Salaam and also on Zanzibar Island, which was situated in the Indian Ocean off the coast of Tanzania.

Our trip included a five-night stay on exotic Zanzibar Island, which was also known as Spice Island due to the abundance and array of spices grown there. The island was accessible by a two-hour ferry journey, which operated frequently between Dar es Salaam and the port of Stone Town on the island. The ferry crossing was a typically chaotic process comprising absolutely no order, but once again it just all seemed to work famously in terms of ferrying hordes of people back and forth between mainland

Africa and Zanzibar. We watched in horror as people scrambled to leap off the ferry onto the ground below before it had even docked. Cars and bikes were all in a great hurry to alight as quickly as possible before the boarding traffic blocked them in. The gates of the pens holding foot passengers opened for about five minutes only and in that time literally thousands of people sprinted to jump on board the ferry before the gates closed again and those left behind had to wait for the next one to arrive.

This same process went on all day with each ferry crossing. The journey was pleasant, and the scenery quite stunning as we passed various tiny, snow-white, sandy reefs dotted about the ocean and on the horizon.

We arrived in Stone Town, the flourishing centre of the spice trade and slave trade in the 19th century, and immediately it reminded Chris and me of Morocco with its very narrow, ambling alleyways and old stone buildings contrasted with big, old wooden doors. It was completely different to the other African countries we had just travelled through; this was an Arabic town, and with the call to prayer regularly sounding out over the loudspeakers scattered around the town, one could easily be forgiven for thinking one had just arrived slap-bang in the Middle East.

It just so happened that when we arrived in Stone Town, it was the end of Ramadhan—the month of fasting for the Muslim people—and celebrations were in full swing. Every evening for a week the small town transformed into a festival filled with incredible colour, vibrancy, and rowdy celebration. Row upon row upon row of exotic food stalls were set up, behind which immaculately attired chefs dressed in crisp white head-to-toe uniforms complete with sky-high chef hats were frantically whipping up the most delectable delights, the aroma and festivities filling the air well into the late hours.

Thousands of families turned out every evening to feast and join the celebration, and we certainly took advantage of being there, taking great delight in sampling the fabulous array of food, and sitting back to watch the beautiful spectacle around us. It was fabulous. People of all ages dressed in exquisite clothing: women were in the most beautiful array of brightly coloured sequinned robes and hijab; men in pristine white robes and hats; little girls dressed in pretty dresses, matching shoes, socks, little handbags, right down to matching hair accessories; small boys in starched trousers and shirts, with immaculately groomed hair. It was a spectacular sight and provided another wonderful look into a new side of African culture.

During the daytime, we joined a walking sightseeing tour of this ancient old city, and in the late afternoon we gathered at a bar overlooking the sea, sitting on the huge balcony sipping cocktails, watching the many dhow boats bobbing on the sparkling ocean against the setting orange sun.

The itinerary for Zanzibar included a few days' relaxation at one of the northern beach resorts, and I don't think there could have been anywhere more perfect than this island paradise to unwind on. The beaches encompassing the island were breathtakingly beautiful and like nothing I had ever seen in my life. The sizzling temperatures, combined with the inviting aqua-coloured crystal clear waters and snow white sands made for idyllic snorkelling and swimming. And at the end of each day there was nothing more fitting than enjoying cocktails at one of the many little thatched bars dotted along the beach.

All too soon, it was time to leave Zanzibar, the warm, tropical Indian Ocean, and take the ferry back to Dar es Salaam, and in complete contrast we proceeded to travel inland to the region of Mt Kilimanjaro. Rich, lush green mountain ranges with tiny villages dotted obscurely amongst heavy vegetation greeted us, the little straw huts and clay houses blending ever so well with banana, tea, and coffee plantations. Changing landscapes, and contrasts of culture and scenery never ceased to amaze us and time and time again I was reminded that it was this very uniqueness of Africa that so captured my heart.

We set up camp in a village nestled at the foot of Mt Kilimanjaro and home to the Chagga tribe. Again we enjoyed the richness, the hospitality, and the friendliness of these people and their very simple lives as they proudly showed us their beautiful surrounds and offered us deliciously cooked home-grown feasts.

There was something very mystical about Kilimanjaro. The magnificent sight of this mighty mountain that stood above the horizon in all its glory, with a dollop of white icing dribbling over one peak, was simply mesmerising.

Our next camp, still in the mountain region, was at a village called Lushoto that also had a spectacular view of Kilimanjaro. We all agreed that the decision to be woken well before dawn to witness the amazing sunrise over Kilimanjaro was without a doubt worth it.

Lushoto was also home to a sponsored village education project, a wonderful centre set up by a British woman some years back, which was now a thriving community school, housing up-to-date technology, including a well-resourced computer room, tailoring classroom, and woodwork shop. The school welcomed many volunteers from all over the world who used the opportunity to experience voluntary work. The ones I spoke with were mainly young British students experiencing a stint of charity work during their gap year. They were having the most amazing time.

We also met an awesome British retired school teacher named Bob who was doing eighteen months of volunteer work for the project. I had absolutely no idea back then just how much of an influence this man was about to have on my own life. Bob took time out from his busy day to take us on a guided tour of the complex, giving us a detailed account of how the project began and how it got to where it was now, what his life working at the project entailed, and how much it had changed his own life. I found him incredibly interesting. We left the village the following day feeling very humbled and pleased that we had been given the opportunity to make a monetary donation to such a worthwhile project.

We also spent a day at a nearby children's home where we simply hung out with the kids, playing football, telling stories, and watching on, amazed, as they demonstrated their gymnastic skills. The children, who were predominantly boys aged between three and seventeen, had been picked up from the streets of the surrounding villages and towns. Typically this children's home was run and sponsored entirely by volunteers who arrived from all over the world and worked in stints from two weeks to six months in duration. Again, most of the volunteers there at that time were students taking a gap year.

After leaving Mount Kilimanjaro, we headed towards the savannah, for a few days of serious safari. Our first stop was Ngorogoro Crater, an enormous expansive dry crater that was home to an abundance of some of Africa's finest wildlife, and also the Masai tribe. Again we ditched our truck for small jeeps as the truck would never have traversed the rugged terrain and steep descent deep down onto the crater floor, and even less so the climb back out again.

The safaris were spectacular and any animals that had been scarce until now were in abundance in Ngorogoro.

This was also our first real sighting of the nomadic Masai tribe who moved freely along The Great Rift Valley between Tanzania and Kenya, herding their cattle and goats in search of water and greener pastures. It was extremely hot when we were in Ngorogoro and the Eastern African countries were in the thick of a three- to four-year drought. The ground was parched, river beds dry, and many rotting carcasses of animals that had succumbed to the severe conditions were scattered everywhere. Now and then we came across small kids standing on the side of the road holding a make-shift bucket or an empty plastic bottle. They waved us down and begged for water. We gave them as much as we could.

Our next destination was the mighty Serengeti Plains, which in Swahili means 'the land that rolls on forever'. This land, covering over 14,000 square kilometres in Tanzania, depicted everything I had ever imagined about the African wildlife and habitat prior to this travel experience. The sheer vastness of the Serengeti and the 360-degree view of the plains was a sight to behold. Every animal documentary I had ever watched, movie I had ever seen, and book I had ever read about Africa and its wildlife, was all brought together in this one-week experience living and free-camping in the Serengeti. The thrill of sleeping in tents with a mere thin wall of canvas separating us from many of the most dangerous animals on the planet was almost infectious.

We pitched our tents in a circle formation all tightly packed together, and we were instructed by our trusted leader that once we were inside our tents for the night, there was no getting out. The nights were hot and we bravely threw back our canvas door and lay with the mosquito net covering the entrance to our tent. We heard hyenas howling, footsteps of other animals, and saw shadows moving outside our tent. In the morning, evidence of a lion's pee, who had obviously come to check us out, was left on the wheel of one of the jeeps.

Oh the exhilaration of the Serengeti with its 360-degree plains of thousands upon thousands of square kilometres of vast parched land, the quintessential African acacia trees sprinkled profusely right out to the horizon, the abundance and variety of animals going about their daily life grazing on the plains, or eyeing up prey, and the sight of the nomadic Masai tribe herding goats and cattle in search of food and water; it all combined to create the incredible uniqueness that so aptly formed the spirit of Africa!

Chapter Nine

Finally we arrived in Kenya, where this trip would sadly come to an end. The mood was dull when we arrived in Nairobi, knowing this could well be the last time we saw some of those awesome people we had shared our lives and our likeminded zest for adventure with for many weeks. We pulled up into the car park of the hotel that was Kenya's finishing and starting point for all the trips, and as we offloaded our gear there was an enormous sadness and lots of talk of promised reunions, and visits to various home countries.

As part of our pre-planned itinerary before leaving New Zealand, we had a couple of nights booked into a hotel in Nairobi before setting off on another, much shorter, camping safari around Kenya.

We checked into the hotel and were instantly overcome with a feeling of opulence. I headed straight for the bath. It felt like a million years since I had the luxury of a bath and I had dreamed of this moment for a couple of weeks now. I wasn't disappointed. We were also filthy and hadn't noticed. The dirt and dust over these last months had engrained in our skin and embarrassingly it took more than one or two showers to rid our bodies of the dirt—particularly noted on the luscious white towels provided by the hotel.

Kenya was a diverse and beautiful country, and in some ways, a culmination of almost everything we had seen along the way from Cape Town. From the lively bustling multi-cultural capital city of Nairobi, to the vast expanse of the Masai Mara world famous for its natural animal migration and prolific wildlife, to the extensive tribal population, to mountains, waterfalls, and deserts, to the exquisite coast of Mombasa and the turquoise Indian Ocean. There was so much to see in this stunning country.

This was the fourth year Kenya was in severe drought, with the countryside and farmland parched beyond any similarity to the lush green flourishing country that it once was. One day we had a very brief downpour which only lasted half an hour at the most, but it was enough to have the local people leaping for joy, ever hopeful that this was just the beginning.

It was pitiful to see dead carcasses scattered over what once would have been fertile land, and skeletal cattle being herded across the barren, dried, and cracked land by their Masai owners, desperately searching for water in dried up riverbeds. Driving through the Masai Mara, again we came across little Masai children standing on the side of the dusty road in the blazing heat holding empty water containers, beckoning us to stop and give them water.

I was sure a book could be written on the roads of Africa alone. It was very noticeable that as we drove north east from South Africa to Kenya, the roads deteriorated increasingly, and so by the time we arrived in Kenya, we were very used to weaving relentlessly from one side of the road to the other in an attempt to avoid potholes the size of craters and the endless kilometres of road works. One day on our trip through Kenya it took six hours to drive 150 kilometres because of the combination of road works, potholes, off-road driving, and police checkpoints. Again however, with much amusement it just added to the accumulation of experiences that combine the Africa that has people going back time and time again for more.

Kenya lay on the equator, and so during this trip we hopped back and forth across the equator many times. Along the main roads were equator billboards, erected to display where the invisible line was supposed to be. The locals took great delight in showing tourists the 'water trick', whereby the water runs down the drain clockwise north, and anti-clockwise south, so they would demonstrate one side, then hop through the other side of the billboard and demonstrate the other. I didn't really know the theory behind this other than it was something to do with magnetic force, but their little demonstration definitely worked.

There were wonderful organisations set up in Kenya to protect the wildlife, struggling to deal with the enormous and heart-breaking exercise of illegal poaching that was prolific in this part of Africa. Everywhere we went through Kenya, we saw animal orphanages, and various other wildlife protection facilities, some set up by the government, but very many set up by overseas NGOs. It was also comforting to learn that Kenya's wildlife was now protected and strict laws surrounding the animals were in place. However, these laws didn't stop poaching, but it was a start.

Sadly, and before we could even really realise it our African trip was all over. I wasn't ready. I still had a whole lot more to do, see, and experience, but for now it was over. Back in Nairobi, we started the painful process of packing up our lives of the last three months, and prepared for the long journey back to New Zealand. Throughout our travels I had managed to collect many beautiful handcrafts to remind us of Africa, and Chris spent hours carefully wrapping and packing the various items, including a full-sized chair, standard lamp, small occasional tables, cloths, fabric, art, and jewellery.

We boarded the first of our many flights, and as we sat back in our comfy seats we could now reflect on our experiences of the last three months. We had crossed the entire width of Africa from the south-west to mid-east and there was absolutely no doubt we had been captured by this amazing continent.

We had met family for the very first time and that to me was completely surreal. How could this have happened? I had since thought very often.

I felt that I now fully understood the power of destiny, and the tremendous pull to go back to my roots. And on top of that, there was such a spiritual uniqueness about Africa that could only really be understood by those who had visited. It got into your soul and called you back. For me personally, I definitely knew I had unfinished business and that I would be back.

PART TWO
RETURN TO AFRICA

Chapter Ten

I remembered the day I received my acceptance email from the volunteer agency that I had selected to work with. I was so excited. I was going back to Kenya for three months, volunteering in an orphanage, and I was filled with overwhelming excitement, tinged with a hint of nerves at the thought of heading off to Africa all alone, and also trepidation at leaving Chris behind. After all, the longest we had spent apart at any one time in over thirty years was six days, and here I was flying off to the other side of the world for three months—to Africa! However, never did I question my decision and not once did I ever feel concerned or worried about living in Kenya. To me it felt like the natural thing to do. I didn't honestly know why I chose Kenya, but clearly something drew me there. I had also decided right at the start that I would make the most of my time there, and really open my whole world to all that was offered. I wanted to soak up the experience as much as possible. I didn't want to go and simply work, I also wanted to absorb the culture. Having that mindset was the best decision I made.

It was my 50th birthday party and all of my nearest and dearest family and friends were all gathered at one time. I thought it would be the best and easiest way of getting my news out in the open, and I knew that inevitably there would be some opposing opinions, but that surely my birthday party would not be the right place to confront me with concerns. The reactions were interesting and varied, but most had a nervous apprehension that I personally couldn't quite understand. Over the course of time leading up to my departure, friends and family felt the need to express their opinions quite freely and openly, and while I appreciated it I had absolutely no concerns whatsoever that this was going to be nothing other than an amazing experience. Not once did I ever feel any of those worries that everybody else seemed to have.

Planning and preparing for the trip involved countless hours of meticulous buying, checking, and ticking off of lists, ensuring I had absolutely everything ... over and over again I checked. It all added to the excitement of the adventure. Once accepted into the volunteer programme, the volume of information that I received on an almost daily basis from my agency was amazing; very detailed and thorough. Aside from the abundance of information regarding my placement, it seemed that everything a volunteer would need or want to know about Kenya; the culture, language, and day-to-day happenings, was also provided to us. However, even with all this information and reading other volunteers' blogs, I still didn't really have much clue what it was going to be like; after all, it was one thing to read information provided, but it would be another thing to actually live it, and our experience of Kenya had been a mere few weeks the previous year, as tourists, travelling around on a safe safari tour with a local tour guide, cook, and driver. It was a very different experience to the one I was about to embark on, and I was beside myself with excitement.

I also began receiving an overwhelming array of donated goods to take with me. Friends and family were dropping off bag after bag of clothing, toys, games, books, balls, and puzzles, and I would find almost every day a bag hanging on the door handle when I arrived home from work.

A final visit to my travel doctor to complete vaccination updates and to receive another endless collection of medical supplies (just in case) was completed, and I felt as ready as I was ever going to be.

Four months after my acceptance into the programme, I left New Zealand with my backpack containing my personal gear, bags bulging with donations, along with excitement I could barely keep control of. The journey was a series of long, interconnecting flights via Sydney and Dubai, but I didn't recall sleeping a wink, I was so excited and simply couldn't wait to arrive in Kenya. I had loosely arranged to meet up with a friend in Dubai who was also travelling on my flight, but then connecting on to France. He was enjoying the luxury of first class travel, while me, I was in economy, or 'cattle class' as it was so often referred to as. We had discovered we were on the same flight a couple of weeks prior to leaving New Zealand, so had decided to try and meet up briefly in the First Class Lounge at Dubai, and I guess I was not dressed appropriately for the first class suite when I arrived at reception looking a little bedraggled and worse for wear. There was a lot of head-to-toe scanning, and secret whispering behind hands amongst staff, before they eventually paged my friend who came to greet me. We caught up only very briefly because by the time I had cleared customs, tried to find my way around the madness of Dubai airport, had a shower, and fought through endless streams of people, there wasn't a lot of time before we were heading off to our different destinations.

As we flew into Dubai I was shocked at the huge amount of dust billowing around. I shouldn't really have been so surprised given that Dubai had evolved from sand and desert, but I guess I just didn't expect to see it in such volume. Flying over the enormous expanse of desert, I knew it was somewhere I would like to visit, and the thought of a camel safari and camping under the stars surrounded by nothing but sand dunes started to conjure up romantic ideas in my mind. I felt like a kid in a lolly shop when I arrived at Dubai airport. I marvelled at the sight of all the glass, marble, and chrome and the extreme wealth of the countless travellers dripping in gold and diamonds and world class designer fashion. People-watching whiled away a good couple of hours as I waited for my connection to Nairobi.

The flight from Dubai to Nairobi was entertaining and fun, as I made a new friend. Leea was her name, she was Kenyan and now lived in Germany with her German husband. Every year she left him back home in Germany working while she made the trip back to her homeland for four months to be with her family. She was a breath of fresh air for me on that last leg of my journey to Kenya, and a joy to have as a fellow flight buddy. By the time we were taxiing down the runway in Dubai I was hearing her life story, and five hours later when we arrived in Nairobi, after barely taking a breath, and leaving behind our untouched in-flight meal, we exchanged phone numbers, email addresses, big hugs, and promises of catch-ups in Nairobi. She was gorgeous and we spent the entire flight either engaging in our life stories or in fits of laughter.

Chapter Eleven

Nairobi at last! I stepped off the plane and walked into the arrivals terminal amid chaos and a sea of black faces all jostling to clear customs and immigration as quickly as they could and get out into the throng of people waiting for their loved ones. In the distance I spotted Leea, who had cleared customs, standing in the arrivals area surrounded by her jubilant welcoming party. I was very excited for her to be back home with her family and friends. I managed to acquire my visa with relative ease, but wondered how long the ink that was now embedded in my fingertips from fingerprint recording, would take to wash off. I was tired, but truly exhilarated, not quite believing that here I was, back in what I fondly called 'my beloved Africa'.

Before leaving New Zealand I had booked the first week in Nairobi at a hotel, and it proved to be one of the wisest decisions I made; all the travelling on and off planes, time zone differences, and lack of sleep had really taken its toll. For nearly a week after arriving in Kenya, I struggled to stay awake during the daytime, and struggled to stay asleep during night-time. Some of the time I spent relaxing by the pool, reading, listening to music on my iPod and generally unwinding, trying desperately to get my body-clock back in sync. I was very aware that once I left the hotel and started my volunteer work, my life in Kenya would be very different to what I was experiencing right then.

I was amazed at how Nairobi rapidly became very familiar to me, and with bursting confidence on the first day I decided to venture into town on foot for a stroll. After being cooped up on planes for two days, I needed a good walk, and was very proud of myself that I actually made it into town and back to the hotel without getting entirely lost. It all seemed so strangely natural to me, almost weird really, and all I wanted to do was immerse myself in the culture.

I had arrived in Nairobi during the 2010 Soccer World Cup, and being a soccer-mad nation, the hype was everywhere. Every conversation that I could understand; every television in every shop, hotel, or bar; every billboard; every vehicle back window; and every flying flag, was all about the World Cup. The city was simply an array of 2010 Soccer World Cup colour and spectacle.

During my first venture out into the big wide world of downtown Nairobi on my own, I set about looking for a computer shop to buy a SIM card for my laptop, and a local SIM card for my phone, and after just a few minutes of navigating my way around the bustling streets I must have looked lost. Within seconds two girls came to my aid and without hesitation walked me to the nearest shop, which was at least one kilometre away. Once they saw me inside, they carried on their way. I thought of home and wondered if I would have done the same—I already knew the answer, no, I probably wouldn't have escorted someone one kilometre in the opposite direction to where I was headed. I realised time was of no real essence here, so a long walk was no big deal. It was a nice thing to do.

Within a very short few days of staying at the hotel, I felt I was making good progress in terms of relaxing into my new environment, and I tried at every possible moment to adjust to the Kenyan way of life. It seemed to come unusually naturally and easily to me. I tried very hard to put my limited Swahili to use, and was pleasantly surprised that I was actually being understood—however I couldn't say it was the same in reverse. The Kenyans had a wonderful, diverse array of mother tongue language, and dependent on the tribe it was often quite unique to that particular tribe. Many Kenyans however speak English as well, some very fluently. As it was now compulsory to learn in schools, many children could also speak some English, although it was as a second language. I wanted to make a real effort to speak some Swahili as often as I could, being very much aware that I was a foreigner in this country and I should try my best to fit in. In my volunteer brief notes, we were told the orphanages may be a different story, as most of the children, especially the little ones, have had very limited or no education, so their language was Swahili or mother-tongue only.

I found the Kenyan people interesting and I quickly became absorbed in their fascinating culture. Kenya was unique in that most of the forty-two tribes still followed some, if not most, of their own traditions. Tribe was very important and they would greet fellow Kenyans for the first time with a handshake, followed by an exchange about which tribe each belonged to.

I would describe Nairobi as a very colourful, bustling, and busy city. There seemed to be two very diverse areas in downtown Nairobi. In one area people were dressed beautifully in all manner of outfits, fashions, and styles. No matter the day of the week you would see the majority of men immaculately dressed in suits or pristine shirts and trousers, and the women dressed beautifully in an amazingly colourful array of African fabrics, sparkles, and heels, with perfect make-up and coiffured hair, mostly braided, or for those with that great longing for straight hair, their heads might be shaved or closely cropped and they would wear fabulous, perfectly turned-out wigs. Then there were the poor areas (or slums) where people were generally dressed in whatever they could lay their hands on. Women wore scarfs on their heads, long skirts with aprons, and men wore oversized pants and jackets. The differences in class were enormous.

I immediately found them to be friendly, helpful people, and took great delight when passing a person in a quiet street in offering a friendly "Jambo!" ("Hello!") to which I would receive a pleasantly surprised reply. I wondered if this was unusual behaviour of mzungu—the name given to describe a white person—to actually speak to a Kenyan first. That was certainly the impression that I got.

I was continually impressed and also amused at the sheer volume of people who were employed in certain jobs, where at home we could not justify the same. For example at the hotel I was staying at, which was probably considered a medium-sized hotel, there seemed to be more staff than guests, all busy going about their work all day and all evening. Every morning I would be greeted in the dining room by at least five waiting staff all hovering around the reception counter, and three or four men who all day, every day maintained the upkeep of the swimming pool. There were countless gardeners, housekeeping staff, security guards, parking attendants, and various other important-looking people walking around the complex clutching clipboards, wearing important-looking uniforms, clearly doing important jobs.

One day I was out for a stroll, and as I passed a petrol station the bustling forecourt caught my eye. I counted thirteen pump attendants and at least two to three other staff members inside the shop. However, with all this seemingly constructive employment, the unemployment rate given the population was still astronomical in this country. According to my new friend Leaa, her view was that those who didn't work were all just plain lazy. I was not quite so sure about that; I met a lot of local people desperate to have a job. I learned that those people who work, really do work very long hours and very, very hard. They were the ones who were fully aware that if there was no job in Kenya, there was no money, and that meant no food for their families. It was a very simple fact of life.

Some, particularly those who lived in the slums where there was a definite culture of uneducated people, were more likely not to have jobs. They lived their lives fumbling their way through life, fighting every day to scratch the surface of basic human survival.

I spent some of my early days in Nairobi with a Kenyan friend we had met the year previous when Chris and I travelled through Africa. I took every advantage of his knowledge, language, and wisdom of the city that he had spent a lot of his life in. To me he was a wonderful asset to have at my side while trying to organise the 'housekeeping duties' as I called them—in other words, all the mundane but necessary tasks that I would need to have in place for my three-month stay in Kenya. He rapidly became my city guide, translator, and computer whizz. As thanks I would occasionally buy him lunch and I would ask him to select a place to eat. I quickly started to get used to the local foods on offer. Most cafes and restaurants offered both African and European menus, but I would try as much as possible to sample the local cuisine. Generally the food was good, lots of meat and vegetable stews, curries, and chapattis with emphasis on 'cheap but filling'. Ugali was Kenya's staple diet and was served with most meals ... however, it took just one small mouthful to remember how much I disliked it when we were there the previous year. Basically it was maize flour and water boiled and stirred to resemble stodgy porridge. I don't think I ever met a Kenyan who didn't like ugali, however. Men almost fretted if they didn't have ugali daily because they firmly believed it made them strong, and wide awake. If a man was tired, he blamed it on the fact that he hadn't had ugali that day. It also had a dual purpose as a spoon, formed by breaking off a chunk, rolling it into a ball, then pressing a thumb dent, which was then used to scoop up vegetables, stews, gravy etc.

One day during that first week I was reminded of how things operate in Kenya. The week before I arrived, a new legislation was introduced that all phone SIM cards had to be registered with Telkom, to try and stomp out the black market trade. This particular day I decided to go and register my phone SIM with

Telkom, so off I walked into town, armed with my registration form duly completed, my passport, and all other relevant documents required. I found Teleposta House after being given many varying directions, and joined the long queue. There were over four million people living in Nairobi alone, forty-four-million in Kenya; the people had four weeks to be registered, and I was certain that on this particular day that over half the population decided to register their phones!

After a very long wait, and a lot of shifting from one foot to another, sighing, and muttering, I finally got to the counter only to be asked by the very sweet young girl in very broken English that I had trouble deciphering:

"Where is passport copy?" She asked me this as she handed me back all my documents.

"Oh sorry, I don't have one, can you please photocopy it for me?" I responded.

"We don't have," she replied, again passing my documents back across the desk.

"Do you know where I can get one?" I continued.

"No," was her final word on the matter.

In New Zealand I may have been forgiven if I started to lose my cool just a little, but I quickly reminded myself that 'This is Kenya, Denise,' and this was the way it was, so I just nodded, smiled, and walked away. After an awful lot of searching and asking locals for directions I finally found a tiny photocopy booth set up on a street. Once again I joined an ever-growing queue, because I was sure all the Kenyans had the knowledge of foresight and were obtaining their photocopies before venturing to Teleposta House. Again, I was quietly entertained watching the complex process conducted by the four young girls all working in this tiny photocopying kiosk. The first girl in the row was clearly responsible for receiving the document, the second girl's job was to photocopy the document, the third girl took the money, and the fourth girl handwrote the receipt. I thought it was beautiful.

Back I went to Teleposta House, to join the queue once more. By now it was twice as long and therefore twice as long a wait required. Nobody was phased by this, except me. This entire exercise took all morning and into the afternoon. This, I decided, was a very valuable lesson and I should learn from it—a lesson on slowing down. What was the hurry?

Chapter Twelve

By the end of my first week in Kenya, I felt rested and eager to get started with the volunteer programme.

The first two days of our programme were focused on orientation sessions for all the volunteer intake for the month. We were picked up from our various locations around Nairobi and taken to a hotel for an extensive information programme, organised by the volunteer agency and led by members of the Kenyan partner agency. It was a very good, well thought-out programme, jam-packed with information, and it covered absolutely everything about living in Kenya, what to expect from our volunteer programmes, and even included some basic Swahili phrases. The second day was more about housekeeping, buying items we might need for our placement such as mobile phones and SIM cards for those who hadn't had any time to organise such things, a quick walk around the CBD of Nairobi, then a visit to the Nairobi Animal Orphanage, and ending with a sumptuous lunch of Kenyan cuisine. There were fifteen volunteers in my intake and we were all going to various placements depending on our skills and our previously arranged volunteer requests.

During this two-day period of orientation, we were placed with host families. I was collected from my hotel that first morning by a member of the Kenyan agency staff, and taken to my host family's home in a suburb of central Nairobi. I knew I would have a roommate, another volunteer, so I was happy not to be alone.

Prior to leaving home, and once our acceptances to the programmes had all been formalised, we had each been sent the complete list of volunteers' names, country, and email addresses in our intake, just to give an insight of who the other volunteers were, and where they came from. Shortly after receiving the list, I had an email from an Australian woman, Caro. She had decided that because we were of similar age and that we were geographical neighbours it would be nice to make contact before we arrived in Kenya. We realised we had things in common and instantly struck up a friendship via email, and looked forward to meeting in Nairobi.

I was the first volunteer to arrive at our host house, and so when the van pulled up outside the house, I went out with the housekeeper to greet my new roommate. As soon as she stepped out of the van, and before we had even introduced ourselves, we both knew straight away.

"Oh my god, you must be Caro!" I picked up immediately from the accent.

"Haha, yeah, and you must be Denise!"

We both laughed.

Our host family comprised a husband, wife, and their two boys aged ten and eleven years. They offered their services to the volunteer agency on a regular basis, as an extra form of income. The family seemed quite well-off; they rented a nice two-storey house in a secure compound, and they had a car. They employed a house-girl to look after the day-to-day running of the home, to cook meals, and to care for the boys before and after school. We soon discovered that Josephine worked every day from 5:00 a.m. till around 10:30 p.m., for very little income. She lived in a tiny servant's quarters room at the back of the property and very much kept to herself. We noticed she never joined the family for meals but ate in the kitchen around doing other chores. It was very clear to us from the first instant, that she was there solely to work, and work she did.

We learned that Josephine was a single mother to four children who lived with their grandmother up-country because Josephine could not afford to care for them herself. Every few months she saved enough money for her bus fare, and took the journey to spend a little time with her family. We warmed to her instantly—she was very sweet, softly spoken, and shy.

On the first morning, once the couple had left the house for work, and Josephine had returned from escorting the boys to the school bus, we invited her to share breakfast with us so we could chat while we waited for our van to arrive to collect us for the day's orientation session. She was initially hesitant to join us, but we soon convinced her that everything was ok. We chatted about all sorts of things, and she really enjoyed the company and the fact that we were genuinely interested in her life. This was where we learnt of her situation, but little did we know at that point how very soon we were to meet many others exactly like her.

As we were packing up and getting ready to leave the house on the second, and last, morning, Caro and I slipped her a bag that we'd filled the night before with a few clothes and toys that we had brought from home as donations, for both her and her four children, together with some cash. She was completely overwhelmed and her beautiful face beamed with thanks.

Once the orientation programme was complete, and we'd visited the animal orphanage, we were bundled into vans along with all of our luggage and taken to our placements where we would spend anywhere from two weeks to six months, depending on individual lengths of stay. It was an exciting time, tinged with a little anxiety about the unknown. We were all completely unaware of what we were heading to and hoped we would have time for occasional get-togethers.

I was the only one from the group that was dropped off at my placement, however I knew I would have another volunteer join me later that evening. She was on a late flight from Dubai, and missed the orientation programme.

When I arrived at the orphanage, my initial thoughts were that it looked nice, in fact much nicer than I thought it would be. Situated in what was classed as a 'rural slum' on the outskirts of Nairobi, and surrounded by typical Kenyan slum shanty villages, the centre comprised an orphanage, one nursery school class, a small high school of two class streams, a carpentry workshop, and a tailoring workshop. At first I was pleasantly surprised; the buildings looked ok, the grounds spacious enough with a playing field, a basic playing area for the littlies, and a vegetable garden.

What I noticed almost immediately as I walked through the iron gates was the loud and boisterous laughter and seemingly happy kids playing and running around the grounds. I admit that it did come as a bit of a surprise—I had been expecting a lot worse.

There were a lot of kids at the orphanage, approximately 160 boys and girls aged between three–eighteen years old. Of the 160, only twenty-six or so children actually lived in the orphanage, while the rest were day students.

From the moment I stepped down from the van inside the compound I was surrounded by inquisitive little people, trying to grab hold of my hands, clasping my legs, and some little boys trying to leap on my back. The older teenage girls were a little more subdued and stood back, waiting for their turn to greet me in a more civilised manner. The older boys looked from a distance— they were a little too cool to be leaping all over me like the young ones.

Once everyone had calmed down, I was escorted to the volunteer house, which adjoined the orphanage quarters. It was a very basic, small brick annex comprising two bedrooms, a lounge, a kitchen, a bathroom, and a toilet. My bedroom had two beds in it; the other volunteer arriving later on and I would be sharing. Some of the children followed me into the house, and stood at the bedroom door, watching. I offloaded my luggage on the floor, and one of the older girls offered to show me around the complex, followed by half-a-dozen or so others. They were lovely, extremely shy—all except for the girl who had offered to show me around, Agnes, who was an outspoken livewire from the moment we met. I liked her instantly, and she had a real spark of mischief to her personality.

The orphanage living quarters were separated into boys' and girls' quarters and it was just how I imagined the inside of an orphanage might look. They lived in a two-storey building, downstairs being the dining and sitting area. There was no evidence of any furniture other than a handful of broken chairs stacked up on a couple of tables. There was also a large bench area with cupboards underneath, which were empty. The bench, covered in soot and dirt, looked like it hadn't been used in a very long time either. Out in a closed concrete yard was an open fire, with huge cooking vessels stacked next to it. This was where all the meals were cooked. We discovered that the children ate their meals sitting on the concrete floor.

Upstairs were the sleeping quarters, with boys on one side of the stairs and girls on the other. The dorms had ten to twelve bunk beds to each room, each bed containing a very thin, well-worn mattress, one thin cotton cover, and a small, flat pillow. The rooms had a small cupboard area where the children stashed their stuff. They were dull and cold, and the smell of urine was foul. I could see where previous volunteers had painted pictures on some of the walls in an attempt to brighten up the dismal surroundings.

Every night a staff member, or 'Mother' as she was referred to, was rostered on to take care of the twenty-six children, to assist with showering, ensure homework was done, and that lights were out at a reasonable hour. She also had to referee fights, nurse wounds, be 'mum' to the children, and organise their chores around the orphanage.

The children helped with all the running of the centre, from scrubbing floors and pavements, to helping with cooking, cleaning dorms, and also with assisting the teachers to teach.

Rachel, my fellow volunteer roommate, arrived that evening and we hit it off right from the start. She was from India, but lived and worked as a teacher in Dubai.

We quickly set up the house as our own; after all, we were the only ones living there at the time. It was perfectly adequate, although I was a little apprehensive about the kitchen, which I'm sure seemed like a breeding ground for rats and mice. It just had that look and feel about it.

We discovered that taking a shower in our house involved rather a complicated process; there seemed to be a problem with the shower nozzle and the water flowed out in a full stream, like a hose without the nozzle adjuster. We put up with this, but one day we discovered someone had fixed the problem by stuffing the hose with a foam earplug, the type given out on long-haul flights. This then forced the water back up and out through the faucet, and vóila, a shower spray—and it worked a treat!

We no sooner settled in than we were told we would be having company at the orphanage. A team of fifteen high school students and teachers from Northern Ireland were due to arrive the following week and would be with us for two weeks engaging in both voluntary work and sightseeing trips. They had just graduated and this was their high school grand finale before heading off to their respective universities. So no longer would we have the house to ourselves. Over the next two weeks, staff busily prepared for the large group, converting disused dorms into bedrooms.

When I arrived in Kenya it was their cool season, but still very pleasantly warm to me, having just left a New Zealand winter. However, it also meant the mosquitoes were out in force, so we had to get used to sleeping under mosquito nets, which for a while I really battled with, waking up at all hours of the night with netting wrapped around my body. I tried a couple of nights without it, but soon learnt that I was far better off to be encased with netting, than being plagued by mosquitoes screeching, biting, and also of course the risk of contracting the malaria that was rife in Kenya.

We had a lovely house-mama Winnie, a lady in her seventies, with seven children and umpteen grandchildren. Winnie didn't live in the orphanage, but arrived at 7:00 a.m. every morning to cook and clean for us. She left in the evening, but not until after our dinner had been served and eaten and the dishes washed and dried. We tried to explain that we were very capable of doing our own dishes, but she wouldn't hear of it. This was her job, and this was what she was paid to do. There was no arguing. She would then go home to attend to her own family; cooking meals, cleaning, and looking after grandchildren.

I decided that the role of women, and in particular grandmothers, was undoubtedly the most important in Kenya.

One day I walked into the kitchen and saw Winnie trying to read a card, struggling.

"Ah Winnie, I have just the thing," I said, pointing a finger into the air, as I hurried off to my room, and hauled out from under my bed the stash of donated items I'd bought with me.

I took out a pair of reading glasses, one of many pairs I'd picked up for $2 a pair back home before I left. I went back to the kitchen and handed them to Winnie, not thinking for a minute that she wouldn't know how to wear them. She looked at them and clearly didn't know how to put them on. I immediately went to her aid and showed her how to wear them and she was absolutely astonished and excited at how well she could see. The next morning when she arrived at work, she rushed in to our room and in her limited English, couldn't wait to tell me that she had spent most of the evening reading her Bible—which she hadn't been able to do for so many years, and which had been the one thing that she longed for. Her little story really touched me, and it gave me great pleasure to give other pairs of glasses to elderly Kenyans who would have been in the same predicament as our lovely housekeeper.

One evening, not long after we had arrived, Agnes, our new friend, came down to the volunteer house and asked if we would hang out in their dorm. Of course we were definitely into that, so after dinner, we headed to the girls' dorm upstairs. We all piled up onto a couple of the top bunks, and spent the evening listening to music on a scratchy, static old transistor radio while the girls talked openly about boys and other typical teenage conversation topics. We let them comb and style our hair. They loved our hair because of its softness, and also being long and straight, they could braid it or tie it into some weird and wonderful creations.

Clearly my hair was something of a fascination to African people, and if I was sitting on a bus I would often feel light fingers running through it, and I would turn around to find a woman or child gently stroking my hair.

And so it became a nightly ritual most evenings that Rachel and I would go and visit the girls' dorm just to hang out with them. Piling up on top of a couple of the bunks became the norm, and as usual, they would get the combs out and braid our hair. The shy ones soon came out of their shells. To be able to forget the hardship of their lives and talk 'girl stuff' for a little while was light relief for them, and we discovered that it was the simple things that mattered most. We loved those evening sessions too—they were such beautiful girls and we had loads of fun with them. Over time we gradually learned of their individual circumstances; many very tragic, and how they came to be living in the centre. For some they had lost both parents, and extended family could not afford to look after them; for others there had been mistreatment in the family home; others had HIV in the home. Every girl had her own story, as did all the children at the orphanage.

Chapter Thirteen

The first day working at the orphanage was a big wake-up call for me.

Being an experienced dressmaker, my placement brief was to assist in the tailoring department, so I left New Zealand full of great ideas of what I could do to help and 'make a difference'. I thought that I could tutor my own sewing classes, and perhaps even hold night classes for adults. I took a couple of very simple patterns from home and with my knowledge, I could teach people how to make basic clothes so they could then utilise their new skills later on and perhaps even start their own businesses. I was really enthusiastic about this project and couldn't wait to start.

Oh my goodness me, how shamed I was to have ever thought that I could teach these young people anything that they didn't already know, and what's more, were experts in.

The moment I walked into the tailoring workshop I immediately realised how very wrong in my assumptions I was. There were twelve students enrolled in the tailoring course, all teens, and all girls but for one boy. They were in the tailoring classroom eight hours a day, five days a week, and the work they produced was nothing short of outstanding, their sewing skills being of such a high standard.

I couldn't figure out how they had developed these skills given the lack of resources they had to work with, and over those first days I became aware of just how little these students had in terms of basic sewing requirements such as fabric, and sewing essentials like scissors, needles, thread, pins, tape measures, etc. To these kids however, life was a simple matter of making-do, and they knew no different. The sewing room was the first example of this, being set up with twelve sewing machines of which only half worked as the others were in various states of needing repair. Most of the tailors in Kenya used manually-operated treadle machines because of the limited or non-existent power. Of the machines that worked, most had problems such as threads breaking constantly, fabric becoming caught in the rusty old plates, or the rubber belts repeatedly falling off.

I had arrived in Kenya with various sums of money kindly donated to me by friends and family to be used either for specific projects or at my discretion. I had made up my mind that I would like to buy at least two sewing machines for the classroom, and from what I had seen that first day I wished I could upgrade the whole damn lot of them.

What astonished me most however was that nearly all garments created by the students were made from heavy-duty maize paper bags because the school couldn't afford, or wouldn't buy, fabric for the students to use. I was gobsmacked to see row upon row of beautifully designed, completed garments hanging on wire, held up with pegs and displayed around the classroom, all produced from paper, right down to buttonholes, buttons, and the linings that were made from plastic bags. It was unbelievable.

There was great excitement when the next day I arrived in the classroom armed with a supermarket shopping bag full of sewing accessories, and when the teacher Jane emptied the bag out on the desk it was like opening a treasure trove. To have such things as pins and needles and sharp scissors was to these students sheer luxury.

One of the girls, Hannah, who was in her final year of the tailoring course and making plans to venture out into the big wide world of employment—somewhere, anywhere—was given what I would call the painful task of teaching me their method of dressmaking;

their process for drafting patterns, mastering the art of operating the treadle machine, and most difficult of all, how to transform this heavy-duty, unforgiving brown paper into a beautifully-sewn garment. I was very impressed with her patience. Drafting patterns in Kenya was all about precise calculations, and these students were well-versed in working out desired measurements off the tops of their heads—definitely no calculators needed in this classroom.

Those first days at the centre went well. I was settling into daily life and very much enjoying the different aspects of my new environment. After school hours we had the opportunity to assist with helping to care for the children with whatever needed doing—homework, cooking, feeding, bathing, teaching, or playing. In the early days I felt comfortable there, where the children's needs appeared to be taken care of.

The orphanage was situated in a lively, bustling shanty/slum area on the outskirts of Nairobi, with gorgeous, peaceful countryside skirting the area. Every afternoon after school, Rachel and I would go for a long walk out into the rural area to escape the craziness and mayhem in the village. We liked the peace and tranquillity and beautiful farmland with lush green fields, banana plantations, and maize crops. Yes, this was a very different Kenya to the one Chris and I had experienced the year before. They had finally had rain ... a lot of rain. In fact, there was so much rain in those first months after we left Kenya, that severe flooding had occurred, washing away riverbanks, houses, animals, plantations, and there had even been human fatalities.

It didn't take long for the locals in the village to get used to seeing us out walking, and often someone would call out or hand us a roasted corn cob as we passed by. This village was a 24/7 constant hive of hustle and bustle and it was difficult to work out if and when the locals actually slept, with a continual stream of people out walking, cooking up food on street-side burners, or generally loitering around open bonfires at all times of the day or night. Ghettoblasters were cranked to screaming pitches, cars and motorbikes roared up and down dirt roads, there were matatu (small buses) shaking and shuddering with near-exploding boom-boxes, and horns blasting constantly.

Matatu were the fourteen-seater beaten-up dungary old Nissan vans generally ready for the scrap heap, or that had been resurrected from the scrap heap, which were used as public transport in Kenya. They were also the police and general driving population's greatest nightmare on the road. There were literally millions of matatu; in fact I could probably safely say that every second vehicle on the roads in Kenya was a matatu. They were a law unto themselves, they ruled the roads, and most of the drivers didn't even have legal driver's licences. Very rarely, if ever, did they carry the correct number of passengers. I counted twenty-two people on most occasions, so personal space did not feature and you were often sitting on another person's lap with a chicken's beak millimetres away from taking a chunk out of your arm.

They each had a driver and a touter who normally reeked of alcohol, look stoned, or were on many occasions, both. There seemed to be an unspoken rule of 'no talking' on matatu, but instead communication just seemed to work via hand gesturing and lots of eye movements.

Fares were handed all around the van from person to person, eventually making its way to the touter, and incredibly he just seemed to know who was owed what change. He hung out the side window of the van, and often out of the side door, touting for fares, and would just about do anything to get you on-board, so the upside was that in terms of reliability, you very rarely had to wait more than a couple of minutes on the side of the road before a van came screeching to a halt beside you, shuddering from the screaming boom-boxes either inside or often fixed on top of the roof.

Many insurance companies actually refused to insure tourists for riding on them because of their phenomenal accident rate and non-licensed drivers. In my first two visits to Kenya, I was involved in three separate matatu accidents, one of which resulted in the van being written off.

In a nutshell, you took your life in your hands as soon as you boarded a matatu, however they were the most efficient form of transport in terms of moving millions of people around Kenya, and the most entertaining and cheap mode of transport—and for the likes of us volunteers who didn't want to pay exorbitant fares, we'd have been completely lost without them.

I noticed that there seemed to be two distinct classes in Kenya—the rare, wealthy high class, with the majority being the extremely poor class. I also saw that areas were not designated to each class as such; for example there were shanty villages intermingled with beautiful, architecturally-designed homes in a hodge-podge type of fashion.

Life at the orphanage in the early days was fun. The Irish teachers and students arrived the following week after Rachel and I, so the centre instantly became alive with energetic, enthusiastic young people. We enjoyed their company and the kids absolutely relished having all the extra attention from us all. The centre was full of activity, noise, games, sports, laughter, and happiness.

Like the majority of the children's centres, many were affiliated with churches, and in fact over the majority of Kenya, people were devoted to their church, regularly attending services. There was a chapel on the premises and the children would start each morning with dedication, and finish with prayer sessions. For most Kenyans, Sundays were dedicated to church, starting with early morning Sunday School for the children followed by church services lasting three to four hours and sometimes much longer. For some the entire day was devoted to church. Services were sometimes in English, but mostly in Swahili and involved a lot of lively singing, dancing, chanting, and drum-beating.

The centre was also involved in community care, and one day we accompanied the manager and another staff member on a home visitation to families who were considered to be at high level crisis point. The cases were tragic and I found it incomprehensible how these people actually managed to survive and battle on in the conditions in which they lived.

We called on an HIV-positive woman whose husband abandoned her with seven children; she lived in her home that was approximately a quarter of the size of a single garage in New Zealand, consisting of four make-shift wooden walls with gaping holes where the timber slats had fallen out. The only items in the house were two old mattresses laid out on the floor where the entire family slept. She paid ksh700– per month for rent, or the equivalent of approximately NZ$9, and if she got behind with payment as sometimes was the case, the landlord came around and locked her out until she rustled up the money.

Another woman we visited was a great-great-grandmother of ninety-two who had been left to care for her great-granddaughter's three children because their mother died and the other family members refused to take responsibility. The care of these children fell heavily on the shoulders of this old lady who herself needed to be taken care of. She could barely walk, and spent a lot of time in bed. These were just a mere couple of the millions of stories like these in Africa.

One of the happier aspects of my job was that I would sometimes look after an adorable three-month-old baby boy Kevin, who's mum was part of a local ladies craft group. The women used an old vacant room at the centre to make their crafts and would meet almost daily. To give her a break I would often carry the little baby around on my back, wrapped and tied on by a kanga while getting on with other duties—or trying to get on with other duties!

In Kenya all babies were securely tied on to their mother's back with a kanga, which was an African cotton sarong, used for a variety of purposes, but first and foremost as baby carriers. Newborns were usually carried in their mother's arms and as they got a little older they were then tied to their mother's backs. I had absolutely no idea how to go about this whole process of firstly balancing a baby on my back, while at the same time wrapping and securing the kanga firmly around both baby and me and then tying it up in the front without him falling out. It was fascinating to watch an African woman go through this whole process with such ease and speed. The first time, Kevin's mum very casually plopped him on my back, threw the kanga around me, tied him in, and as I gingerly stood up I could not believe how secure he felt. The ladies all laughed at me as I walked with a very pronounced stoop, frightened that he would drop out and on to the floor. African simplicity—and it worked perfectly.

We quickly became used to Kenyan ways, Rachel and I, and it didn't take long before we felt at home and comfortable with our new surroundings. We settled into life at the orphanage, and loved having the Northern Irish crew around. We all found living and working with the kids very rewarding and it helped that we appeared to be living in a relaxed, casual environment. We usually worked Monday to Friday, but I often took Fridays off, and we made good use of our free Saturdays and Sundays to unwind, shop, and explore the area. It also provided us with the opportunity to head out of Nairobi for weekend safaris or to the coast for rest and relaxation if we wanted to.

We loved the kids at the centre, and we used to laugh when they would call out our names as Lachel and Dee because they had difficulty pronouncing our names properly. They loved the attention we gave them, especially when we pulled out the board games. Snakes and Ladders was a real hit, and Kenya being the soccer-mad nation that it was, an after-dinner game of football, 'Mzungu v Kenya' was always one of the highlights of the day. The Kenyan kids would always win, barefoot and all. A couple of the boys showed outstanding skills and we recognised enormous talent, and we couldn't help think that these were the kids with the potential to become future stars if only given the chance.

We found being a 'mzungu' in Kenya amusing and got very used to the constant attention and the continual stares wherever we went, whether it be walking around our local slum village, shopping in the fruit and veggie market, travelling on the matatu, or wandering around town. White people were very seldom seen in the slum areas of Kenya, and because Rachel and I would shop at the local markets for our supplies, barter at fruit and vegetable stalls, catch local matatu transport, and actually take the time to stop and chat to the locals, people were always very friendly towards us. Mzungu simply don't walk the slums, shop in the slum markets, and would never take their lives in their hands and catch the matatu. So, to the local Kenyan, we didn't quite fit the stereotypical image, and it was puzzling for them.

Sadly, and much to our immense disappointment, it didn't take too long before stories about the centre of a not-so-pleasant nature started filtering through and we slowly began to form suspicions that perhaps things were not quite as rosy as they seemed on the surface.

One morning I went to see the ladies in the craft group and I was promptly asked if I knew a certain British mzungu who had been volunteering at the centre some months before we had arrived, and could I please find out what happened to the money she had agreed to send them. Of course I had no idea what they were talking about, so the ladies proceeded to explain how a few months before Rachel and I had arrived, a former volunteer from Britain had established the women's craft group, setting them up in the vacant classroom at the centre where they could come with their babies and small children every day, make their craft, and then on-sell their goods in the local market as a form of income. This woman sponsored the ladies by paying for fabric and all the materials they would need to produce their craft. She returned to Britain with the promise of sending funds on a monthly basis to provide the women with all their craft needs. With the women's help, I discovered that the volunteer had indeed sent the funds, but it had not gotten to the recipients for whom the money was intended. I immediately started feeling a little uneasy that sadly perhaps things weren't quite as they seemed here.

I had arrived in Kenya with a lot of donated funds from family and friends back home and I decided that whenever I wanted to buy something for the people, or children there, that I would most certainly organise it myself and not involve the staff, particularly the management. I applied the same rule to the donated clothes, and other things I had with me.

Chapter Fourteen

Depending on the placement, volunteers generally had weekends off as free time, so when our first weekend at the orphanage came around, we decided to venture into town. We had planned to catch up with some of the other volunteers who were at other placements, to visit the craft markets and have lunch together. We were a little unsure about public transport to begin with as we were quite some distance from the CBD, so we decided to play safe and catch a taxi into town. We were shocked at the cost—it was astronomical! As we quickly learnt, there was local price, and then there was mzungu price.

We met up with the other volunteers and decided to take a visit to Kibera, one of the largest slums in the world. We weren't entirely sure why we wanted to visit, maybe just out of simple curiosity to see first-hand the terrible squalor that some human beings were forced to live in. On the other hand, we didn't want to make these residents feel they were living constantly in a fish bowl. Visiting Kibera had to be arranged through our volunteer agency, as it was certainly not a place to stroll around unaccompanied by a local. For a small fee, local resident John took guided tours through the slums, so our agency assigned him to look after us.

Kibera was like nothing you could ever imagine; the conditions that approximately one million people live in were horrific. We wandered through filthy, dirty, narrow alleyways, weaving our way amongst shacks no bigger than two metres squared, jam-packed together, sewage seeping through the ground, and little children playing in filthy, contaminated water. Everywhere we went, women were busy with laundry, bent over buckets of water, scrubbing and squeezing and wringing. I was amazed at the obvious strength of these women as they single-handedly managed to wring the last drops of water out of heavy blankets with what looked like no bother at all. Laundry was left to dry anywhere there was a space, whether it be strung over makeshift clothes lines, sprawled out over concrete walls, or laid out on dusty rocks. The homes were generally made of either wooden slats with newspaper lining to keep out draught, and dirt floors, or quality houses were made of iron sheets and possibly had a concrete floor. Most had curtains dividing the small sleeping areas from the living area, and the furnishing was extremely basic—sometimes a couch, or a couple of chairs, and sometimes a narrow bed, depending on the size of the house. Some had nothing but bedding on the floor. These homes all had families housing from four to seven or eight people, and in many cases a whole lot more, all living together. The one thing that firmly stuck in my mind was that these so-called shacks were home to these people, and they clearly tried to make the most of the awful situation in which they lived. It was obvious that they took great pride in their personal, humble haven.

Situated amongst all these houses was a medical HIV/AIDS clinic, and an adjoining maternity unit. Once again the buildings were made of concrete and iron sheets, with basic facilities. There were beds lined up against walls in the maternity wing, but very little else. Hygiene did not even feature. At the back of the maternity unit was a shed housing a burner, where all number of things were disposed of, including placenta, syringes, needles, and other sanitary items. Grubby rags that resembled towels and filthy hole-ridden sheets hung overlapped on a single washing line. While we were in the maternity unit, a heavily pregnant woman came staggering into the clinic barely able to put one foot in front of the other. She was supported either side of her by two women who were carrying her weight. She was on the verge of collapse and bleeding profusely, her clothes soaked with blood, and leaving a trail behind her. It was absolutely shocking. We left at that stage, and over the next few weeks, I often wondered what happened to that woman and her unborn baby. To us, it was horrific; to the residents, it was just another day.

After the shock of Kibera, and generally feeling a little downhearted, we wandered about town, familiarising ourselves with our new city. We stopped for a traditional Kenyan lunch and visited the Masai craft market, where we all bought up wee African treasures while also battling a fair amount of guilt that we were so lucky to have this privilege when so very many didn't.

The day ended with great amusement for Rachel and me however, when we decided to catch a matatu home. It was one of those memorable experiences, and whenever I thought of Kenya later, I was instantly reminded of the infamous matatu.

Matatu were banned from the Nairobi city centre, so there were designated matatu junctions at various spots skirting the CBD area. This was also a congregation point for buses and motorbikes. So after weaving our way through town, often having to stop and ask someone if we were heading in the right direction, Rachel and I finally made it to the matatu junction. It was getting on towards peak hour so the junction was absolute mayhem—totally chaotic and completely shambolic. There were literally hundreds of these old heaps parked in absolutely no order at all, while others were moving slowly, any which way; touters screaming out for people; horns blasting; boom boxes so loud that the vans were shuddering; and of course the mish-mash of thousands of people all fighting their way to their matatu. We finally spotted our van in the distance, and made a beeline for it, weaving in and out of crowds, before confirming with the touter when we arrived that this was indeed the correct one, because even though the matatu number was displayed on a board in the van front window, one could never be too sure.

"Yes, yes," he roared, while grabbing us both by the arms and shoving us right into the seats directly behind the driver.

The vans left only when they were full, so we had no choice but to sit and watch, with wonder and amusement, the activities going on while we were waiting for our van to fill up.

The matatu vied for position, all wanting to get out of the junction gridlock first, so they were constantly nosing in front of each other, reversing here, u-turning there, mounting curbs to overtake other vans—it was purely and simply, a total shambles.

While we were watching all the action take place, one van caught our eye. Fully laden with passengers, the driver decided to mount a curb and drive over a concrete path that was jutting out onto the dirt road, to get out of the jam. Unfortunately for him, this particular curb was much higher than he had obviously anticipated, and his van got firmly stuck. He tried accelerating with his foot flat to the floor in an attempt to force the van to move, but with wheels spinning furiously and smoke pouring out of the back, the van was still firmly lodged by its under-chassis. A lot of bellowing and hand movement followed, at which time a bunch of guys came to the rescue, and with their combined effort managed to push the matatu off the curb. It came crashing down with a large thud, parts of the chassis flying off as it hit the ground. The driver simply crunched it into gear, and away it roared, leaving debris in its wake.

If that wasn't enough commotion for one day, right in front of our eyes a three-van pile-up unfolded, and this happened without even leaving the junction. What amazed us with this altercation was that the drivers barely batted an eye as they all made an attempt to prize their vans off each other, which were by this time locked together, and then proceeded to roar off into the distance. My thoughts turned to home, and the stock car races I had been to as a teenager.

Meanwhile, while we were completely distracted, our van was getting full—and I mean *full*. This fourteen-seater was, by the time the touter decided we couldn't possibly squeeze another soul in, jammed pack with twenty-two of us. There was an art to fitting twenty-two people into a van built to hold fourteen, and in this particular case the touter had it down pat. The first passengers, except us, were herded in and pushed to the back of the van, and then starting from the back, working towards the front, the touter proceeded to fill up all seats in what seemed a normal, fairly orderly fashion. Then, when all seats were taken, more people were pushed in, again to the back to sit on the knees of the backseaters, then a plank of wood was placed across the aisle to fill up the gap and at least two more people in each row sat there, then the final couple of passengers were pushed in and held in place until the side door was slammed shut to prevent them from spilling out. Bearing in mind most passengers had at least one shopping bag, sometimes sacks of wood or vegetables, and then sometimes chickens as well. I tried to avoid sitting anywhere near anyone with chickens; they terrified me and I knew it would be just a matter of time before one decided to take a wee peck at an unfamiliar mzungu arm. I didn't want that mzungu arm to belong to me.

The whole process of filling up a matatu was extremely impressive and it was very obvious that personal space was definitely not an issue in Kenya. Without any windows open however, the smell of body odour from twenty-two people squashed into such a confined space without ventilation was foul.

Finally we were off. The ghettoblaster bellowed out with the bass turned right up to the max, so our van shuddered and vibrated and I couldn't help wonder if it was going to explode at any second. With so much weight on board, the exhaust pipe was hitting the ground every time we ran over an uneven spot in the road—which could account for 99.9% of the journey. This matatu seemed to only have 1st and 2nd gear, and occasionally the 3rd gear working, so for our entire forty-five-minute journey, we drove with the gears screaming.

We had all been warned about the trials, tribulations, and dangers of riding the infamous matatu at our orientation session, however, after the expensive ride into town by taxi, Rachel and I felt the risk was worth the very small cost. Of course, the old adage 'you get what you pay for' applies in every situation, and we discovered the vast difference between a taxi ride for ksh1,000/– and a matatu ride for ksh30/–.

Our journey involved a lot of weaving in and out of every other vehicle in front of us, and the one-car-per-lane theory ... forget it! On those roads, it was each man or matatu for themselves, so one lane very rapidly turned into two or three or four lanes, which in turn inevitably caused a gridlock.

About ten minutes into our ride, and just as we were slowly starting to relax a little, the van suddenly swerved over to the side of the road, screeched to a halt, the touter quickly grabbed a handful of passengers—the last ones to get in, as well as Rachel and I—and pulled at our arms, indicating we were to get out of the van, then promptly pushed us towards another matatu that had pulled up behind us, all the while thrusting coins into our hands, and beckoning us with a lot of sign language to hurry along and get inside the other matatu. He then ran back to his van, jumped aboard, and roared off ahead of us. We followed suit in our new van and continued on to our destination. We had no idea what had just unfolded, or why, but we looked at each other in amazement with a 'what was all that about' look and simply burst out laughing.

As it turned out, this same practise happened several times in those early days of living in Kenya, and we started getting very annoyed at continually being thrown out of the matatu, until we understood one day exactly why this was happening. Police very regularly set up random check points to try and alleviate the overloading issue in matatu. However, most often a driver was notified of a police checkpoint ahead by fellow matatu drivers, so they pulled over, offloaded as many passengers as required (of course, whoever was closest to the side door). The driver then drove through the checkpoint, and once safely past, the process of overfilling started once more. Sometimes the touter hopped out of the van, ran past the checkpoint on foot while the driver was put through the check, then once safely past, the touter hopped back in the van and on they went. We found this highly amusing and somewhat impressive that they had discovered this way of avoiding trouble by the police.

Alighting the matatu also required a certain level of skill. The vans barely stopped moving; in fact they more or less just slowed right down, while passengers, clutching at their bags, chickens, and parcels struggled to squeeze past all the other bodies and hopped down on to the road before the van roared away. Precision timing was of an essence.

Chapter Fifteen

The early morning call I received from Chris delivering the news that my dear mother-in-law had passed away back in New Zealand was not the news I ever expected. I'd received a text from Chris asking if he could phone, but I sent one back telling him to wait a few hours as it was early in the morning and I was afraid I'd wake up the house. Next minute, the phone rang, and it was Chris. He said he couldn't wait another few hours, and told me the news. I was totally shocked. In hindsight, because of previous health issues, it shouldn't have been quite so unexpected, but it was something I was never prepared for—especially when 20,000 kilometres away.

I was immediately consumed by an overwhelming feeling of being at the other end of the world, and apart from my own sadness I was also feeling immense guilt at not being at home to support Chris who had just lost his beloved mum, and also our children Craig and Hayley, who had just lost their beloved grandmother. In spite of Chris insisting everything was fine, everyone was ok and were all supporting each other, and his repeated requests not to contemplate coming home, along with messages from friends and family advising me the same, I could barely stop myself from walking into a travel agency and booking the next flight despite the two days of flying it would require. I eventually agreed to stay in Kenya on the promise that we would all keep close and frequent contact.

On the day the funeral was to take place back in New Zealand, I felt the need to be somewhere very special, and the nicest place I could think of to spend the day was at an abandoned baby centre situated not far from my orphanage. It was a fantastic project, that was set up and was 100% funded by an American charity to provide temporary care for abandoned babies and toddlers. The setting was stunning, with pristine conditions, gorgeous gardens and grounds, and high-tech facilities, including a fully equipped newborn assessment clinic where all babies initially entering the centre spent the first week. Once the doctors were satisfied, the baby was then transferred to Cottage 1. He or she would remain at the centre until such time as they may be fortunate enough to be adopted.

The Centre's main objective was to provide a nurturing environment for newborn abandoned babies and toddlers, and would have to be one of the most well-run institutions I had ever experienced, with staff who were completely dedicated and devoted to the care of the babies and children.

There were four cottages and the babies moved through the cottages as they grew. There was also a wing for disabled adults and children, and included a small but highly impressive rehabilitation centre complete with nursing staff, an occupational therapist, a physiotherapist, and the very latest equipment. It also ran a day clinic for local villagers.

I chose to spend my day in Cottage 1, for newborn to six-month-old babies. There were thirteen babies in the cottage when I was there, although some were about to graduate to Cottage 2 for six-month- to eighteen-month-old babies. I helped with feeding, washing, bathing, and providing lots and lots of cuddles. It was lovely to see how healthy, happy, clean, and well-looked after the babies were, and I thought how wonderful it would be if there were more institutions like that in Kenya.

The day I was working, a two-day-old baby was brought into care. She was found in our village, abandoned next to a rubbish bin, and was gravely ill. She was immediately put into the assessment unit with twenty-four-hour around the clock intensive care, and remained there for seven days. During that period she underwent extensive medical checks and assessments. I was allowed to go back to see her two weeks later, and she had been transferred to Cottage 1. Another lucky one rescued from potential death. This was life in the slums of Kenya.

While I was there at the orphanage that day I was offered a baby to take back home to New Zealand. Whenever I mentioned to the staff just how absolutely adorable they were, one would say, "You take to your country. You fill out form and you take." I was pretty sure it was not quite as easy as that; I had heard that prospective parents had to spend at least three months in Kenya bonding with the child, and rightly so. However, I can understand the frustrations for the staff at centres, and any slim chance that a child may have a better life outside was ever hopeful.

Chapter Sixteen

After staying in the orphanage for a month, I started to learn a lot of what was going on behind the scenes and it was both terribly disappointing, and also quite shocking. I had learnt that the directors had been pilfering a lot of the donated goods and money that volunteers had sent regularly to sponsor a child after returning home, and also overseas funding including staff salaries, and so after years of this, they were now very wealthy people.

The principal donor pulled their sponsorship immediately when they were alerted to the misappropriation of their funds, which had apparently gone on for quite some years, so this left a major hole in the funding of the organisation. This happened while I was there. Almost immediately, the funding had stopped, and there seemed to be a lot of activity going on at the centre with various mzungu coming in, walking around the premises armed with clipboards, interviewing staff, and writing reports. They were representing a British NGO and were thinking of taking on the sponsorship, and so of course they had come to investigate the operation thoroughly before committing. The sad part of all this was that the children were the ones who primarily suffered, so the deception of just a handful of very greedy people potentially had a detrimental effect on these kids' lives.

We had noticed little incidents over the previous two weeks that started to arouse suspicion amongst us volunteers. The alert started when the Irish volunteers arrived. They had each brought a suitcase bulging with donated clothes, shoes, books, and toys and had emptied them all onto a row of trestle tables, in large piles, in an empty dining room. A couple of days later, the children were brought into the room in groups and were instructed by staff to choose one item of clothing each only—there were twenty-four kids. Not even the slightest of dents was made in this enormous pile. The remainder was bundled up in boxes and stashed away in a corner of the room, and I was told by one of the staff that they would be sold off in the markets. Meanwhile the kids were still running around in disgusting old threadbare rags, shoes that were falling apart, some with soles ripped off, and in many cases, no shoes at all. One of the older boys wore an old pair of soccer boots that a volunteer had specifically given to him. They were his only footwear.

We had been told at our orientation class that we were not to hand out donations at our placements and that there was a process to follow. All donated items, money, etc. was to be given to management, who would distribute it appropriately amongst the children.

I decided not to enter into that arrangement, and instead, stashed my bags under my bed until I felt the timing was right to hand out my goods. There was absolutely no way I was going to hand over donated cash.

One night after the staff had left for the evening, we called all the children to come down and visit us in the volunteer house. They had no idea what we had planned. We dragged my bags into the lounge, opened them up, and let them go for it. They had the time of their lives, screeching and leaping around with sheer delight, rummaging through mountains of clothes, hats, and scarfs and taking whatever they wanted. And the astonishing thing was that there was no squabbling over things! I was amazed by what excited them most—brand new underwear, socks, and beanies. And it wasn't just the small children who were excited; the teenaged boys and girls were equally thrilled to pieces to be given a brand new pair of undies or socks, and to have a new skirt, top, or pair of pants was to these kids just the icing on the cake.

I had also been given various amounts of money and it added up to quite a substantial amount. I decided not long after arriving at the orphanage that I wanted to buy sewing machines for the tailoring workshop. One day I took the tailoring teacher Jane into town with the purpose of buying two brand new manually operated treadle sewing machines. After dragging out my most hardened bargaining tactics, we settled on two lovely machines and tables at the local sewing machine shop. We hailed a taxi van and loaded up boxes, machine tables, and all the other paraphernalia and headed back to the centre. The students had no idea that we had been in town buying sewing machines, so when we arrived they were simply beside themselves with excitement, and had the machines out of their boxes, assembled, and operating at lightning speed.

Kenya was a developing country and the poverty was huge, and we were confronted with this every time we stepped out of the volunteer house and witnessed people struggle to survive with even the most basic human needs. People of Kenya were tough, very tough. They had to be. But they seemed almost genuinely happy with their lot. There was always lots of laughter, music, singing, dancing, and they just got on with life.

One day I went into town to buy fabric, lots of it. When I first arrived at the orphanage and saw the budding young tailors making garments out of brown paper bags, I decided immediately that these kids were going to make a real garment, using real fabric. I wanted each of them to make something just for themselves.

I meandered about town for most of the day searching for fabric and agonising over choices. Florals, checked, stripes, and colour—such a dilemma! I settled on a few pieces of patterned cotton print that I thought would be ok; I was not entirely happy but nevertheless they would do. I also bought a piece of checked shirt fabric for our only male student.

When I took the materials back to class later that day, I hadn't anticipated the euphoria that broke out. It was only then that

I discovered that not one of them had ever sewn a garment for themselves, and my agonising over choosing fabrics was totally in vain because they loved all of my choices. In fact, I realised that if I'd arrived back with a whole lot of tea-towels to sew into an item of clothing, they would have been equally as thrilled.

Within minutes, fabrics were chosen, tape measures whipped out, and pattern drafting was in progress. By the end of the next day each student had a finished garment that they were truly proud of.

I organised a fashion parade on the playing field for the following day where the students got to model their finished garments. I didn't invite the staff, however a couple of the teachers came and watched. We had such a fun afternoon, and of course they couldn't help but act out crazy poses as I took photos of them all. I had them printed off and presented a photo to each of them so they could see what they looked like in their beautiful garment, and I wanted them to understand just how clever they were. They were immensely proud of their new skirts, dresses, and shirts, and all looked simply beautiful.

Chapter Seventeen

One beautiful, warm, sunny Sunday I went hiking with a Kenyan friend high up in the Ngong Hills, which fringed the outskirts of Nairobi and were still inhabited by a few Masai and animals. It was a beautiful walk, meandering through little narrow red dirt lanes, with thick coffee and banana plantations encompassing the area, crop farmers dragging small donkeys who were attached to heavily laden carts, and elderly women lugging huge loads of maize-filled sacks on their heads and backs. We headed on an almost vertical climb through scrub and bush to the summit, which provided the most stunning 360-degree views of the Great Rift Valley, expanding right out to the Masai Mara, down to Nairobi, and then further out to Tanzania and the outlying areas. It was absolutely stunning and very peaceful. I sat up there on top of the world and pinched myself at the beauty and serenity of this place, just a mere few kilometres from the hustle and bustle of Nairobi.

I had been noticing billboards and banners appearing all over town, advertising the upcoming Africa Track and Field International Games to be hosted by Kenya at the national stadium in Nairobi. Thinking back to my flight to Kenya and my decision to embrace as much of the culture as possible during my time there, I decided to go along. I was so pleased that I did—it was a true spectacle. Watching and cheering the top of the elite of African runners competing against each other was fantastic. I was one of a very few mzungu sitting alone amongst the 40,000+ cheering crowd, and it was a wonderful experience. Everybody was so friendly, waving banners, blowing vuvuzelas and a few comedians provided between-event entertainment to the crowds. The games were awesome, complete with medal ceremonies, national anthems, and flag-raising triumphs. I absolutely loved it. Initially I had only planned to go on the Saturday, but I went back again on the Sunday too. I thought this might be a once in a lifetime opportunity; there were fifty-one other countries competing, and if they all had a turn at hosting, it might be another fifty-one years before they were hosted again in Kenya.

Meanwhile school holidays were looming and this meant many of the children at the centre would be returning to their rural homes for the month of August. Most of the children had at least one member of their extended family to go to, so the centre would essentially be closed. As my volunteer buddy Rachel was going back to Dubai and I would be alone, I was given the opportunity of moving to another placement, this time to a teenage boys' detention centre. I knew I would miss Rachel and I really didn't fancy staying at the orphanage on my own so the opportunity to move on and try a new environment was appealing. The detention centre also appealed to me for some unknown reason.

We decided to throw the children a big leaving party on the last night of school term, which also coincided with Rachel's and my last night also. We brought up ridiculous amounts of party food, drinks, balloons, banners, and other treats, and once again, when the staff had left for the day, we assembled all the children and had a fantastic, fun evening eating, playing games, and just making that last night an extra special time for them all.

The next day was very sad, as we said our goodbyes with tears and promises of return visits to the centre to see the children.

Rachel left Kenya and I moved into my new abode in a leafy, rather affluent suburb in a rural area of Nairobi. In terms of living standards, I felt I had gone from pauper to princess in the space of the time I was picked up from the orphanage and delivered to my new house, which took all of an hour.

The living standard contrasts in Nairobi were extreme and I had the experience of both. I had come from the slums where crime was rife and an everyday occurrence, with no security and where people battled to survive, to a wealthy area with its palatial homes, magnificent gardens, and with what seemed to be an overkill of security.

The new home was situated in a private lane with steel gates and a communal security guard housed in his gentry at the entrance. There were seven residences in the lane, each alarmed and with private guards at their gate. One of our neighbours was a government politician, or had been, and he had his own armed guards who walked about in camouflaged uniforms, machine-guns slung over their shoulders.

On our property lived a dear little old man named Muli, who was eighty years old. Muli had been employed for the last forty-plus years as the gardener for the property, and lived in his tiny wood-slatted, tumbling down, two-metre squared shack all that time. He still cooked over an open fire inside his little smoke-filled hut, with his battered up little transistor radio for company. He spent his days pottering about in the beautifully manicured garden, just as he had done all those years, and every afternoon he would hobble up the road to collect tree branches to keep his fire stoked. I don't know where he actually got the wood from, but clearly he had his secret source.

The volunteer house was full of women—there were nine of us from various countries around the world, ages ranging from eighteen years to late fifties, all staying for varying periods of time. We were all there for the same like-minded reasons, so I knew instantly I was going to fit in well in this new environment with these lovely women.

A few days after moving into my new house, Kenyans went to the polls and voted on a new constitution, which had the potential

109

to erupt into violent riots as had happened in previous elections. Consequently everyone in Kenya was advised to stay at home for both election day and also the following day just in case of any outbursts. And so it was perfect timing for me to get to know my fellow housemates, being holed-up in our property for two days.

During the days leading up to the election, we had stocked up on supplies of food and drink, and judging by the copious quantities of alcohol and snack foods that were stashed in our pantry, we had a fairly good idea of how we would keep ourselves entertained. Consequently, many an hour was spent sitting out on Muli's beautifully manicured lawn soaking up the warm sun, swapping interesting personal stories, sipping wine, and nibbling on delectable delights. The time passed quickly and by the end of the second day I felt I was getting to know my new housemates well, and that I would really enjoy my time in the new house.

Chapter Eighteen

My new placement at the teenage boys' detention centre was
a twenty-five-minute walk from our volunteer house. It was
a centre for boys aged between eleven and eighteen years who
had been taken into custody by the police and been through the
court process, and were ordered to spend up to three years in the
detention centre. The reasons for the boys being sent to detention
varied; many were street kids who had run away from home
because their lives were so terrible that living on the streets seemed
a better option, many had also been involved in crime, others had
been sent to the centre because their families could no longer look
after them. When I was there, 106 boys were living there.

The facilities were basic and shabby, but this was the boys' home,
and although during daytime hours the gates were open, they were
not allowed to leave the compound unless they had permission,
and this was strictly adhered to. There was a school on the premises
with trained teaching staff, so they had daily lessons, along with
counselling sessions. They had to help with the responsibility of
the day-to-day running of the centre, and were assigned designated
duties including everything from tending crops, herding cattle,
helping in the kitchen, cleaning and scrubbing rooms, and fetching
water in jerry cans from the nearby bore.

I took a real liking to the boys almost immediately, and formed
a special bond with a handful of them who were soon to become
my friends and helpers. They were boys I could rely on during my
placement period.

When I arrived it was school holidays, but of course the boys
weren't allowed to leave the compound. They still had to wear

their school uniform, they still had to report for assembly every morning out on the quadrant, and they still had to tend to their daily chores whether it be school holidays or not.

Initially my placement brief was to help teach the boys basic tailoring skills, but as soon as I saw the poor state of the one and only treadle sewing machine and the non-responsive reactions from the staff on having it repaired, even at my own cost, I knew this was probably not going to eventuate. I went home that afternoon thinking of what other use I could be to these boys.

I decided to become involved in the set-up of a recreational library project at the centre. I liked the whole concept, and decided this project was something I would really get in to. I got quite excited and thought about how and what I could do to make the library a really cool place for these kids.

I arrived the following day full of enthusiasm and informed the headmaster of my plans and ideas I had come up with. He enlisted the help of one of the teachers, Ano, to advise and assist me with everything I needed for the project. I liked him instantly; he was friendly, helpful, and genuinely seemed to have a good rapport with the boys.

We were allocated an old dis-used classroom with an adjoining small office. I thought we could transform the office into a library and the classroom into a reading room. The classroom was in a disgusting state and when I first walked in, I was completely overwhelmed and wondered where and how on earth we might begin to start clearing it out. By the enormous amount of old broken furniture, rubbish, obsolete resources, books, old wood, and mountains of papers it contained, it was very clear that the main purpose of this room had been as a dumping ground. Ano, having sensed my trepidation, immediately enlisted the help of three boys who were to soon become invaluable to me during the project.

Together we all mucked in and started the laborious task of clearing out the classroom of all the junk; the boys took great delight in building huge bonfires out on the field to dispose of the rubbish and debris. Just about everything that came out of that room was thrown on the fire. The clearing out process took nearly two weeks.

Next, we set about cleaning and scrubbing the room from top to bottom, so we could then paint it a bright sunshine-y yellow. I'm ashamed to say that it didn't occur immediately to me that water might be a problem; but of course it was—this was Africa. There was no tap we could simply walk to, turn on, and fill buckets from with an abundance of water. No, water was fetched from a communal borehole some five-minute walk each way, and there was only one bucket! There were also no cleaning products, or cleaning cloths, so I made a quick dash up to the nearby village store to buy all the cleaning products I could find amongst the very small range. I came back armed with half-a-dozen buckets and cleaning detergent but no cloths. There didn't appear to be such a thing in this little village. I relayed this news back to the boys.

"No problem Madam, wait," said my young friend Elvis as he promptly ran off with two of the other boys, coming back a short time later with old newspapers, which they scrunched up into balls demonstrating how they would use these balls as scrubbing brushes. Very soon more boys appeared and together they all headed off to the water bore to fill up the buckets. I couldn't quite get my head around the newspaper cleaning cloth idea, especially once they rapidly became sodden blobs of mush, and I also couldn't cope with the wet newsprint being smeared all over the walls either, so I decided to leave them to it, and I concentrated on less frustrating jobs such as writing further shopping lists for paint, curtain fabric, posters for the walls, etc., then went off to town, leaving the boys to get on with it. When I came back a couple of hours later the walls were all cleaned down, and the boys were busy mopping up the excess water off the floor. I knew that they would be invaluable to me, with their high energy and ability to make do—something I personally struggled with in Africa. Improvisation by thinking outside the box didn't come naturally to me there.

We moved onto the adjoining office area, and once again the boys repeated the process of cleaning and scrubbing with their trusted newspaper cloths. Ano arranged to have broken cabinets repaired, locks put on doors, and broken glass panes replaced in the windows with small one-man operators in the village.

When the walls were clean and dry, I gave the boys the task of painting the rooms. They loved the painting job, and considered it a real treat. The inconsistent paint application by the boys made a slight marble effect—unintentionally of course, but nevertheless it looked fantastic. While up in the village one day I noticed a small tailor shop, so I bought a piece of lightweight sheer fabric in town, took it to the lady in the shop, and asked her to make some curtains. We hung them up on wire, and they looked great. The rooms were starting to look fresh, bright, and ready to be transformed into a library.

I decided to spend some of the donated money I had been given on books for our new library, so Ano and I spent many hours trolling book markets, buying large quantities of suitable second-hand books for the various age groups and reading abilities of the children at the centre. One of the benefits of buying in Kenya was that we could buy so much for our money, and knowing the money would stay in the village was also an added bonus.

Slowly we started building up the book collection with a variety of both Swahili and English books. English was now compulsory to learn in schools in Kenya, so Ano said it was very important to have books in both languages. I spent hours cataloguing, alphabetising, and displaying them on shelves. It started to look really good, and the boys were excited at the prospect of having story books to read.

When the word got around that the library was opening on a particular day, there was a mad flurry of boys who had come to borrow books, all crammed into the library, and it very quickly got out of control. We couldn't keep up with the recording aspect, and therefore had no idea who was taking books, and how many. We immediately had to instil some order, so we introduced a rule of allowing two boys in at a time, and when they had selected their books and had them recorded in the register, they had to leave and allow two more to come in. This seemed to work, although the queue outside was often long, and this continued all day, every day. Sometimes I noticed the same boys coming in two or three times a day to drop off books, and to take new ones out.

The library was my main focus at the centre, and rapidly became the boys' as well. It kept me very busy and I enjoyed it. It gave me great satisfaction seeing how much the boys thrived from having simple things such as books to read.

I started to notice from my register that some books were either slow to be returned, or just not returned at all, which annoyed me. One day I complained to two of my helpers, David and James, about the books going missing. "We'll find them, Madam," said David, so I gave them a list of books that had been missing for five days, and off they went. Sure enough they returned some time later with all the books on the list. From then on they had a new job as 'book police' and every day I would give them a list of books that were either overdue or deemed missing, and inevitably they came back every time with the books that they were sent out to track down. It didn't take long before we worked out that some of the boys were very shrewd, and when recording their name and book in the register, would make up a fictitious name so it was hard to track them down, or to figure out which classroom they belonged to. What they hadn't thought of though, was that my book police knew all the boys' 'other names'.

Chapter Nineteen

Meanwhile back at the volunteer house we were all becoming a nice little group of friends, and started planning a small holiday break to Mombasa, the southern coastal town of Kenya, situated on the Indian Ocean. The journey consisted of an eleven-hour overnight bus trip from Nairobi to Mombasa town, then a five-minute ferry ride followed by a thirty-minute tuk-tuk drive to Diani Beach on the south coast. We were all looking forward to it, and had heard the coast was gorgeous.

The weekend soon came around and we excitedly departed on our five-day mini-holiday. The bus ride was hilarious; a rickety old vehicle jam-packed with people, chickens, and luggage piled high up on the roof. We left Nairobi and the bus shook and rattled for the entire journey; sleep was almost impossible because of the crammed conditions, but at some stage during the night I must have dozed because I woke to find myself semi-sprawled over a poor young guy who was sitting on a cardboard box in the aisle next to me, and who was clearly too polite to nudge me upright into my own seat. Feeling embarrassed, I apologised to this poor man, but he was nonchalant about it, and not fazed at all that I had invaded his personal space.

The bus arrived at the busy port town of Mombasa at dawn, and as we alighted we were immediately swamped by local touters pushing and shoving and wanting our fare to escort us across the river on the ferry, and then the thirty-minute drive to our destination at Diani Beach. We chose two three-wheeled tuk-tuks because they looked like fun. However they turned out to be anything but fun as we were cooped up inside the canopy, unable to sit up straight, and with all our luggage piled on top of us for the thirty-minute ride, trying desperately to hold on to our bags as they teetered on the verge of falling out all over the road.

We arrived at our accommodation, a group of cute little cottages that we had found in a travel guide, situated right on the beach and nestled amongst beautiful palm trees and lawn. It was also home to a variety of monkeys, including the protected Colobus monkey who lived in the trees and roamed the property, entertaining us with their antics.

The coast was picturesque, with palm trees, snow-white sandy beaches, and very warm, aqua-green water. We checked into our rooms, dumped our luggage, and by 9:30 a.m. we were lying on the beach basking in the beautiful, fresh sea air thinking that life couldn't get much better than this at that point.

The following four days were spent in pure low-cost indulgence. We swam and snorkelled in the tropical Indian Ocean waters, had long early morning walks along the deserted beach, and sat around a table on our patio in the late afternoon sipping cocktails, playing board games, and soaking up this little taste of decadence.

Mombasa was a predominantly Muslim community and we noticed most of the people wearing the traditional dress of robes and head coverings, and in contrast there was also a large population of the Masai tribe living on the coast whose traditional dress comprised a selection of cloth, carefully draped over one shoulder, and lots of beaded jewellery and sandals made out of rubber tyre. They were a familiar sight on the coast as they herded their cattle and goats across the land or walked the beaches baring beautifully handcrafted beaded jewellery, leather sandals, and engraved wallets for sale.

The time passed quickly and before we knew it we were boarding a matatu back to the ferry, and then to the bus for the long journey back to Nairobi. It had been a great idea taking this short holiday, and had cemented our friendships very firmly, and the much-needed break away from our hectic lives in Nairobi was perfect.

The longer I was in Kenya, the more comfortable I felt, and the more it became my second home. My confidence in moving around Nairobi increased rapidly and I was feeling very happy and at ease with my new surroundings. Of course I missed Chris and the kids, but with such fantastic technology as skype, email, text, and phone, the world was a very small place now, and we never really felt too far away from each other.

I also made some wonderful new friends, and even though from different cultures, different backgrounds, and different circumstances, the friendships I made would forever be treasured.

With my new Kenyan friendships came invitations to attend important celebrations, so I was very excited the day I received an invitation to attend a Kenyan wedding. The grandson of one of my newfound friends Winnie, who was the housekeeper at the orphanage, was getting married and she invited me to attend. Weddings in Kenya were very grandiose affairs, with bridal parties of huge numbers, and it was not uncommon to have ten to fifteen bridesmaids, flower girls, and an equal number of groomsmen. No matter what the status, no expense was spared. Guest lists generally numbered around a thousand people or more. Entire villages turned out sometimes.

The wedding I attended was in a slum area of Nairobi, the families being extremely poor. The villagers all combined to contribute and assist with the wedding arrangements, preparations, and costs as best they could. I was just one of approximately 1,000 guests invited to Winnie's grandson's wedding, and I was also the only mzungu, so I felt extremely honoured to be part of such a truly extravagant occasion. I went into town to buy a gift, and decided on a beautiful wall clock. The service, held in a church deep inside the slum interior, was to commence at 11:00 a.m. (or so the invitation read), so of course I planned to arrive about twenty minutes early as we would in New Zealand. My friend Jane, the tailoring teacher from the orphanage, was also attending, so we arranged to meet up and go together. She was late, so I waited for her by a market, and as we walked to the church, I was worried we would be late too. No, I needn't have worried, it was some two hours later at around 1:00 p.m. that the bride and her party of attendants arrived at the church, and the service was finally able to begin.

The ceremony lasted two-and-a-half hours; it was a very lively celebration of traditional, formal proceedings interspersed with lots of singing, dancing, and loud clapping by both the wedding party and guests. Various groups of musicians performed items while women hollered and children bellowed at the top of their lungs. Guests wandered freely about, taking photos, swapping seats, and chatting with other guests during the ceremony. When it came to the exchange of rings, there were so many people crowded around taking photos of the couple that the rest of the congregation couldn't see a thing. It was fabulously loud, boisterous, and happy, and the church was full of joyful celebration.

When the service had finished, guests were invited to make their way to the reception which was a half-hour walk through meandering narrow lanes to the grounds of a children's orphanage, where clusters of exquisitely decorated marquees were erected on the lawn. The marquees were beautifully draped in orange, brown, and white tulle, and ribbon and enormous overflowing fountains of stunning flower arrangements cascaded down walls, over tables, and formed archways under which the bride and groom and the entourage of the bridal party traditionally walked through when arriving to join the reception party.

In Kenya it was tradition for guests to eat first before the bride and groom arrived at the reception, and so we feasted on beautiful

African dishes of beef and chicken curries, vegetable stews, and sweet soda drinks, while we listened to live entertainment.

There was an embarrassing moment for me as I joined the back of the long queue for dinner. I suddenly felt two hands grab at my arms, and before I could turn around, a lady promptly marched me down the line to the tables, thrust a plate into my hands, and pushed me to the front of the queue, insisting the staff serve me immediately. I was mortified, and proceeded to put up a mild protest. Nobody took a blind bit of notice and implied that it was a huge honour to have my presence at the wedding and asked me to allow my friends to treat me as an extra special guest. I relented, had my meal served, and quietly slumped back to the marquee to be with my friends.

It was Kenyan tradition that when the bride and groom arrive at the reception, they were greeted at the roadside by all the female guests, including wee children. As soon as the newly-weds stepped out of the wedding car, they were completely engulfed by women singing loudly, chanting, wailing, and dancing, and in a wave of slow movement they gently ushered the bride and groom up towards the reception area to be greeted by the other guests.

The festivities went on well into the early evening and I was not entirely sure when it finally finished, but at the time I left the reception, the party was in full swing. It was a wonderful occasion and one that I was truly grateful for having had the opportunity of experiencing.

I also had the privilege of attending a dowry ceremony during my time in Kenya. My friend Elizabeth's sister's dowry ceremony was taking place one weekend, and she invited me to go along. So, once again I jumped at the opportunity for another wonderful experience.

Dowry payments were debts incurred by a husband-to-be to the father of his new bride; in other words, it was payment for the privilege of marrying his daughter, and could consist of all manner of items from goats, cattle, camels, suitable gifts, and money, and could be on-going debt for several years depending on the agreement reached between the two families. Dowry played a very important part in Kenyan culture and was marked with a big celebration and ceremony. During my stay in Kenya I heard wide debate and media discussion over the dowry issue, that because the size of the dowry could be so crippling to a man and his family, many young people were opting not to go through with a marriage in order to avoid the dowry debt.

We set off from Nairobi early one Saturday morning squashed in the back of Elizabeth's brother's Toyota Corolla, and after a picturesque three-hour journey we arrived at the family shamba (meaning farm or plantation) high up in a remote mountain region north-west of Nairobi. The setting was breathtaking; a compact shamba with an immaculately maintained plantation of crops growing profusely in this obviously perfect climate, cows and goats wandering freely, and a small cluster of tiny clay houses nestled among plantations of banana trees.

Inside one of the houses, women were busy preparing the feast, with huge cauldrons of meat stews and vegetables bubbling away on an open fire, and sky-high stacks of chappati kept warm on hotplates. Meanwhile the men sat around outside in what appeared to be very important conversation.

I received an exceptionally warm greeting from all members of the family and although the language barrier was huge, as these people spoke no English, we somehow managed to communicate fairly well with the help of a lot of hand gestures.

Throughout the day, I was treated with nothing but the utmost respect, but again I felt uncomfortable. This celebration wasn't about me, and yet I was made a huge fuss of. Once again the women were fascinated with my hair and the young girls took great delight when I allowed them to brush and style it. I could tell I was obviously a big topic of conversation to them, and for many it was their first ever contact with a mzungu.

I was fascinated by the culture of these people, and I doubted that much had changed over hundreds of years. They were completely self-sufficient; they had to be in this remote location, cooking over open fires inside their homes, and they lived entirely off their land, including growing and processing their own tea and coffee. They bathed in, washed clothes in, and drank the water from the rivers and streams.

Women were, in my opinion, the backbone of Kenyan culture, and I could only describe them as super-women. They seemed to do everything. They fetched water in twenty-litre jerry-cans and then clambered up very steep embankments to their shambas with a jerry-can balanced on top of their head, plus sometimes another one in each hand; this process was often repeated half-a-dozen times or more a day. They tended the crops; they milked the cows; they chopped and carried firewood; they cooked; and they cleaned. This was just the way it was, and talking with many of the women during my time in Kenya, very many agreed they wouldn't have it any other way. I wondered if perhaps the women didn't think the men capable of such chores.

While I was on a tour of the shamba by Elizabeth and some other members of her family, I heard the faint sound of singing, chanting, and whooping way in the distance. It seemed to gradually get louder, and closer. Approximately fifteen minutes or so later, a procession of women, men, and children appeared through the thick forest and out in the lane, shuffling and swaying along to their singing, coming closer towards the shamba. This was the dowry procession. Almost all the women were bearing gifts either piled high on top of their heads, or secured to their backs by way of leather strapping looped around their foreheads. There were huge crates of soda drinks, enormous bunches of green bananas—that incidentally I tried to pick up off the ground, and couldn't even move them—there were sacks of vegetables, ugali, sugar, rice, and of course the sacrificial goat. And these were just the gifts to start the dowry offering; there would be much more to follow.

The bride's family and guests, including us, all gathered at the imaginary boundary line, where an exchange of greetings, words, and shaking of hands took place. This was a welcoming gesture by the family who then invited the procession onto the shamba for the traditional ceremony and thereafter the celebratory sharing of food and drink.

The goat was slaughtered and promptly thrown into another big bubbling cauldron and was left to boil on the open fire. Thankfully I was excused from witnessing the slaughter; I definitely could not have watched it. I stayed inside the house.

When the goat was cooked, the meal was served. The goat was carved up and the big cauldrons of beef, chicken, and vegetable stews were served from the fire. The goat was completely devoured, and all that was left was a mere handful of its very large bones. And even then, those remaining bones had been completely stripped of all flesh.

Once the meal was finished, it was time for the menfolk to proceed with the meeting to discuss the dowry. They retired to a private room where they closed the door and sat for several hours negotiating the dowry and whether it was sufficient or if further payments would be required, which was quite often the case. Meanwhile the womenfolk gathered the dishes, washed them in big tubs outside, re-organised the kitchen, and then set about preparing the food for the next meal that would take place when the men had finished their negotiations.

When the men emerged a few hours later, they celebrated the successful meeting with more food, and home-brewed beer, and proceeded to celebrate late into the evening. There was no mention of what discussion took place inside the private room, however. That was definitely not for the women to know.

As the evening wore on, the rains came suddenly and furiously, which signalled our departure, with great frenzy too I might add; apparently if we'd stayed much longer the rain would have made the dirt roads impossible to use and we could potentially have been holed up for days.

As it was, the drive home with nine of us piled into the Toyota Corolla, was somewhat hair-raising enough; however, after experiencing the constant ducking and diving, dodging ditches, potholes, ravines, and never-ending lumps and bumps in the road, not to mention the close encounters with other vehicles, mixed with the sheer blackness of the night, it didn't take me long to figure out that this was still most definitely the better option as a means to get home. I was told the original plan was to catch public transport from Nairobi and then back again, which would have involved chugging along in a rickety old bus for two hours, then hopping onto a boda-boda (small motorbikes used as transport on the mountain tracks) for the remaining journey up into the mountains to the shamba, and then the same process back home again. I was quietly very grateful that Elizabeth's brother came to our transport rescue at the 11th hour with the car. By the time we left to come home, it was raining hard, and very dark. Apart from the odd fire burning or lantern flickering through the bush, the night was very black, and thoughts of riding on the back of a boda-boda in the dark filled me with fear.

I loved to talk about the immense admiration I had for the women in Kenya, and here was just a typical example of why I was constantly astounded by their resilience and tough attitudes to life. As we were driving hurriedly away from the shamba to escape the rapidly increasing sodden dirt roads, we spotted a very elderly woman walking along the road in the pitch black night, guided only by a tiny lantern; she had been at the dowry celebration and was heading to her home. We stopped the car and she squashed into the back seat, the door not able to close because of the congestion; there were already nine of us. A good four or five kilometres later, we arrived at the foot of her shamba, which was situated at the top of a very steep embankment. She insisted we leave her at the bottom, and got out of the car. As we drove away I watched her through the back window, heaving herself up the steep slope to her wee hut, with just her tiny little lantern to guide the way. Had we not pulled up beside her and offered a ride, this elderly woman would have walked in the torrential rain.

I found the dowry celebration fascinating, and it was yet another one of those amazing African experiences I had the privilege of encountering, and it was very easy for me to see that this was one of those age-old traditions that make African culture so rich and important.

Chapter Twenty

Meanwhile back at the detention centre the library was proving to be a big hit with the boys. With Ano's help I had bought a cool selection of around 100 books to add to the dismal collection that already existed and it was building up nicely. I thought that if future volunteers could continue building up the library book collection, it would be a fantastic asset for the centre and the boys who were very enthusiastic and eager to read.

It also became a gathering point and soon many of the boys would come to choose a library book and just hang around wanting to chat with me. I learnt a lot of their situations and how they ended up being in a detention centre during these sessions. For many of them it was from simply running away from home, living on the streets and being picked up by the police. Others had got involved in crime, some serious, some minor, but enough to be charged and sentenced to up to three years at the detention centre. For some, their parents simply couldn't afford to look after them, so they had voluntarily placed them in the centre.

I also enjoyed listening to them talking of their plans and dreams, and the huge importance of what education meant to them, being fully aware that their futures would be very bleak without education. Some were also very smart and not a day went by without at least one of the boys coming and asking me if I could provide some financial assistance either with their education, to buy clothes and shoes, to pay for a bus ticket if they were given a home leave pass, or even just to buy a treat. I also learnt that many were very shrewd, and I became wary of those who tried to take advantage of my supposed wealth and generosity.

I was happy to help the kids who I decided were worthy of my assistance; namely the boys who had become my invaluable helpers, but I couldn't help everyone. I got pleasure from seeing that my little bit of help whether it be my time, or the odd donation of money to help with exam fees or transport, was impacting directly on the child. For example, I paid for one of my boys Elvis, who I had become very fond of, and an accompanying teacher to travel home to central Kenya because he needed his birth certificate to register for his final exams. The post was apparently too unreliable so the only sure way for him to acquire it was to physically go and collect it, but his aunt who was also Elvis's guardian couldn't afford the transport cost. Without the birth certificate this boy wouldn't have been able to complete his final graduation exams, meaning he wouldn't be able to move on to high school, and he was a very bright boy who had the potential to have a successful future.

He was so thankful and excited that the morning following his return to Nairobi he waited out in the lane for me to arrive so that he could show me his birth certificate and he had made a bead bracelet as a little thank you present. I was really touched.

I had to keep reminding myself that to a lot of Kenyan parents, who were earning an average wage, essentials such as transport costs, school fees etc. were an enormous struggle to pay, and more often when it came down to priorities, kids would simply have to miss out on education opportunities when there was not enough food on the table. There were many kids in the detention centre, and of course all other schools in Kenya as well, who missed out because their families simply could not afford the exam fees or other related costs.

Most of my Kenyan friends were paid a very low salary, though having said that, they were also very grateful to have a paid job; but when comparing salaries to costs of living, it was very hard to make ends meet. For some, 60% to 80% of income would go on rent alone, and the rest spent on their staple diet of rice, maize, and beans, with no allowance for extra costs. Parents were fully aware however that the single most important thing other than food that they could offer their children was education. So while I often found it annoying and frustrating to be constantly approached for financial help, the longer I was living in Kenya, the more I understood that these people were simply desperate.

Teaching was one of the lowest paid of all professions in Kenya; also teaching positions were more often obtained on a 'who do you know, and how much can you pay me if I employ you' basis. One of my teacher friends applied for a job at another school, but missed out on an interview because he couldn't pay the ksh20,000/- the school management was asking. My teacher friend Ano was teaching without receiving any pay at all even though he was lured to the school with attractive salary promises. He decided that teaching for no pay was better than not teaching at all because one day someone may put him on the payroll.

That was life in Kenya, and most Kenyans, while they were very proud of their country in terms of its people, culture, landscape, wildlife, and agriculture, were very frustrated with systems that seemed to continually keep the poor very poor and the rich very rich.

In spite of the frustrations of corruption, poverty, large population and chaos, there was a certain magic about Kenya that simply could not be explained, and inevitably left people always wanting to go back. You just couldn't help but love this country and its beautiful people.

Chapter Twenty-One

My new home away from home was lovely, and I felt settled and happy for the duration of my two-month stay. Volunteers were all staying for various lengths of time and so during my time, I saw many comings and goings. With every new intake, those of us remaining would speculate on the new arrivals. Although it was a sad time saying goodbye to newfound friends, it was also exciting having new flatmates and in our house I often described us as a melting pot, because we were all from different countries, different cultures, and were different ages. As we all worked at various placements around the vicinity of our house engaging in a variety of different lines of work, many evenings were spent sitting on our lush lawn offloading the days' events over a glass of wine or two … and sometimes, three or four. We each valued the opinions and input of the others and this was a great way to vent. Our days were tough, and we all had our stories to share.

A couple of the women were working at one of the orphanages close to where I was at the rehabilitation centre and becoming increasingly frustrated at the lack of medical care and treatment of the children who lived there. Most of the kids were plagued with ongoing skin infections and diseases, and so of course while not being treated, they were spreading like wildfire throughout the institution. We collectively decided to pool together some of our donated funds, buy medical supplies, and start a treatment programme for the kids. One of the volunteers from Australia was a registered nurse, so under her guidance we bought supplies of basic medical treatments such as antiseptic lotions, scalp treatments, and all sorts of creams for this and potions for that, as well as a supply of sterilised equipment to work with. We agreed that every Friday afternoon we would all get together at the orphanage for 'treatment time'. Although we could only manage to get together once a week, it was worth it, not just for the children, but also to show the staff that with continued regular care, the spread of some skin infections might well be brought under control very easily. Every child at the orphanage had, at the very least, ringworm and scabies, many of them covering their entire bodies, while others had horrific festering sores that needed urgent treatment. It was amazing how quickly these infections were brought under control with repeated care.

So every Friday afternoon we met at the orphanage and set up a temporary treatment centre outside on the grass. We would form a production line with each of us having a specific job, then organise the seventy-plus children into lines, and set forward with our process. We stripped, washed, disinfected, dabbed, blotted, and band-aided every child at the centre. Tending to the children was the easy part—trying to keep the wee ones under control while they waited their turn in the queue was the nightmare, and it took at least two volunteers to keep them from pouring tubes of antiseptic cream down their throats, drinking disinfectant, stuffing used cotton ball swabs into their mouths, and picking at treated scabs. It was exhausting, but worthwhile, and the exercise most definitely helped the children as we saw rapid results from what was really very little effort.

Kate, our registered nurse volunteer also spent a lot of time writing up good detailed notes and reports for the benefit of future volunteers who might replace us when we left Kenya, with the hope that the treatment programme would continue. Sometimes it takes very little to make a difference.

Chapter Twenty-Two

By late September my three months in Kenya was rapidly drawing to an end, and the final week was eventful, starting with an unplanned tooth extraction.

It was quite an ordeal because the roots to my tooth had been badly crushed weeks earlier while crunching on a barbequed corn cob I'd bought from a street hawker. I was apprehensive about going to a dentist in Kenya so I left it, thinking I could hang on until I arrived in Thailand, where I was to meet Chris, but it became seriously abscessed so I had no option but to go and get it sorted out.

My reluctance to visit a dentist in Kenya was largely due to pre-conceived ideas that I might die—or at the very least be forced to endure the worst pain imaginable because for some unknown reason I didn't think pain relief would be very high on the list when undergoing surgical procedures. I also worried about the state of hygiene and dental care. Well, I could not have been more wrong.

I lay there in the comfy dental chair, my eyes focused on the plasma TV attached to the ceiling, surrounded by all the gadgets and state-of-the-art equipment, with the marvellous dentist and his four lovely assistants dressed in pristine white uniforms and matching white face masks lined up and waiting to tend to the dentist's, and my, every need. There was an upmarket coffee machine, a water cooler, immaculate chrome and glass décor, and of course a marvellously cheap bill at the end of it all—this all contributed to my conclusion that a visit to the dentist could never get any better than that. I couldn't help but let out a little whimper however when the dentist informed me that my tooth was so badly infected that I would need to have it extracted right then and there, before proceeding to growl at me in an ever-so-kind sort of a way for leaving it so long, and that I was lucky I hadn't contracted meningitis and died.

Then there was another drama, this time at the rehabilitation centre. A small burglary had taken place in the deputy principal's office and management immediately suspected the boys to be responsible. They were made to drag their personal trunks out of the dorms and on to the grass playing field, where they were ordered to empty the contents out in a pile. They lit a fire and forced the boys to throw every personal item such as photos, clothing, shoes, letters, and other treasures onto the blaze. It was heart-breaking; for most of these kids, their treasured trunks held every personal possession they owned. The children were devastated and so was I and also some of the teachers. At the time of my departure from Kenya, they had still not found the culprits.

Meanwhile at the children's orphanage, four siblings aged between nine and thirteen years had arrived. They had been rescued by police from living on the streets in a town in Tanzania and were in a devastating state. They had been maimed since babies by their parents and had spent their entire lives being forced to beg on the streets. Their parents would go to them every night and collect their cash. I don't know why they were taken to an orphanage in Kenya, but their emaciated bodies and stick-thin legs from muscle wastage had doctors doubting they would ever walk again; it was horrific. I had never known anything so shocking. They spent their days clinging to each other in a room set aside for them, and that's where they remained for the duration of my stay in Kenya.

I spent my last weekend high up in the mountains of remote eastern Kenya, having been invited by one of my helpers at the detention centre, fourteen-year-old David, to accompany him on an overnight home-visitation to his family's shamba. This trip had been weeks in the planning because he was cared for under the Department of Corrections and was not allowed to leave the detention centre. However, after a lot of consultation between social workers, court, and the detention centre management, he was granted special leave, provided he was accompanied by a teacher and abided strictly by the rules enforced on him. Permission also had to be granted to allow me to go with them. Ano was the teacher appointed to accompany David.

In the very early hours of Friday morning we set off on a matatu. However this was just one of the many forms of transport we used to travel to David's family's shamba, which was in a very remote region of Mt Kenya some seven hours away. The journey was amusing and consisted of two matatu rides, two off-road dirt bike rides, incidentally with three of us including luggage and the driver jammed onto one small bike, and then to finish the journey we piled into a quarry truck, which delivered us to the shamba.

The setting was stunning, and the shamba consisted of the usual cows penned up in tiny little cow-sheds, chickens, dogs, puppies, and goats all running free amongst lush crops and banana trees. From the property was a spectacular view of Mt Kenya and surrounding mountain ranges, forests, and waterfalls. David's parents with their typical Kenyan hospitality made us very welcome and no sooner had we arrived than the customary feast of chicken broth followed by stew, vegetables, ugali, and chappati was set down in front of us.

After the meal David's parents Gladys and Matthew proudly showed us around the shamba, and we meandered among crop plantations, fish farms, and waterfalls. We piled on to two motorbikes and headed to the nearby village to stroll the markets and mingle with the local villagers. Gladys and I were on one motorbike, with a driver, and suddenly high up in the mountain pass, we ran out of gas. It was stiflingly hot, and there was nowhere to shelter from the blazing sun while we waited for help to come our way. What seemed like hours later the driver's friend came and rescued us, bringing a can of petrol with him, and so we proceeded on our way. For the first time I tried miraa, a legal narcotic plant grown profusely in that region of Kenya and widely used by many Kenyans. I didn't like it at all and wondered what all the fuss was about.

I had noticed upon arriving that there didn't appear to be a lot of room at David's family's shamba and I wondered where we would sleep. I quietly suggested to Ano that perhaps we should find some accommodation in the village, but he would have to broach the subject with Gladys and Matthew, mindful of not offending the family. After a lot of persuasion they finally agreed to the guesthouse idea, but weren't satisfied until they had found something they considered very suitable. As long as it was safe, secure, and provided clean rooms, then it was ok by me.

After finally finding a nice guesthouse and booking the rooms, we went for a meal in a local makeshift bar, then headed back to the guesthouse for a cup of chai. Upstairs was a communal sitting room, right next to my room, with a badly crackling and screeching TV, a small kitchenette area, and comfy chairs. We made chai and sat chatting. Shortly after, Ano retired to bed, and Gladys, Matthew, and myself stayed up for a while longer and had another cup of chai before they prepared to go home. I went downstairs to say goodbye to them, then after pottering about in the bathroom I went back upstairs to go to my room. Two armed police were now sitting on one of the couches in the sitting area almost directly outside my room, AK47s propped at their sides. We exchanged greetings and I went into my room, bolted the door, and wondered what these cops would possibly be doing there. I wasn't unnerved; in fact I felt almost at ease knowing they were directly outside my room. I heard them chatting to each other in low muffled tones, but I must have drifted off to sleep because I didn't hear them leave.

In the morning I met Ano out on the street as we were being picked up by motorbikes to be taken back to the family shamba for another meal before departing for Nairobi. I mentioned the police being at the house after he had gone off to his room and asked him if he knew why they would have been there. He said that being the local village police chief, Matthew would have organised them to act as my security for the night.

I hadn't given any thought to the fact that I might not have been in the safest environment, but felt pleased that my visit and security had been taken seriously. To me it was another area of rural Kenya that I hadn't seen before and I was happy soaking up the experience.

Ano pointed out that many of these people had quite possibly never seen a white person before, and that it was important to provide the utmost security for me. In hindsight I probably should have thought more about where I was going, but at the time it just didn't cross my mind that I might be a potential target. And I must add that I never once felt that my safety was in jeopardy. I felt very free in Kenya.

That morning when we arrived at the shamba, after exchanging greetings, David had rushed out to the yard, announcing he was going out to kill one of his chickens in my honour. Several minutes later he brought the poor plucked, bedraggled looking bird into the house, threw it in a pot, boiled it up furiously until it fell from the bones, and then served it up in bowls—mine first. The family sat and waited for me to eat before starting their own meals. I felt uncomfortable with this; eating home kill was not one of my most enjoyable pastimes, and the thought of devouring that poor little chicken that only an hour beforehand had been happily waddling around content in his little world, made me feel sick. I managed to force some of the meat down, and when the family went into the kitchen, I offloaded the rest to Ano.

After the meal, we got ready to leave for our journey back to Nairobi. David came inside with another chicken, this time a live one. He had bound his legs together and put it in a plastic bag, leaving just his head poking out the top. He had decided to take a chicken back to the head teacher at the rehabilitation centre as a thank you for having a major influence in allowing him to take the trip home. He had told me earlier that he wanted to take a chicken back to head teacher—it never occurred to me that he meant a live one.

The trip back to Nairobi was entertaining as David spent the entire journey trying to keep, by this time, a highly disturbed chicken from flapping and squawking around the matatu. The poor thing had to endure hours and hours of travel with its legs bound up with string, and semi-stuffed into the plastic bag. I was a little worried about its wellbeing, forgetting that in this part of the world chickens were placed on this earth for two reasons; eggs and meat. Any care or concern for a chicken would simply never occur. At one stage David had put the chicken on the ground at his feet, but it had wriggled its way under the seat in front—the one I was sitting on. I was scared it was going to attack me, so I spent some of the trip with my legs tucked up by my body, too afraid to put them on the floor. The only time I felt relaxed was when David had the bird beside him on the back seat.

My last days in Kenya were spent on goodbyes; mopping tears interspersed with farewell dinners, drinks, and parties at local nightclubs. In the early hours of my departure morning, there was a knock on our front door, which woke up the volunteer household. Apprehensively we opened the door, and standing there looking immaculately dressed, with a tiny little suitcase, were David's parents Gladys and Matthew. They had travelled all night from

138

their rural home by public transport, the same as we had taken the weekend before, to escort me to the airport, wait until my plane had departed, and then they would go to the matatu terminus and go back home again. This was one last moment in Kenya that I would never forget.

And so it was with sadness that the time came to bid farewell to what I fondly called my beloved Kenya, and one of the most amazing experiences of my life. An experience jam-packed with culture-shock; hard work; happiness; fun; laughter; at times immense sadness; exciting adventures; and above all the privilege of meeting and sharing three months of my life with some of the most beautiful people I was probably ever likely to meet.

Africa had changed me, without a doubt. Things that used to be important, were no longer an issue in my world. Leaving Kenya had quite a profound impact on me, and I just knew that I would be back again. The goodbyes were more 'until next time', because this wasn't the last time I would see these people who had become my Kenyan family, and who had had a major influence on how I now saw the world.

Chapter Twenty-Three

I was reunited with Chris at Bangkok airport. The plan was to meet in Thailand where we would spend a month backpacking through the southern islands before heading home to New Zealand. Chris's flight had arrived from New Zealand twelve hours ahead of mine, and he decided to stick it out waiting at the airport, so by the time my plane landed, there was much relief, not only from Chris but also the airport staff who had continuously checked on him, made sure he was ok, and reassured him my flight would arrive on time.

It was exciting seeing each other, of course. We'd missed each other a lot, there was no doubting it, and three months was a long time to be apart, but thankfully made much easier with the help of modern technology. We had so much to catch up on and we were both thankful to have the next month just to ourselves.

One of the first conversation topics to come up was Chris's keenness to return with me to Kenya in the near future so that he too could work with the teenage boys at the rehabilitation centre. After hearing me describe my experience there, the idea of working with the boys really appealed to him and he felt he had a lot to offer. And so, it didn't take us very long to start making plans for a return to Kenya the following year, 2011. Of course we had to really focus and save hard, but we thought it was an achievable plan. We could do our own travel arrangements, and by then I knew enough about Kenya, and had direct connections with the management at the rehabilitation centre and orphanages, which meant we could bypass the necessity of connecting through a volunteer agency, and thus save on the associated fees. I also knew that I could find accommodation easily enough.

We arrived back in New Zealand and I immediately swung into action, searching cheap flights and budget accommodation for a three-month stay in Nairobi the following year.

I joined budget travel and local websites and posted forum requests for temporary housing. I managed to secure a short-term contract at a guesthouse not too far from the detention centre, and it sounded perfect for our stay. I also made contact with the manager of the detention centre and together we organised a three-month plan. A friend of ours in New Zealand, Mandy, was also looking to do something a little different, combined with a trip overseas somewhere, so we invited her to join us for a couple of weeks. She jumped at the chance. I contacted the guesthouse owner and booked another room and organised a placement for her at the same detention centre. At the same time my cousin Nicole also expressed interest in doing some voluntary work so again I contacted the guesthouse owner and added another person to the booking. She wanted to work at an orphanage, so I organised a placement for her at the orphanage very close to the detention centre.

During this period of planning for our next trip, a 'beanies for Africa' knitting campaign was started, by accident really. Various friends and family had asked me for ideas for donations of clothing we could take back to Africa and I suggested beanies. I had remembered when I was working at the orphanage the year before how much the kids had loved the handful of beanies I had in my collection of donated goods.

The beanie project escalated and soon we had beanies rapidly overtaking a room in our house. Sometimes I would come home from work and find supermarket bags hanging on the front door, bulging with beautiful, brightly coloured hand-knitted beanies. Bags were dropped off at my work, through friends of friends, and I was soon receiving them from complete strangers. It was overwhelming and soon became a dilemma as to how we would be able to transport them to Kenya given our strict luggage allowance. We were also spending a few weeks backpacking through India en route to Africa, so the thought of dragging them with us was daunting.

I started by contacting the airlines with which we were flying, requesting lenience on our luggage allowance, but to no avail. We investigated courier and post but the cost was astronomical. We looked into sea freight and once again it was costly. A friend, Gary, who worked for a freight company came to our aid and agreed to help us out just a week prior to our departure from New Zealand. By this time we had well over 500 beanies.

We hastily bundled them up in solid tea chests and Gary collected them from our home in Wellington. A couple of days later, I received a phone call from the Auckland port saying the chests would be returned to us for formal identification and description cataloguing. Seemingly they needed full and detailed descriptions of each individual beanie, from strict colour detail to exact measurements. The task seemed enormous, especially when all this happened just a few days before we were due to depart for Africa.

We had no other real choice but to unpack our luggage, and re-pack, adding as many beanies as we could fit. Every pocket and every nook and cranny of our backpacks was bulging with beanies. Thankfully they were lightweight, and pliable, and we managed to pack in 350 of them, leaving a good 150+ behind. They would have to wait until the next trip. Thinking ahead, I emailed the guesthouse where we were staying for a couple of nights in Mumbai asking if we could leave the bulk of our luggage there while we travelled through northern India, with the promise of staying an extra two nights on our return before flying out of Mumbai for Nairobi. That worked a treat, and the owner was most obliging. The dilemma was solved.

Family connection – me and Edgar, South Africa

Sharing the braai cooking – resort holiday, South Africa

145

San Bushmen, Namibia

Okovango Delta, Botswana

African sunset, Chobe River, Botswana

Etosha Salt Pan, 130km long and 50km wide, Namibia

African 'angels', Tanzania

A Masai tribesman, Kenya

Great excitement at the orphanage
with the arrival of the brand new sewing machines

Completed garments from the talented girls at the orphanage. These garments
were all made from paper sugar sacks because they couldn't afford fabric

My library 'helpers', Detention Centre

Baby orphanage day visit

'Beanies for Africa' – over 500 beanies were hand-knitted by wonderful generous New Zealanders for us to take to Kenya as donations

Masai women standing by their manyatta, Masai Mara, Kenya

Bearing dowry gifts

Koha School

Our beautiful greeting from the school children, the day we arrived in Kenya

Not too late for Chris to change career

153

A basketball hoop – an old motorbike tyre and a tree is all that's needed for innovative African children

Beautiful children, Uganda

154

Two little girls who came running down a bank when they saw us walking in the lane. They were collecting water for their orphanage, Uganda

Jinja, Uganda

155

Tamariki Learning Centre, Kenya

Playtime at Tamariki Learning Centre, Kenya

A place we visited often. Waiting for our connecting matatu to our favourite hideaway, Lake Naivasha

Dancing like the locals – Malawi

Only in Africa – Victoria Falls, Zambia

PART THREE
UNBROKEN SPIRIT

Chapter Twenty-Four

We finally arrived into Nairobi after a long flight from Mumbai. Thankfully we breezed through Kenyan customs without a hitch, and the beanies were with us. I was a little worried that if they asked to check our luggage and found the mass quantity, it may have set off alarm bells, which could well have caused a problem. We could have faced a hefty fine, or perhaps even the possibility of having them confiscated at customs. We breathed a sigh of relief as we wheeled our luggage out into the waiting area of the airport—mission accomplished!

We strolled outside and hailed a taxi. With the help of the taxi driver's local geographical knowledge, we found our guesthouse with relative ease. As we drove from the airport, through Nairobi CBD, I felt overwhelming excitement to be back to what had begun to feel very much like my second home.

The guesthouse was gorgeous, and I was relieved to find it was just as I had imagined from viewing the photos on the website, but with so much more. A very large and spacious villa set in a beautifully manicured garden greeted us. The grounds were immaculately kept, and added to the high electric fences enclosing the property was a security guard at the gate providing twenty-four-hour security. There was also a housekeeper, cook, and gardener in residence to tend to the guests in the house.

The house was already occupied by some African university students from Zambia, Tanzania and Burundi. Two others, a guy and girl from Rwanda, who were cousins, were staying in the guesthouse for two weeks. The girl, Clarisse, was applying for a green card to work as a nurse in USA and her cousin Prosper had accompanied her to assist with the process. We took an instant liking to them all; they were friendly and fun. Some of them spoke English, but the others were difficult to understand, although we still managed to communicate really well. A few days later, Mandy and Nicole were due to arrive followed by Astrid a veterinary intern from Germany, and the house would be full.

In my luggage, along with the beanies, I had wool and knitting needles that had also been donated. I wondered if they were donated just in case we ran out of beanies and we could whip up a few more in our spare time. One evening I hauled the wool and needles out of my pack and asked two of the girls in our house Lwimba and Clarisse if they would like me to teach them how to knit. They were very keen, and took to it very easily. Clarisse, who decided to knit a scarf, was completely hooked. She couldn't put her knitting down and it grew at a rapid rate of knots.

Chris was keen to start work at the detention centre, so the following morning after arriving, we set off for our first day of work. I was really excited to see the staff and the boys again, and most importantly Ano. I wanted Chris and Ano to meet; they had both heard a lot about each other and I knew they would be eager to finally meet in person. However, to our disappointment, he was no longer there—the manager informed us he had moved to teach at a private school. I was instantly happy with that news because it meant that finally he would be receiving a salary. He gave me Ano's phone number, I contacted him, and we made arrangements to meet for lunch in a café.

It was really good to see him, and I mentioned that it was great news to hear he had changed jobs and was finally getting paid for his work. He explained that for the first couple of months he was being paid and all was well, but that had soon changed because there was no further money for salaries. So, Ano and his family were back living as before … from hand to mouth, day to day. They still lived in the derelict old shack behind the detention centre, with no power, no water, and very little food. They washed in the stream behind their house; collected tree branches for firewood; used the fire for cooking and heating; used an old kerosene lantern for light; and an old broken long-drop toilet was used for ablutions.

We spent the afternoon catching up on all the news of the last twelve months, and then when it was time to go, we sent him on his way with an enormous bag of groceries I had gathered together prior to meeting him.

Chris and I stayed on in the café, and over another coffee we started discussing Ano's circumstances and the reality that he was just one of millions living in the same poor conditions.

With a hint of meaning, I casually said to Chris, "Wouldn't it be cool if we could build a little school in a big slum for fifty kids, and we could have Ano run it?"

I went on to say that if we could afford it, we could pay his and one other teacher's salaries and also pay for the basic running costs of the school. That way we would be helping Ano considerably, plus providing fifty children the chance of an education.

I expected Chris to scoff at the idea, and dismiss it as just another one of my 'pie in the sky' ideas, but he didn't. He actually quite liked it and suggested we first find out if it was something we could do here in Kenya. We didn't know anything about Kenyan laws, and certainly nothing about education, setting up a school or running a school. Neither of us came from an education-related background, so the idea of establishing a school was possibly a little far-fetched, but nevertheless once the seed was sown it was very hard to back away.

Of course, at that stage, we also didn't even know if we could afford it.

Hesitantly we had to tell Ano and run our idea past him to find out if it was something we could potentially do. We also had to be careful not to get his hopes up, especially if we suddenly realised we couldn't afford it.

Ano, as expected, was extremely excited by the idea, and immediately tracked down a couple of builders to give quotes to build three classrooms and two toilets, which on top of renting land, and buying equipment such as desks, blackboards, and school resources, all added up to making it a do-able project.

We agreed to be directed and guided by local community in the construction of the school. After all they lived there, and knew best. It had to be an African school, and we also agreed that Ano would be responsible for running the school.

Meanwhile our two Kiwi visitors, friend Mandy and cousin Nicole, arrived the following weekend, and we were very excited to see them and swap news stories. Of course, big in our news was the plan for the new school and we didn't hesitate in asking them if they were keen to come on board with the project. They both said yes they were, so after doing the sums, over and over, we decided we would go ahead. Chris and I pledged to financially support the school on a monthly basis once the initial set-up was complete and operational. Funding two teachers' salaries and the general costs of running the school with fifty kids amounted to very little in our world, and we decided that this was going to be our contribution to helping fight poverty in the world, which up until that point had consisted of a few coins thrown into a collector's bucket out on the streets of Wellington.

Suddenly everything became very exciting and moved at a rapid rate. Ano had to firstly receive written approval from the village chief to have a school built in his constituency. He then had to find suitable land on which to construct a school. This he found within twelve hours of receiving the approval to go ahead from the chief. We met the landowner and after agreeing to the rent payment, we secured the lease. The plot was in the slum of Kawangemi, a very large community situated on the outskirts of Nairobi with an estimated 500,000+ residents (nobody knew exactly for sure).

It was a nice site, in a semi-rural location, and had been used for growing crops and bananas. Ano managed to track down three builders to give quotes, and selected one to go ahead and build the classrooms. Literally within minutes of giving the builder and his labourers the go ahead, they started stepping out the estimated building site, picking up machetes and clearing the vegetation. After a short time of this they stopped, processed in their head what materials they would need to get started, and set off on foot to the local builders' merchant. They arrived back an hour later with all sorts of building materials piled up high on their heads and shoulders, followed by a young boy pushing a hand-cart loaded with bags of cement and sand. Within a couple of hours the holes were all dug for the stone foundations and the construction of a three-room building was underway.

Very many of the residents of Kawangemi didn't have jobs, and so it wasn't altogether surprising that we had endless offers of help from locals who had nothing better to do with their days than to come to the mzungu building site, pick up a machete, and start slashing vegetation, or pick up a hammer and start hammering nails.

The site was a hive of activity and within twenty-four hours the framework and trusses, which all consisted of tree branches, were erected, and the concrete floor was prepared for laying. The floor caused an element of intrigue in the local community because apparently most other schools and churches in the vicinity consisted of a dirt floor, so concrete was considered a luxury.

Meanwhile back at home we had swung into action and drafted a constitution, formed a Trustee Committee, typed up an agenda, conducted our first preliminary meeting, and had the minutes typed and distributed.

Chapter Twenty-Five

Chris, Mandy, and Nicole were starting to feel settled at their placements at both the detention centre, and orphanage, so their time spent at the school site was limited to after work. Chris really enjoyed his time at the detention centre where he promptly initiated teaching basic carpentry skills to the boys, making wooden frames for the soccer posters he had brought from New Zealand, and fixing broken school chairs, desks, and cabinets—but his mind was also on the construction of our new school.

Life at home in the guesthouse was fun and we all became good friends. We enjoyed having our young flatmates around; they were mostly all university students who took their studies very seriously, sometimes up till the wee hours with their noses in textbooks. The house was gorgeous with large, spacious grounds, and we spent hours lounging around on the grass after being at our projects all day.

We decided that as my voluntary role for the year was going to be more ad hoc, and I was not specifically assigned to any institution or placement, I would forego a few days each week to assist Ano in working on the administrative side of establishing the school. My plan for the three months in Kenya was to teach a few girls dressmaking, pattern drafting, and knitting, so that they could be resourceful by setting up their own little businesses and selling their handiwork. So, this way I could work my timetable to fit in where needed.

Ano asked us if we would give the school a name, and also write a motto, vision, and mission statement, so considering the New Zealand connection we chose 'Koha School' as the name, and the motto as Kia Kaha, meaning 'stand strong'.

We started the process of formally registering the school with the Education Department and I quickly learnt this would be a long and lengthy process compared to building the school. The school was rapidly taking shape but the process of formally registering the school and dealing with bureaucracy and government was a different story. I understood the registration process would take time, however I felt the more we could achieve while we were still in Kenya, the better.

My patience however was tested to the max one day when we had to go to the government offices to sort out some of the requirements of the school curriculum. There didn't appear to be an appointment-making process in Kenya so we arrived super early this particular morning, thinking we would be extra clever and get ahead of others who planned on visiting the office that day. However it seemed many other Kenyans had the same idea, and by the time we arrived there was already a long trail of people starting from the counter inside, trailing outside, down several steps and along the path. We joined the queue and proceeded to wait. And wait. All through the morning we waited. At 12:00 noon the office door suddenly banged shut and an office clerk promptly slapped a notice on the door announcing they would reopen at 2:00 p.m. Still we waited, the doors reopened at 2:00 p.m. and we continued to wait. 4:30 p.m. came along and I had well and truly had enough, especially as the offices closed for the day at 5:30 p.m., and the thought of having to repeat the process the following day was unbearable.

I spotted a very important-looking young office clerk walking around with a clipboard. I committed the ultimate sin and asked Ano if we might be able to pay him a small amount of cash to fast track our time in the queue. Ano called him over, and asked him if there was any way he could help us with our paperwork and in return we would give him ksh100/-. He promptly marched up to the counter, butting in on the customer standing there, spoke to the counter clerk briefly, came back to us, and ushered us to another counter where we were served and out of there in five minutes. I felt ashamed and annoyed with myself that I had stooped to the level of bribery and corruption, the very acts that had helped to cripple that country and of which I had a very strong adversity to. I declared right then and there, that I would never do it again, and to this day I haven't, although the temptation was very hard to resist at times.

And so this pretty much became a daily routine at whichever office Ano and I had to go to. The queuing and waiting for endless hours to speak to the 'right people' became very much a normal day, and I have to say the Kenyan people were extremely good at waiting … for anything ... they just simply waited.

I remembered a time the year before when I was doing my voluntary work and my visa was due to expire. I went into the visa office to have it updated. The offices were packed with Africans all just waiting, so I too proceeded to wait. After about two hours I started pacing a little. This went on for about half an hour when suddenly it dawned on me that there were two of us quietly pacing the room—another mzungu, and me. We could learn so much from African people in the art of patience.

Meanwhile the school building was progressing quickly. It was interesting to watch the construction developing, and the materials used; twigs for stakes and pegs, tree branches for the framework and roof trusses. Quarry stones and cement/sand were used for the foundations, which also served as a dual purpose in stopping ants and termites that seem to be the biggest problem that faced buildings in Kenya.

All materials were bought as locally as possible, and transported sometimes two to four kilometres by head, shoulders, and hefty wooden push cart usually operated by two men; one pushing from behind, and the other positioned in front, leaning back against the cart to act as a brake. Men would often walk through crowded lanes with long lengths of steel rod protruding for many metres in front and behind them, and one had to be very careful to steer clear of these lethal weapons. The quarry stones arrived by a battered up old truck that rattled and rolled through the village, and down to the school, often getting stuck in loose dirt and sand, wheels screaming, smoke billowing.

Once the framework was up and we could see the school building starting to take shape, Ano could stand it no more, and decided to share the news of the new school with his extended family. He knew he only had to phone his mama to be sure to have the news spread around his sisters and brothers who were scattered throughout Kenya.

Within a few hours of hearing the news, they were on their way from their rural areas to gather at mama's shamba in remote western Kenya to celebrate the good news and to each call us to express their gratitude and excitement. There was a goat slaughtered in our honour, in our absence.

Next morning, Ano's brother Peter was headed for Nairobi to meet us and see this exciting new school project. It was nice to meet another member of Ano's family and good to have someone to assist and accompany us when we went to visit the Education Department to discuss paperwork and also the cabinetmaker to discuss having desks and blackboards made.

We started to get really excited. I felt this was going to make a big difference to a small number of kids, not just for the time we were in Kenya doing voluntary work, but also in the future.

For me, I appreciated that the single most important thing parents could provide for their children was an opportunity to have an education, and knowing the situation with the scarce, over-crowded public schools, and the difficulty in obtaining a place in one, it created a very special feeling for me that we were able to offer this opportunity to a few more kids who would otherwise have more than likely missed out.

Meanwhile, the emails and text messages of support, plus monetary donations to our bank account from friends and family, started pouring in from home, and it was amazing, truly amazing. It suddenly gave us more options in terms of setting up the school and the resources we could afford to buy. People also offered to send stationery and other items to us, but we reluctantly had to turn those offers down, as the chances of the parcels actually getting to us was doubtful. We explained that if people wanted to donate, then money was by far the best option and we could then buy as much as possible, such as the stationery items and other resources needed, in the local community, which would help them greatly.

I decided to teach Ano's wife Everlyne to knit. She had admired the beanies we brought with us, and this gave me the thought of her possibly starting a little business for herself. So one morning, armed with knitting needles and wool, I visited her and we spent the morning sitting out on the grass under a tree and I taught her to knit basic stitches. She picked it up almost immediately, and by the time I got back to see her the following week she had well grasped basic knitting stitches. I had many balls of wool with me, which I thought I would give to her to get her beanie supply going. I also researched a couple of NGOs in Kenya where she could possibly get wool donated. She loved it and got very excited when I suggested that maybe one day she could have enough beanies to start up her own little market stall.

Chapter Twenty-Six

After a couple of weeks we were all getting tired and in need of a small break. Mandy and Nicole only had a short time with us, so we decided a weekend escape to the beautiful coast of Mombasa with hot sun, snow white sand, and warm, clear Indian Ocean waters was just what was needed. We also talked one of our housemates Michael from Zambia into coming with us. He'd never been to the coast and had never seen the ocean before.

The twelve-hour journey to the coast was a new experience for the others and for me it was equally as chaotic, scary, and tiring as the trip I made with the volunteers the previous year. However the coast was so beautiful, the journey was very much worthwhile. I had booked us into the same place that we girls had stayed at the year before, right on the beach and very cheap, but comfortable and clean.

We all really enjoyed Michael's first beach experience, him having never seen or touched sand, sea water, or sea creatures. He had never seen surf and waves. It was a whole new world for him and he thrived on the new experience. Chris took charge and had him out in the water splashing and frolicking about in the waves, and he absolutely loved it—so much so that we had difficulty getting him out of the water.

We also booked a boat ride out to a small sandy reef. The crystal-clear waters beneath the glass-bottom boat were perfect for viewing life under the sea, and when we anchored at the reef, we dived into the water with masks and snorkels and saw the most amazing sea life; fluorescent coloured starfish and small fish, unusual shells, and crabs.

We spent many hours strolling along the miles and miles of open beach, chatting with the locals, in particular the young men and Masai who were often lingering outside the various beachfront hotels, resorts, and guesthouses waiting to pounce on unsuspecting tourists in an attempt to sell their local handcrafts and trinkets.

We discovered a small bar that had been set up in the sand, comprising a few tree branches, with the universal plastic tables and chairs scattered under a large tree. It became our 'local' where we went to have a bite to eat and enjoy a couple of beers when the sun was too hot and we needed a rest. One late afternoon we were enjoying a drink and we noticed a skinny, neon green snake slithering its way up a tree and across the top of a fence. Of course, being Kiwis, we were not at all familiar with snakes and we closely watched the direction in which it was headed. Our trusted African friend Michael reassured us it was not dangerous and we need not worry. However, to our horror we discovered later that it was in actual fact a deadly green mamba snake.

It was a perfect few days, and before we knew it, it was time to pack up and head back to Nairobi. We felt rested, refreshed, recharged, and ready to get stuck into our projects once again.

We arrived back home and couldn't wait to visit the school to see what had developed since we'd been away. It looked amazing, like a proper building, with the walls and roof enclosed, two little windows, a doorframe cut out, and a nicely laid concrete floor. Meanwhile excavation had also started behind the building, which we learnt was the toilet pit. Toilets in the slums were just a large hole dug in the ground, with a concrete floor laid over the top comprising a small round hole, and a framework of iron sheet walls and roof. In the slums there was no sewerage connection which meant that when the pits were full, Ano would have to call a sewage company, who would send a pump truck to come and pump out the waste.

Building a school in the slums of Kenya was not only an exciting experience but also a major learning curve. It really highlighted our different cultures in many ways and we had to make a conscious effort to remember that this was Africa, not New Zealand. The buildings were not going to be the same, and building standards were definitely not going to be the same, and also the meaning of the word 'quote' was not necessarily going to be the same either. We found out the hard way that it really means more an estimate, which started to cause us all sorts of frustration when dealing with the builders.

At the very beginning we had specifically requested a firm quote—that what was written on the quote, was what we paid. We thought we made it very clear. We also asked that they include absolutely everything needed to complete the school building and toilet block as we were on a tight budget and it was essential we accounted for everything before starting. With their limited but satisfactory English, the eager nodding of heads, and shaking of hands, we had thought the builders had fully understood the importance of this. Apparently this was not so.

Soon after starting the building, we were asked for money for basic items like nails and screws because they hadn't allowed enough in the quote. Then we had to buy a handsaw and a hammer because one hammer disappeared and the handsaw was blunt. They also took it upon themselves to extend the building by another two metres, because hey, why not? This of course meant more building materials and then more labour costs because they had roped in another couple of builders to help out. Then they asked for money to pay cousin 'So-n-So' because he had helped cart materials through the village, and also a couple of the builders' friends too because they had helped in slashing maize crops away. Not that those particular maize crops were anywhere near the building site, but nevertheless, they just decided to clear them.

Chris had to call a meeting to say enough was enough. Fortunately we had a contingency slush fund, but its purpose was not for paying out every Tom, Dick, or Harry who decided they needed some cash for the day. If it wasn't for the fact that we were somewhat amused by all this, then I'm sure we would slowly but surely have started to go quite mad.

Then there was the workmanship, and the beautiful uniqueness of our little school that had the builders, Ano, and the community beaming with pride, and then there was us who just smiled while shaking our heads in amusement. There were crooked doors—or was it the straight doors fitted into the crooked frames? There was the tree branch framing still covered with twigs, leaves, and bark; the gaps between the walls and the roof so large that birds flew in and set up home; and of course the window shutters that actually did close, but only if you heaved them into place and bolted them quickly into the frame. We loved it all and added a very unique flavour to our little piece of Kiwiana in the middle of an African slum.

The community was abuzz with talk of the new school and how beautiful it was looking … after all, it had a concrete floor! That was one thing we insisted on, a good solid floor, unlike many houses, schools, churches etc. that had dirt floors. A couple of small schools close to Koha School had dirt floors, and the children had no desks, so they sat on the floor, and instead of having exercise books to work in they used the dirt to write their lessons in.

Apart from the concrete floor, we were very careful when we decided to build the school not to charge in with our western ways and gung-ho ideas. We were very mindful that this was an African school and we wouldn't have it any other way.

We discovered there were three very important things essential in registering a Kenyan private school: (1) A uniform must be worn, (2) A photo of the Kenyan president must be on display in the school office, and (3) the Kenyan flag must be raised on a Friday and Monday with a formal ceremony. We had numbers (2) and (3) sorted, but no uniform.

We agreed we wanted something special and unique for our school, and settled on a short-sleeved dress with white trim and black waistband, black jumper, white socks, and black shoes for the girls, and the same dress fabric for a shirt, black shorts, black jumper, red socks, and black shoes for the boys. It sounded so smart.

One day I asked Ano to take me to look for fabric. We caught a bus to a suburb called Eastleigh, which was the home of textiles and a wonderful place to go to in search of something a little different to the normal run-of-the-mill fabric shops in downtown Nairobi. We arrived at Eastleigh and as soon as we alighted the bus, I felt a little overwhelmed and clutched at Ano's arm as tightly as I could while we ploughed our way through hordes of people for fear I might lose him in the chaos. We walked along the street and through an arcade that had hundreds of kiosks all selling fabrics of every description, colour, texture, and pattern. As we walked by, a colourful fabric caught my eye and I knew instantly that it was perfect; a red, white, and black diamond-shaped pattern that reminded me of New Zealand. I loved it, I thought it was gorgeous. We bought the three rolls the shopkeeper had in stock and asked him to perhaps order some more just in case. We then bought some of the contrasting black and white fabric trim, popped into a uniform shop along the road, and bought a couple of pairs of shorts and jumpers.

We went back to Kawangemi and Ano went in search of a tailor to sew some dresses and shirts so that we could display a couple of completed uniforms at a planned open day for the school the following weekend.

They looked beautiful when finished and very different to anything else we had seen anywhere. The school uniform was very important in Kenya and Ano said ours was so unique that it could have been a lure for parents to bring their children to Koha School.

Nicole left Kenya and Mandy went on a trip to Ethiopia, but came back to Kenya for a few days before flying home to New Zealand. We still had another six weeks before we too would be leaving and we were hoping the school would be open before we left.

So, one month after signing the lease on the land, with the structure all but complete, Ano put an invitation out to twenty families in the immediate surrounding area to attend an open day at Koha School one Saturday morning. The aim of this was to get a feeling of interest more than anything. We had by this time purchased some curriculum text books and small stationery items, which we put out on display along with a set of both boy and girl uniforms. We printed off a few flyers outlining basic information about the school as well as our motto, vision, and mission statement. We hired some white plastic chairs from a local church, blew up loads of balloons, and set up a party atmosphere. We also decided as a goodwill gesture to give out a beanie to every child who attended the open day.

Ano had invited the families to arrive at 10:00 a.m., so Chris, Mandy, and I got up extra early to catch a matatu to Kawangemi Village to be sure of arriving ahead of time. We got there around 9:45 a.m. expecting to find everything set up, chairs out, displays set up, uniforms hung up, but no, instead there was not a soul around and nothing remotely organised at all. We found Ano down at the stream behind the school plot, filling a container with water so he could water his newly planted cuttings. We promptly sent him off to gather all the display items that were being stored at his friend's house for safekeeping, but he came back a couple of minutes later unable to contact the friend who had evidently gone off to collect all the chairs to bring to the school and whose phone had run out of battery charge.

By 11:00 a.m. a handful of people had arrived, but we still had no chairs for them to sit on, no textbooks, no display items, and no tables to display them on. Nobody minded except us of course—they were happy to wait for everything to fall into place, as Kenyans were very clever at doing. Of course we should have remembered by this stage that time means absolutely nothing in Africa, and the only people showing any signs of mild stress were of course us three.

By 12:00 noon everything was in place, the school building was packed out with more than fifty parents, and we had a very successful event. One parent took a register of interest from parents, and by the end of the session we had received forty-two registrations for when the school officially opened. We knew then that we were on track to have our planned fifty children enrolled as our first intake of pupils at Koha School.

Chapter Twenty-Seven

The school was situated on the outskirts of Kawangemi slum and from where we had to alight the matatu it was an approximate two-kilometre walk through the village and down to the school. The walk was always highly entertaining and not a day went by without something attracting our attention. There were what seemed like a million people, mostly walking, not entirely sure where to, or where from, but everywhere people were heading somewhere. The slum was a mixed blend of thousands of knocked-together tiny wooden or iron sheet shacks, often two metres squared in size, that served many purposes e.g. as houses; churches; worship centres; kiosks; shops; tailoring workshops; mechanic workshops; butchers; carveries; and schools. Together with the hundreds of thousands of residents, it was very difficult to decipher what was what. Ghettoblasters with speakers screeched out all over the village 24/7, belting out an eclectic mix of music that was African, traditional drumming, reggae, 70s/80s, and back to Elvis and the 50s/60s.

Careful attention had to be paid at all times when walking down to the school as there were very many obstacles that could easily end in tears. For one, there were lots and lots of people sitting or sleeping; women bent over scrubbing and washing clothes in plastic basins; men squatting on the ground assembling furniture, fixing bikes, or welding metal; butchers carving up animals and cooking them in enormous cauldrons; kids playing in the dirt; girls braiding hair; and people peddling bikes laden sky-high with all sorts of things, ducking and diving amongst the men pushing hand-carts laden with bags of cement and timber. Cows, goats, chickens, and dogs also roamed freely, rifling through rubbish looking for scraps to eat. And then there was the very real possibility of being knocked over from behind by a speeding motorbike, or a battered up old matatu. I always walked through the village constantly checking my surroundings to make sure I didn't trip over a body, be snapped at by a rabid dog, or get run down by a vehicle. But we loved it. The atmosphere was electric and we thrived on chatting to the familiar locals as we regularly passed by.

We hadn't seen any other white people in the village and we were clearly a source of intrigue to the locals. We got very used to them making a point of coming up and saying hello or shaking our hands, or the children constantly chanting, "Mzungu, mzungu, how are you? How are you?" in a tune that became very familiar. This would continue until we were well out of sight.

The beanie dispersion went very well and we often spotted one of our beanies perched on top of a local head in the village. We had started taking bags of them when we left home in the morning and giving them out to people along the way to school. It was extremely satisfying to be able to give people something that I knew they would really treasure.

Claire, my friend from Ireland, had arrived in Kenya for a month's voluntary work at an orphanage on the other side of Nairobi, so we arranged to meet up and also for her to visit the school. It was really exciting to see her again, and we had a lot of fun reminiscing about our time in the volunteer house the previous year, and enjoyed a couple of nights out in a local nightclub, which we both knew well. Claire came and spent a day with me at the school and helped with painting the classrooms; one yellow, one blue, one green, and they looked beautiful.

The school was coming along nicely and I was really longing to get stuck into the painting. We decided to paint the exterior a dark red/brown and I was ultimately responsible for that project.

However, the novelty wore off very quickly, and one day as luck would have it, a young man who I had spotted on a couple of occasions hanging around with the builders approached and asked if he could paint for me in return for some food for his family. It was a done deal. It meant I got let off the hook with the paint brush, and this young man had a day's work and food on the table for his family.

It was one of the cool things about the school project, being able to involve the community as much as possible. I was constantly impressed by the amount of people who fronted up asking for work—security guards; teachers; cleaners; cooks; gardeners; and caretakers.

One afternoon a young man wandered on to the site clutching a folder under his arm containing art. He had a dreadful speech impediment and couldn't string a sentence together; however he proceeded to proudly show me his artwork examples and I gathered he was looking for work. His art was beautiful and I hired him on the spot to paint some design work around the door frames and windows of the school. That evening we played around with a few designs on the internet until we were happy, printed it off, and the next day when our budding artist turned up for work we produced a printed version of what we wanted. He cleverly copied the exact replica onto the door frames and window frames and we were thrilled to pieces with the finished look. And he was extremely happy, because he had money.

We also hired one of the parents who had enrolled her daughter at Koha School to make the school uniforms for the pupils. She lived across the road from the school and so we were able to send parents directly to her when they came to enquire about the school uniform.

Everything was coming together nicely and was on track for the official opening day of the school on 5 September 2011. We had brought over a lot of stationery that had been donated by kind-hearted friends and family in New Zealand, which came in very handy for kick-starting the resources cabinet that we had bought in the village one day.

Ano and I had acquired a list of National KCPE (Kenya Certificate in Primary Education) curriculum text books and set off on a hunt for the best deals at the teacher resource shops.

We had hired a cabinetmaker in the village to build two mobile classroom dividers so that our building could be split into three separate classrooms but could also be used as one large room for assemblies and parent meetings. We also contracted him to build three blackboards and twenty-four combined desks/seats, each desk to accommodate three children. The day all the furniture arrived was exciting, and suddenly the building was really starting to look like a little school. In my opinion the classrooms still lacked colour and brightness so I went up to the village shops and bought colourful alphabetical and numerical charts to hang on the walls. I found fluorescent paper in a stationery store in Nairobi, so I bought various colours and cut out large alphabet letters, placing them around the rooms. Suddenly the rooms were looking bright, colourful, and cheerful.

One morning we arrived at the school and Ano informed us his eldest sister Jermima and husband were on their way to Nairobi from Kitale, near the border of Kenya and Uganda. We had spoken on the phone a few times so I was really excited to be meeting her. The trip would take them eight hours and they were due to arrive mid-afternoon. They would spend the remainder of the afternoon with us at the school, then catch a matatu back to Kitale in the evening. We had a nice time together and Ano was proud as punch showing off his new school. Everything was starting to take shape and really all that was missing were children.

The rains came suddenly and furiously late one afternoon, lasting all of about half-an-hour, and they seemed confined to one area of Nairobi. This one sudden flash flood caused mayhem, with mudslides, collapsed power poles, and horrendous traffic problems. The school suddenly had a torrent of water running through it, and it was at that stage we counted our blessings that the builders' levelling accuracy was not quite perfect, because the slight lean on the building allowed for good drainage. I was not entirely sure this was purpose-built for this reason, but it certainly paid off in the long run. The flash storm caused power outages off and on for days afterwards.

One afternoon shortly after when we were walking to the school, Chris decided to pop into a local barber's kiosk that he had spotted en route. He was desperate for a haircut so announced he would stop off there, and then meet us at school. No more than about five minutes later he appeared looking slightly sheepish and bemused, and took off his cap to reveal a somewhat disastrous looking new hairdo. He looked exactly the same as when we had left him at the barbers, except for a strip shaved down the centre of his head; an aircraft landing strip sprang to mind.

We all laughed hysterically and asked what on earth happened. Apparently the barber had no sooner set to it with the electric clippers than the power suddenly went out, so the barber simply packed up his clippers and told Chris to come back the following day and he would finish his hair cut. Hakuna matata—no problem! Fortunately the power did come back on a couple of hours later, so he raced back up to have his haircut finished off before the imminent power cut once again.

Chapter Twenty-Eight

O n 1st August 2011 we opened the school for our first operational test run. It was school holidays and Ano had offered a holiday tuition programme to children who wanted extra study. It was a chance to see how the school would run and to iron out any teething problems that may have cropped up. Ano had employed two trained female teachers and everything was pretty much all set to go.

We arrived at the school early on this day expecting to be busy with greeting parents and taking holiday enrolments, but surprisingly we arrived to a very calm, orderly school in full operation; two classrooms full of kids sitting at their little desks, books open, pencils in their hands, reciting the alphabet, doing sums, and teachers writing on the blackboards at the front of the class. However, the sudden realisation that in one month we had built a school and it was now already semi-functioning, with children sitting at desks, with textbooks and qualified teachers was almost hard to comprehend. We still had a little way to go before the school was ready for its official opening day on 5th September 2011, but nevertheless, everything was falling into place and the holiday programme was proof that the school would work.

It was a huge learning curve. I suddenly realised how precious the most basic of stationery was to the children. Simple things that we take for granted in the western world like a sticker placed on a page in their exercise book brought squeals of delight, as did the skipping ropes, balls, and card games we had brought with us. Most of the kids had never seen stickers or skipping ropes before. Skipping ropes were made from vine pulled from trees in Kenya, not tailor-made ropes with handles. Children who lived in the slums struggled to survive on the most basic things in life, so this was all very foreign to them and a little overwhelming to begin with.

A couple of days after opening for holiday tuition, we received an official visit from the government offices, as part of the registration process. I had been a little nervous about the upcoming visit, and hoped everything was ok and we had things in place correctly. It went very well and apart from a few small issues we had to sort out, it was all really good, positive feedback that we received.

The following weekend after opening for holiday tuition, we were invited to travel to western Kenya to meet Ano's family. We were really excited about it; another adventure to a remote place we had never even heard of.

We left Nairobi very early in the morning and travelled eight hours by matatu, crossing the equator, passing through Eldoret to the rural town of Bungoma. From Bungoma town, we took a boda-boda for approximately forty-five minutes, right into the thick of rural Kenya to Ano's mother's shamba. Again it was one of those experiences where we were clearly a novelty to the local people.

Western Kenya was beautiful, with expansive green farms of lush banana, maize, sugar cane, and coffee plantations dotted with small mud huts and brick houses. Everywhere there were donkeys pulling carts laden sky-high with crops, and being guided by tiny little boys who looked no older than about seven years. The majority of farming communities were very poor and literally existed day to day by selling their crops to the markets and to Nairobi. The shamba housing generally consisted of either grass or mud huts or derelict shacks made from clumps of clay with cow-dung floors, and there was the occasional brick house in the mix. The shambas didn't have running water or power, so water was generally collected at a borehole or the river. We noticed a small simple pump with a hose attached to it, hanging on the wall in Ano's mother's house, and she explained it was a water filter contraption for purifying the water pumped from the well. An American NGO had come to Kenya and gone door to door where they supplied one to every single household in rural Western Kenya.

Meals at the shamba were prepared outside, whether rain, hail, or shine, and so was the washing of dishes. Cooking was done over an open fire set up on the ground in a smoke-filled separate room. Most shambas contain a cluster of little buildings—one as a sitting room/bedroom, one for the cooking, one for the bathroom, and one for the toilet.

Ano told us that once sons had gone through their circumcision ritual as an adolescent, for the rest of their lives they could no longer sleep in their mother's house, so they had their own little outhouse bedroom to sleep in. Bathrooms consisted of a concrete box with a basin of cold water and the toilets were, of course, a hole in the ground.

The toilet/bathroom at the shamba was quite a distance from the main sleeping house and I knew that getting up to go to the loo in the middle of the night was going to be completely out of the question for me. The mere thought of ploughing around in the pitch black night in deepest Africa with just a small torch, was just too scary to contemplate.

We arrived at Ano's mother's late on Friday afternoon and the plan was to stay one night with her, before moving on to Kitale to see Ano's sister Jermima, who we had met in Nairobi.

Ano's sisters and his brother, their families, and neighbours arrived from nearby to meet and greet us, making us feel very welcome. We had a wonderful time with them all and of course we were fed … and fed! Food was of huge importance in African culture, particularly in welcoming guests to the shamba. It was customary to serve guests a meal and quite offensive for the guest to decline the meal or leave food that was placed in front of them. The amount of food and the many different dishes prepared for us was simply mindboggling, and because they were farmers, they lived entirely off the land. If more meat was required, they simply went outside and killed another chicken, or slaughtered another goat, or picked more vegetables. Meals traditionally consisted of the same type of food every day; lots of beautiful meat or vegetable stews, chappati, fruits, and of course, their staple food, ugali, the thick porridge-like maize flour and water combination that Kenyans simply could not live without, particularly menfolk. Ano and his brother could both talk for hours and hours on the wonders of ugali.

We spent just one night at the shamba before once again taking a boda-boda and heading to Jermima's shamba in Kitale. No sooner had we left Bungoma than we got caught in a sudden downpour of rain, and in a flash the dirt lane became completely bogged and impossible for us to drive the bikes on. We hopped off and proceeded to plough through the thick sludge, pushing the bikes as best we could until we found shelter under a makeshift verandah of a makeshift hut. After about fifteen minutes the rain stopped, the sun shone brightly, and we carried on our way, feeling drenched and sodden, but everything dried out very quickly when the sun came out in Kenya, so it wasn't too unbearable for long.

We arrived in Kitale amidst a flurry of locals who immediately descended upon us, and by now we were getting very used to this reception wherever we seemed to go. We headed straight to a marketplace where we knew Jermima was working at her little fruit and vegetable kiosk. She was very surprised and delighted to see us, not expecting us for a further few hours, and in a fluster, promptly closed up shop, took off her pinny, hailed a couple of boda-boda, and off we went to her shamba about ten minutes down the road on the outskirts of town.

The family of six, all adults and teenagers, lived in a gorgeous little shamba with a cow named Jenny, a couple of dogs, and loads of chickens. Her children were all lovely and seemed to spend the entire time we stayed cooking for and fussing over us to enable their mum to spend as much time with us as possible.

As usual our evening meal consisted of a banquet of various dishes the girls had prepared and set before us, and as usual we were expected to devour it all. I wondered where we would all sleep because space was so tight but nothing was a problem for the family; Chris and Ano slept on couches in the living room and I shared a bed with his lovely sister Jermima. At 5:00 a.m. she was awake and up to prepare the water and the girls to cook breakfast, before hopping back into bed where we talked for a good hour. She expressed over and over, her eternal gratitude for our assisting her brother with his life.

After a hearty breakfast, we headed back to town where we were packed into a bulging matatu and driven eight hours back to Nairobi. We briefly stopped off along the way to Eldoret to visit another of Ano's sisters and to meet her family before continuing on our way.

It was a very hair-raising trip home and for me personally, with all my experiences of riding in matatu, it was by far the worst and most scary. Matatu were of course nerve-wracking at the best of times, but this trip was made much worse by the fact that very frequently during the trip home there were sudden deluges of rain, resulting in vehicles weaving all over the road to avoid potholes and patches of flooded road, and everybody seemed to be in an enormous hurry; us included. Our driver appeared to have a bullet-proof attitude, overtaking and ducking and diving with absolutely no thought given to oncoming traffic or the fact that visibility was at a minimum. I found comfort by plugging my music into my ears, sitting back, and closing my eyes for as long as possible. Chris survived with his heart firmly embedded in his throat.

We arrived back in Nairobi and decided we really should consider our transport options in the future, especially on long trips, but the local public transport was such a normal part of our life in Kenya that we never really thought about the danger aspect.

Chapter Twenty-Nine

With two-and-a-half weeks to go before the opening day at Koha School and just another further couple of days before we were due to leave Kenya for Uganda, the pressure was well and truly on to have as much of the project completed as possible.

Priority was firstly given to building a fence around the perimeter of the school. It was very important to secure the compound; both for the children and also from potential robbers who may have taken a liking to the iron sheet cladding, or absolutely anything else that could be sold on the streets for a little cash. Such was life in the slums of Kenya.

This also highlighted the issue of extra security once the school was opened. I suggested a big ferocious guard dog but that idea was firmly squashed, the reality being that this most definitely wouldn't work with a whole bunch of kids around during the day. Ano talked about hiring a security guard to watch over the school at night time when burglary would most likely occur.

One day all the materials for the fence, including ninety fence-posts, wire, cement, sand, etc., was delivered on-site so a tribal warrior who lived nearby offered to come and guard the fence materials overnight until it was built, for a few Kenyan shillings per night. He would arrive at 6:00 p.m. and stay till 7:00 a.m. in the morning. We decided this was a perfect solution to the worry of having the fencing materials being sold on the streets of Nairobi, so we agreed.

The warrior turned up for duty that same night armed with a panga (machete), spear, and bow 'n' arrow, and promptly informed us he would use them if he had to. This didn't sit very well with

Chris and I, and we voiced our opinion disapprovingly that we didn't think using weapons was the appropriate way of handling intruders, however having them on display may well have been a deterrent for any would-be robbers.

Ano and our Masai guard had already followed the correct procedure and informed the village chief, notifying him of his weapons and intentions if confronted. At least we could now leave the school at the end of the day knowing the materials were safeguarded.

It highlighted however that a night guard would be the best solution for the safety and security of the school once it was operating; that a mere wire-netting fence might keep children in, but wouldn't keep robbers out. We asked the Masai if he wanted a permanent job, and he jumped at the chance.

Meanwhile Chris decided that with little time remaining in Kenya, and still a lot of finishing to be done, namely the fence for starters, that he would have to finish up at the detention centre and devote his time solely to the school project. The fence was going to be an enormous job, and he wanted to oversee the construction because this was one area the builders didn't seem too familiar with.

So with a lot of help from locals, the fence rapidly took shape and it was good to see a boundary defining the school compound. A lot of attention was given to the gate, which had also been built from heavy posts, but the weight of the posts was dragging it on the ground and making the gate hard to open and close. With the help of a few old rubber tyres wound around the posts, the gate was lifted securely in place, making it easy to swing back and forth.

The community were clearly amazed to see Chris hammering and sawing, and lugging posts and big coils of wire netting, and often there were hordes of people standing on the lane just watching in fascination. Apparently it was not a familiar sight to see mzungu doing hard manual labour and they were very impressed and somewhat amused.

"Why you doing this work?" was a question repeated several times a day by locals.

"Because in my country, this is my job there," Chris would reply.

We also received fantastic news that we could have water connected at the school. This was something that worried us and we always thought we would have to buy in water supplies for the children to drink, and also for sanitation, but the city council came by one day and said we could have it tapped into existing water supplies.

Meanwhile holiday tuition was going well and every day more and more children turned up, especially since the word was out around the community. Seeing the children react to the most simple things such as having paper and colouring pencils, crayons, and felt pens to draw with was a real pleasure to see.

One day a little boy Jeffrey promptly started to help me gather up library books, tidying up paper, putting away the pencils, etc. and at the end of the day I wrote him out a small school certificate that we had printed off a template from my computer, thanking him for his help, and I put a few stickers on it for added decoration. The next morning Jeffrey's mum waited at the school for me when we arrived, ready to thank me for the certificate, and explained what a treasure it was for the family.

While the fence construction continued well into the weekend, I decided to take my friend Elizabeth and her three children into Nairobi to spend the day picnicking in Uhuru Park, one of my favourite places to hang out on the weekends. It was a beautiful, hot, sunny day, and even I, who absolutely loves the sun, desperately searched for a suitable tree that we could sit under out of the hot blazing sun. We had a lovely afternoon, the park was, as always, alive with activity; a place many families tended to congregate to after church. There were all the usual fun activities like bouncy castles, merry-go-rounds, swings, paddle boats on a manmade lake, and even camel rides. Lots of hawkers wandered around selling balloon animals and head crowns, and offered on-the-spot ear piercing, hair braiding, and nail manicures. Elizabeth's kids loved it and spent hours on the bouncy castle and merry-go-round. Her eldest son however was a little too cool and spent most of the day lying on the grass.

Back at the school, one week out from opening day, we felt almost ready. The fence and gate were all secure, and the gate was now working well. Fifty uniforms, a mix of both boys' and girls', of varying sizes had been made by a local tailor, with pullovers and socks bought in the village to complete the outfits. In Kenya, size was not important, so the age of the children didn't really matter. One size easily fitted all, and possibly for a few years to come.

A long, skinny, particularly straight tree branch that Ano had selected out as a flag pole for the school at the local timber yard arrived onsite and with the aid of many men they managed to concrete it into the ground just in front of the school building. Fortunately they remembered to attach the rope to the pulley system before setting it upright, or that would have caused problems trying to attach it when it was standing many metres up in the air, cemented into the ground.

Next day when the concrete was set the menfolk arrived back to try out the flag pulley system to make sure everything was in working order for opening day ceremony the following Monday. They attached the flag and hoisted it up the pole to the very top. Much to everyone's amusement, the locals noticed the flag had been attached upside down. Everyone laughed.

When they tried to release the pulley to bring the flag down however, the cord somehow slipped off the wheel and got stuck in a groove and wouldn't budge. There was no way anybody could climb up and fix it, so one of the builders went off into the nearby bushes and came back with a long piece of vine that had a natural hook of bark on the end. He thought it would work as a lever to try and manoeuvre the cord into place on the pulley.

In the process of hunting for the vine, he had gashed his foot open on broken glass and arrived back with his foot wrapped in a piece of cloth that was by this time soaked in blood. His foot needed immediate attention but first of all he wanted the flag issue sorted out.

After umpteen attempts of trying to lever the hook under the cord, finally there was success; the cord was lifted into place and the flag was lowered down, taken off, and reattached the correct way up.

Meanwhile, I insisted the builder with the seriously bloodied foot go to the nearby medical clinic, which he did. He came back an hour or so later sporting an enormous padded bandage and hobbling on crutches and proceeded to pick up his hammer and continue with the last finishing touches to the school building. A cut foot was not going to hinder him in any way.

A local church group asked Ano if they could bless the school by holding their Sunday service at Koha School and also asked if we would attend. It was a lovely gesture and we didn't hesitate to accept.

On Sunday morning Chris and I were up early. We didn't want to be late to the service, thinking that would be very disrespectful. We arrived at the school and the entire building had been emptied of desks, and the partitions that divided the classrooms were pushed back against the walls to make one large room. All the furniture was stacked up outside the classrooms which was a little alarming because it looked like imminent rain. The thought of our beautiful new desks getting wet caused concern.

The service and school blessing was beautiful and the sounds of singing, chanting, hollering, and drum-beating bellowed out of the school and across the village. It was a special time and we felt honoured to be a part of this moment.

We got the impression the service was going to continue well into the day so we quietly excused ourselves after a couple of hours.

We learnt the next morning that the service didn't finish until about 7:00 p.m., and when Ano went to the school in the evening to get everything back in order for opening the following morning he was greeted with large piles of chicken feathers, bones, and the remains of an open fire pit that had been built clearly to cook the chickens on. It didn't impress him one little bit.

A couple of days before the open day at the school I had pre-arranged to take Elizabeth to lunch because it was her birthday. She had particularly requested we go to a lovely little restaurant she had seen and heard about. It was a couple of boda-boda rides for me to get there, but nevertheless, I agreed to take her. Chris and Ano were busy finishing the last touches to the fence, and so I hailed a motorbike to take me over the hill into another large neighbouring slum. From there I had arranged to meet Elizabeth and we would take a matatu together to the restaurant.

I arrived at our meeting point, a very busy and chaotic marketplace, and while waiting for her to arrive, I decided to go in search of a flower kiosk to buy a bunch of flowers for her birthday. I was slightly early and wandered around the market to fill in time. When Elizabeth arrived we jumped into a matatu and headed to the restaurant.

We had a lovely afternoon, dining al fresco under a sun umbrella on a beautifully manicured lawn. The food was fabulous, and Elizabeth was thrilled to be indulging in such decadence on her special day.

When it came time to pay and leave, my wallet wasn't in my bag. It had disappeared and immediately a sick feeling in my stomach surged up in my throat. My gut feeling was that I'd been robbed. After explaining the situation to the staff, with a promise to return as soon as possible with cash to pay for our meal, Elizabeth and I immediately set about retracing our movements; back to the market, back to every kiosk that I had wandered past, but to no avail.

I called Chris and asked him to send a boda-boda for me, I wanted to get back to the school as soon as possible to confirm I hadn't left my purse there. No, I hadn't left it at the school.

By this time I was frantic, and the timing for being robbed couldn't have been any worse. We were leaving Kenya in a few days and heading off to Uganda for the next part of our travels. I had broken a strict rule that day, I had carried all my bank cards with me, something I never ever did. And the reason I was carrying all my cards was because we had to withdraw a large amount of cash from the ATM to pay the builders out and buy the last of the materials and in Kenya you can only withdraw a maximum of ksh20–40,000 per day. We needed at least ksh100,000, so we used various cards to reach that amount. However, the big mistake I made was deciding that rather than stopping off at home to drop off the cards, I carried on to school, delivered the cash, then I would go back home before meeting Elizabeth but I didn't end up going back home. I was so angry with myself for being so stupid.

To make things worse, Chris greeted me with the familiar 'how could you be so stupid' look that I had seen a few times in the past thirty-three years. Of course I could see his point, but it only added fuel to the already raging fire. I then had to go through the painful process of phoning New Zealand banks to have the cards stopped, which was lengthy and frustrating.

The major problem was that as a result of having my cards stolen, we were left with just Chris's one credit card to use for the remainder of our trip of another six weeks, and unfortunately that particular card wasn't as widely accepted in some countries in Africa.

This meant a huge disruption to our plans of backpacking through Uganda and Rwanda. We were led to believe Rwanda didn't accept the card at all, and because we were limited on what we could withdraw in Uganda, the worry of not having enough money and being stranded forced us to cancel our trip to Rwanda. This was really disappointing because we planned on meeting up with our mountain gorilla researcher friend and former flatmate Prosper and hiking with him in the mountains.

Of course yes, it could have been a lot worse—I could have been also carrying the recently withdrawn cash, but thankfully I'd given it to Chris. That didn't solve matters for us though.

Chapter Thirty

It was the opening day, 5th September 2011. Ano asked us to arrive early; he said the parents and children would all want to meet us. We aimed to arrive at around 8:00 a.m., thinking that would be sufficient time to get there to welcome new parents and pupils. We got that wrong, very wrong.

As we walked down the hill towards the school we could see a flurry of activity around the compound with people coming and going through the gate. As I walked into the school building, I could not believe my eyes. It was absolutely jam-packed with children, and body heat literally radiated out of the rooms. All three classrooms were bulging with kids: four or five of them crammed into desks built for two to three; some children sitting on plastic chairs that were obviously borrowed to accommodate the overflow; and the baby class, which instead of having desks, had two long bench tables and bench seats that housed at least twenty to twenty-five kids. There were little school bags lining the entire length of one side of the fence and what looked like hundreds of shoes scattered around the doors to the school.

Meanwhile, classes were already in progress, with teachers standing at the front of each class and children all attentively listening and writing in exercise books. There were 117 kids all enrolled at Koha School by 8:00 a.m. on that very first morning, and, of course, having over double the number we hoped for immediately caused all sorts of problems. There was not enough room to begin with, not enough teachers, not enough textbooks, not enough stationery, not enough desks, not enough school uniforms … and so it went on.

Chris and I turned around and walked back outside, stared at each other with a look of alarm and wondered, what were we going to do now?

Turning around, he looked at me and said, "Ok, there's nothing we can do now with only three days left in Kenya, but there's only one thing for it. When we get home to New Zealand, we'll hold a fundraiser and send the funds back to Ano to build a further three classrooms to spread the pupils out into more comfortable conditions."

No sooner had I nodded my head in agreement than he had turned and walked out to where he thought the new classes could go and with the help of a couple of builders who had brought their children to start school, they immediately started pacing and pegging out the next lot of classrooms. Chris figured that if he at least helped with the digging of foundations, it would be a start. So, while school was going on inside, Chris and his gang of men were busy digging a trench that would house the foundations for the new building.

My immediate reaction was one of panic about funding. How were Chris and I ever going to be able to fund this school on our own now? Ano had already informed us way back at our first planning sessions that most parents wouldn't be able to afford to pay school fees, so the school's survival would rely heavily on Chris's and my support, which we had previously agreed on. However that was the agreement for fifty children, and two staff members. Now we had 117 children.

We agreed that we really needed to talk and come up with a plan. Then we had to have a meeting with Ano as soon as possible. I was worried, and this was day one! We decided that in order for us to enjoy the six weeks remaining of our travels, we had to put all thoughts of the school's future on hold until we got back to New Zealand. We told Ano this, and promised that as soon as we got home, we would hold a fundraiser for the new set of classrooms, and that would at least alleviate the congestion in the classes. That would be a start. We then ordered him that under no circumstances was he to enrol any more students.

So, we spent the remainder of our time in Kenya enjoying Koha School, the staff, the parents, and the pupils who had rapidly turned this building into a beautiful little school.

From where our guesthouse was situated, we had to walk a good 500 or more metres down a lane, and around a corner past a cluster of roadside kiosks, to catch a matatu. This was the same route, whatever direction we were headed in. Because we did this at least twice daily, we became a familiar sight to the local stall owners and slowly over the course of time there developed a good deal of banter and joking between us. Chris had his friend Robert, a young fruit and veggie vendor who every day Chris would complain to about the price of his bananas. But every day regardless of the fuss he made, he would buy three bananas.

There was also an elderly man in dirty, raggy clothes who sat every day on a small square of matting on the ground, holding one deformed hand out in a begging gesture. He never made eye contact so we were never sure if he could see or not. Begging is strongly discouraged so every day for three months we walked right past this elderly man, never once dropping any money into his hand, or on to the mat. It bothered me, so I made a plan that on the last day we were in Kenya, I would give him all my surplus Kenyan money. So, on our very last morning as usual we walked the same route to the matatu, only this time I had a fist full of notes and coins, all ready to drop into the old man's lap. I was almost excited about it, I'd planned it for weeks, and it was my opportunity to show him that we actually did care. As we rounded the corner, sure enough, he was sitting in exactly the same spot as always and while continuing walking, I just casually bent down and placed the money on to his mat, without so much as slowing down, or uttering a word. The look on his face when he realised what had happened was priceless, and I'll never forget it.

Chapter Thirty-One

Three days after the opening day of Koha School we boarded a bus bound for Uganda. Time to move on and continue with our travels; six weeks in Uganda and then on down to South Africa to spend ten days with my cousin Edgar and the beautiful family.

We sat back in our seats and thought back over the last three months. It was completely surreal to both Chris and I that we had flown into Kenya, and just three months later, we left having built a fully operational primary school. It was crazy! Where on earth and in which part of our life plan was the bit about establishing a school in a slum in Kenya? Heaven knows.

It didn't take very long before I was missing the action at the school, and wished we were back there to continue what we had started. I didn't feel comfortable with just getting up and leaving the way we did. However, we had no choice, our visas had expired, and it was time to continue our journey. In my head I was already planning to go back to Kenya, and I was thinking sooner rather than later. In the meantime we felt we had left the project in very capable hands, and that was at least comforting.

The eight-hour bus journey to the Kenya/Uganda border was surprisingly uneventful except for the parts where road diversions were in place due to recent flooding. Some of the potholed, deeply rutted dirt tracks our bus driver manoeuvred the coach through were definitely not meant for buses, and a couple of scary moments when I thought our bus would tip over on its side had my heart in my throat. The upside to this though, was that we got to see some pretty rural areas, landscapes, and villages that we wouldn't have normally seen had we not been forced to make the diversions off the main roads.

The border crossing went smoothly, except that when we arrived it was teeming down with rain and every person crossing the border had taken refuge under the verandah of the tiny office, causing mayhem. We fought our way to the counter for visa processing and then made a beeline back to the bus as quickly as possible.

We arrived in Jinja just before dusk and stepped off the bus into a crowd of boda-boda riders all touting for fares. We had a lot of luggage, including two huge backpacks with sleeping bags, boots, and other paraphernalia hanging off the pack straps, plus two small day packs.

We made our way over to two guys standing away from the crowd, leaning on their bikes. The drivers leapt to our aid, grabbed our luggage, and directed us to sit on the back. They proceeded to pile the bikes up with our backpacks and daypacks, and promptly hopped on and roared down the road, with our luggage balanced precariously, making me too scared to move a muscle for fear of toppling under the weight and bulk.

First stop was an ATM because of course we had no cash. We didn't realise that finding an ATM that accepted our one and only card would be so difficult as we had been assured before leaving Kenya that in Uganda we would have no problem, as there were not the same issues as Rwanda. I started to feel a little anxious that every bank we stopped at only accepted the one we did not have. Finally, after much searching, we spotted a large bank displaying the logo on a post outside and I breathed a sigh of relief when the ATM accepted the card and duly delivered my notes.

Once we had sorted some cash we were keen to find the camp and get settled. Our driver dropped us off at the camp I had pre-booked into before leaving Kenya, however they didn't have our booking and there were no rooms available except a four-bed bunk dorm. We didn't have much choice so we took it anyway. The room was empty at that moment, so everything was fine.

After offloading our gear, showering, and freshening up, we headed for the camp bar. We were absolutely blown away by the breathtaking view; the camp perched high on a hill top overlooking some furiously flowing rapids on the River Nile. There were a couple of overland trucks in camp and by the time we arrived at the bar, they were well into party mode, so we promptly made friends, joined in, and spent a really fun evening socialising with the tourists, which included a couple of Kiwis.

Our bunk beds were comfy and we both had a good night's sleep. After breakfast we hired a little boda-boda of our own and went off exploring the little town and surrounding rural area. It was beautifully picturesque and we had a lovely time chatting to local farmers. Suddenly, out in the middle of nowhere, the bike died. After a lot of tweaking of this and that, it was surely not going to start and we realised we had no choice but to leave it at a nearby mechanic's workshop and start walking in the direction of the camp. We walked for miles and miles down a long straight road, which created interest amongst the locals who were intrigued as to why we would be walking, particularly in the blazing heat of the sun. Many came over to greet us, and little kids appeared at our side and tagged along for a walk.

After about an hour of walking, and by this time, in desperate need of water, we came across a little road-side kiosk that sold soda straight from the crate, but there was no room for fussiness so warm soda it had to be. We sat down under the shade of a tree to have a rest—it was so hot and we were tired. As we got up to leave, we heard a boda-boda spluttering down the road, and it seemed to slow as it got closer. We recognised the driver as the mechanic and the bike as the one we'd not long ago left with him. He stopped, we both climbed on the back, and we roared off down the road to the camp.

Initially we decided to stay on one further night but then decided to stay longer; the room remained empty so it suited us just fine.

We started to relax and unwind and really enjoyed the serenity. We pored over our travel guide and decided the next destination would be Lake Bunyoni, high in the mountain region of south-western Uganda, close to the Rwandan border.

After a further three nights at Jinja, we decided it was time to move on. We had a very long journey ahead, which included a bus interchange in Kampala, Uganda's capital city.

We arrived in Kampala after an uneventful journey and everybody got off the bus. As expected, it was chaos. This was the main interchange for Uganda, and buses by the hundreds lined up one after another going in all directions throughout East Africa and beyond.

We got off our bus, and were immediately swarmed by touters. It was hot, we'd just travelled six hours, we were thirsty and hungry and not altogether in the mood for fighting off the hordes. However, we also had no idea where to find our bus to Lake Bunyoni, so we hired the services of a young boy who clearly assumed he had secured a job by the mere eye contact that exchanged between us and him, promptly picked up my backpack, placed it on his head, then picked up Chris's pack, which he held on to with his free hands.

"Where to, where to?" he shouted before heading off into the throngs with our luggage.

"Lake Bunyoni, mate," replied Chris.

With that, we chased off after him, keeping our eyes firmly fixed on my backpack that was rapidly disappearing into the crowds of people.

We finally arrived at a brightly decorated bus, with flowers and colourful artwork, among what looked very much like local buses. Our guide dropped our packs, held out his hand into which Chris duly thrust a few shillings, and he was gone.

After negotiating the price with the driver who was checking passengers in, and loading luggage into the under-carriage, we took our seats up the front of the bus across the aisle from the driver's seat. And then we waited … and we waited … until we finally discovered the buses didn't leave until every seat was occupied and with our particular bus, this took hours. As we sat watching neighbouring buses pull in, load up, and leave, we were feeling a little anxious that with the late departure our arrival time into Lake Bunyoni would be quite late in the evening, it would be dark, and as we had no accommodation booked we hoped we wouldn't be forced to stay overnight in some dodgy hostel. It was nearly four hours before the driver finally climbed aboard, closed the doors, started the engine, and drove off out into the crazy traffic

The bus ride started off ok and we settled back and relaxed. However, this wasn't to last, and an hour into the journey, after we'd passed through the city and were at last out into the country, things drastically changed.

The driver started behaving very carelessly and it was almost as if once he was out of the city rat race he could just sit back and relax. At one stage I looked over and he was punching in numbers on his cell phone, and then proceeded to sit back in his seat, leaning half-heartedly against the window and talking on his phone with one hand while steering the bus with the other.

It started raining heavily and we could barely see one metre in front of us for the rain battering at the windows but this did not deter this crazy man whose driving was nothing short of insane. He was overtaking other vehicles on mountain passes, sometimes so far across on the other side of the road that the wheels were in the dirt; overtaking on blind corners; driving on the centre line; and all of this combined with heavy rain and darkness, was in my mind a recipe for death. Meanwhile the cell phone was almost fixed permanently to his ear.

This went on for hours, and I became more terrified.

"Oi, you! Slow down, or you'll have us all killed," I bellowed across at him, glaring into his eyes. "I'll have you reported to the police," I screamed.

He glared back at me and sniggered. I saw red. This prompted other passengers to also speak up, yelling at the driver in Swahili in anger.

"Right, that's it, I'm out of here at the next police checkpoint," I snapped at Chris, continuing that I would ask the police to call me a taxi and that I would take the remainder of the journey in that.

Chris glared at the driver, then back at me, who by this time was reduced to tears. He tried very hard to calm me down, agreeing that we would get off the bus. As luck would have it however, there were no more checkpoints, even though we had been stopped every few kilometres by road blocks up to that point.

I had no choice but to sit cowering in my seat, all the while working myself up into a terrible state, entirely convinced that our two children would be orphaned that night.

We finally arrived at the destination much to the relief of everybody on board the bus. It was a small town called Kabale at the base of the mountain ranges and Lake Bunyoni. From there we had to take a taxi up and over the ranges, to the lake situated high up in the mountains.

We got off the bus and into the familiar swarm of taxi drivers touting for fares. The bus driver was unloading luggage from the under-carriage, and as he threw my pack onto the ground, I snatched it up, gave him one last glare, and muttered, "You were a bloody idiot," before storming off to Chris who was negotiating a taxi fare.

He settled on a price, and I marched off to the taxi, slung my backpack into the back seat, and slumped in beside it. I couldn't stand the sight of that bus driver's face and I needed to get out of there because I was pretty sure I would have slapped him.

As we were about to drive off in the taxi, the driver suddenly announced that he needed petrol before we could proceed up into the ranges. He set off in the direction of the petrol station, however it was by now 11:00 p.m. and the petrol station was closed. Parked on the forecourt, he sat pondering what to do.

"Just take us back to the bus stop and we'll get another taxi," I snapped.

But he asked us to wait a moment and then got out of the taxi, instructing us to stay put and lock all the doors, reassuring us he would be back very soon.

Finally, about fifteen minutes later, the driver returned with a petrol can, emptied the contents into the tank, the taxi roared into life, and off over the mountain range to our destination of Lake Bunyoni we went.

We finally got to the summit of the ranges, and there before us was one of the most picturesque, idyllic mountain-lake village hideaways I'd ever seen. It was simply breathtaking. The lake, an enormous, expansive glass mirror, reflected the full moon in all its glory.

The taxi driver stopped at a small camp, suggesting this as a good place to stay. Thankfully for everyone, there was a vacancy in one of the banda huts. It was an adorable little round, whitewashed mud hut with a grass-thatched roof, perched overlooking the lake. By midnight we were at last sitting with a beer and a vodka outside our darling little hut, in the most exquisite garden setting right on the lakefront, soaking up the stillness, smells, and full moonlit view of this enormous Lake Bunyoni and its tiny islands, high up in the mountains of Uganda. It was simply breathtaking and I suddenly felt we had been transported to paradise, albeit via a rough journey, but finally we made it.

We slept soundly that night and were woken in the morning by the sound of monkeys chattering in the trees, the most beautiful bird-song, and the twittering of thousands of small birds outside our hut. There was the distant sound of children singing and drums beating, which we soon discovered was from a little school situated on the bank across the other side of the lake.

We spent several days in Lake Bunyoni; it was beautiful and we weren't in any hurry to leave. Many hours were spent exploring the rural plantations, strolling through the nearby villages, chatting with the local 'lake people' as they were called, and enjoying the company of other backpackers who wandered through.

Transportation on the lake was by dug-out canoe, or in other words, a dug-out tree trunk. Our first experience in the canoe was disastrous and it was a lot harder to manoeuvre than it looked. Somehow we managed very easily to direct our canoe to either go round and round in circles (commonly known as the 'corkscrew' by locals), head for the banks of smaller islets, or we found ourselves paddling furiously while moving absolutely nowhere. However we persevered and soon managed to find our way to a nearby tiny islet where we moored up and had lunch in a beautiful little lodge nestled in amongst the trees overlooking the lake.

We had read in our travel guide about a tribe of pygmies who lived in the lake region, very close to the Uganda/Rwanda border, and so one afternoon we decided to go and visit them. We initially thought no, we had visions of some sort of circus attraction, but then locals told us that the pygmies liked mzungu to visit them and they had set up a relatively thriving little business selling their crafts and wares to visitors, so we agreed to go.

It was quite an ordeal to get to the pygmy village; firstly we had to take a small motorboat some forty kilometres up to the furthest point in the lake, followed by an eight-kilometre walk, which in hindsight we had not really taken enough notice of.

Surprisingly, at the agreed time, the tiny motorboat came puttering around the corner and pulled up to the jetty of our camp.

It was already full of locals, many of whom commuted daily back and forth between islands to the mainland to sell their wares. The boat operator gestured to all the passengers to move close together to make room for us, and off we went on an hour-and-a-half boat ride. We cruised past many tiny islands, some so small they were more little bush-clad blobs dotted on the water, dropping passengers off at various places along the way. Boat or canoe was the mode of transport for the lake people getting from one place to the other.

We finally arrived at our destination, and we were glad to get out and stretch our legs. Little did we know that the eight-kilometre walk was ahead of us, and we were totally unprepared with just small water bottles, and sandals on our feet.

We were met by a young guy who nominated himself to be our guide. We were grateful to have him because we were in a very remote area and had no idea where we were supposed to go.

The walk was long and made less pleasant by our inappropriate footwear, but the scenery and landscape were stunning. Every bend we rounded brought with it a different view and we were simply astounded by the beauty. The land contour and terrain immediately took me back very many years to a visit to Switzerland in the summertime, with sheer, almost vertical lush green hillsides, contrasted with deep, deep valleys. Small round, grass-thatched huts; tiny little churches; and the occasional school built right into the hillside dotted the landscape. Every inch of land was cultivated with crops and we could see tiny specks moving in the far distance. These were the workers.

We arrived at the pygmy village, situated just a few hundred metres from the Rwandan border. As a small settlement nestled into the hillside, the self-sufficient pygmy tribe also relied heavily on tourist visitors to buy their handcrafts. Some of the girls entertained us with dancing, singing, and drum-beating, which was fantastic, especially as the music rang out and echoed over the entire valley.

No English was spoken, but through all our travelling through Africa, we had become very adept at communicating with hand and arm movements, and our guide also translated for us.

We spent an hour or so with the tribe, before it was time for the trek back to where our boat was moored, another eight kilometres back. By the time we got back to the camp, we were tired, and our feet sore, but it had been well worth the effort and we were glad we'd decided to go and see the pygmies.

We had been staying at Lake Bunyoni for about five days, and one morning decided to take a boda-boda down the mountain to Kabale town to buy supplies and find a cyber café to catch up on emails.

We found a café that also had wifi, so we ordered coffees and sat outside on the small porch in front of the shop, watching the world go by up and down the street of this small town. A man stepped up onto the porch to walk into the café, and lo and behold we recognised him instantly as the bus driver from hell. He spotted us at the same time and proceeded to come over to our table.

"Hello," he said. "Do you remember who I am?" he asked, grinning, and holding out his hand to shake Chris's hand.

Chris just sat there. "I aint shaking your hand mate, you nearly killed us the other day," he said in a calm but firm tone.

"You were an idiot and you should not be on the road, especially carrying passengers in a bus!" I butted in.

The driver stood there looking shocked and astonished, listening to the verbal attack that I continued to unleash on him.

"I was sorry for that. Yes, yes, I will be more careful. Thank you for telling me those things," he said, nodding his head.

There was a bus parked up on an empty plot across the street from where we were sitting. The whole front was smashed in, the sides crushed, and wheels torn off.

Chris pointed over the road, and continued, "That could have been us."

With that, he nodded, waved farewell, and hurried on his way down the street, no doubt wanting to get away from us as fast as he could.

We spent many more days soaking up the beautiful, tranquil Lake Bunyoni, occasionally taking a boda-boda over the ranges down into the town of Kabale for supplies. One day, we were riding back up to the lake and our bike came puttering to a stop on a remote mountain hill road. The only sign of life was the sight of quarry workers way in the distance, working on the mountainside. A young man came riding up on his bicycle, stopped, and tried to help, but the bike was dead. Suddenly a car came up and stopped beside us, an American woman driver and a younger woman in the passenger seat. They asked if they could give us a ride over the mountain to the lake, which we promptly accepted. Meanwhile the bike's driver stayed with the bike, and he had radioed through to a friend to come to his rescue.

The American woman had a similar story in that she had arrived in Uganda some years before to work as a volunteer, fell in love with Africa, then went home to the US and sold up everything and went back to Uganda where she now lived. The difference being however, that we weren't going to be living permanently in Africa … as much as the thought often did cross my mind.

Chapter Thirty-Two

Travelling was, I'm sure, at times meant to test us and throw out a few challenges every now and then. I also think Chris and I unintentionally invited a little drama to shake us from complacency.

After our beautiful week at Lake Bunyoni, and then a couple of fun nights at a gorgeous camp just outside of the capital city Kampala, we decided to head for the Ssese Islands, a cluster of small islands on Lake Victoria.

It was our last few days in Uganda, and the thought of a beautiful tropical beach setting was exciting. We had to go firstly to Entebbe, a one-and-a-half-hour bus ride from Kampala, and stay the night there before boarding the ferry to the islands the next day.

Fortunately our bus ride back was uneventful this time, and although I was dreading it there was absolutely no drama at all. We stayed in a lovely camp, sleeping in a tent on a perfectly manicured lawn, and the owners kindly offered to store the bulk of our luggage while we visited the islands.

We packed just a few small items into our daypacks, hailed down a boda-boda driver to take us to the ferry and asked him to stop at an ATM on the way so we could get cash as there were no ATMs on the islands. Entebbe was home to the only international airport in Uganda, so we were totally unprepared for the one ATM that would accept our card to be out of working order.

With just one hour till the ferry was due to depart we did a quick count up of our remaining cash and also a quick calculation of how much we thought we might need for the three days on one of the islands, not really having a clue, but nevertheless we were both really keen to go and wing it. We'd read our travel guide and worked out the accommodation costs, and had a fair idea we would be ok. We had the sum total of NZ$40 to pay for the return ferry trip, accommodation, and food. As long as we had enough for those basics, then we could forego anything else that might be considered a treat.

So we boarded the ferry and set off on the three-hour boat trip. We munched our way through a very small packet of groundnuts and a couple of bananas I had brought with me, enviously watching the locals tuck into enormous lunches served on board. We laughed—it was way too early in this trip to start indulging in such luxuries, we could save the best until our return ferry ride in three days' time, provided there was money left of course.

Poring through the travel guide on the ferry, we found the cheapest campground on the island that was within our pathetic budget, so I phoned from the ferry and booked two nights' accommodation ... perfect!

The ferry ride was lovely and we passed many beautiful little islands in the Ssese Group along the way to our destination.

The ferry finally arrived at the island and we stepped straight onto pristine, snow-white sand, with crystal-clear water, and following directions printed in our travel book we proceeded to walk along the beach some fifty metres until we spotted our camp. It was set up in the most perfect setting right on the lake with its own private beach, with the camp accommodation nestled in amongst beautiful native bush and forest.

The camp looked hilarious. It was owned by an eccentric middle-aged German couple who evidently seventeen years previous were backpacking around Africa, fell in love with the small island, set up camp, and had never left.

Both artists, the camp accommodation comprised of tiny straw-roofed wooden huts scattered through the bush, in all manner of shapes and sizes, painted up with crazy artwork and colours, some perched high up on piles of perfectly placed rocks, and others built into the bases of large trees. It looked crazy but fun.

We were greeted on arrival by screeching music coming from a little portable radio that was belting out old-school rock. The couple were clearly waiting for us, having seen the ferry arrive into dock, so as soon as we walked along the beach, they both came down to greet us.

"Hey, and welcome," the guy said, before proceeding to run around playing his air guitar, occasionally blurting out weird and random stuff that we couldn't really understand.

Meanwhile his wife sort of floated about, dream-like, while chatting to us in both English and German, with the occasional burst of laughter thrown into the mix. Chris and I both just looked at each other and laughed, thinking that this was going to be a fun few days.

We discovered we were the only guests in the camp that night and the couple seemed very keen to have us for company for the evening, inviting us for drinks at their outside bar. They were very friendly and so after being given a grand tour of the camp, we decided to unwind a bit in our little hut before joining them for a couple of drinks. The setting seemed bizarre, but we really liked it.

The little huts, on first glimpse, looked really funky and fun but it didn't take long for us to figure out they were overdue for repairs. The walls were made of thin wooden slats and lined inside with grass matting. There were large, gaping holes in the floorboards, roof, and windows.

That night when we got into bed, we discovered we had visitors and I stayed frozen in my bed, listening to creepy crawlies scratching at the walls, running across the floor and over the roof. I was terrified.

Luckily that first night I hadn't seen the large snake holes pitted all over the sandy ground, but by night two I was quite scared.

However, with our financial crisis the way it was, we had no choice but to stick it out. We couldn't afford to move onto something better. On a positive note, as we were the only guests at the camp, we were treated well and the meals they served were fabulous.

Daytime on the island was awesome and no sooner had we gotten up in the mornings and had breakfast, than we went off exploring. We walked miles and miles, through tiny villages, chatting to the locals and swimming in the beautiful, warm, waters.

Apart from the sleeping accommodation, which continued to terrify me with weird and unusual scuffling noises, our time on the island was magic.

After two nights and three days, we boarded the ferry back to Entebbe with NZ$4 still in our pockets. We were quite chuffed that we had survived, and with money to spare. However, we still had one more night in Uganda before flying out to South Africa, so our $4 had to provide us with food, but $4 went a long way in Africa, so we were ok, and it was surprising what we could get that was filling and cheap. You learn something new every day when travelling.

Chapter Thirty-Three

Meanwhile all the time we were in Uganda, we were in constant contact with Ano back in Kenya, and all was going well at Koha School much to our relief. Children were learning, he informed us. That was all we really needed to know for now, until we got back to New Zealand and organised a fundraiser for the new classroom block.

We left Uganda for the final leg of our trip back to my beloved South Africa. We arrived into George, a small airport not too far from Mossel Bay, and were ecstatically reunited with Edgar, Denise and Nadia. This time there were no first-time greetings, barriers were down and we were absolutely thrilled to see each other again. It was as if time had stood still.

Everybody was so excited, and no more so than me, I'm sure. Such was the tightly formed bond between us, it was very natural that we simply picked up where we had left off two years beforehand.

One of our first visits was to Edgar's mum who, sadly, had been widowed since the last time we'd visited. Her husband, Edgar's dad, had passed away, which meant another family link had passed. It was so lovely to see her again, and over the following few days we caught up with many members of the family and friends who we had met on the previous visit.

This time Chris and I had decided to take Edgar, Denise, and Nadia away for a few days to spend some quality time together and also as a treat for them. Edgar and Denise chose the resort, and so one morning we piled our belongings into the car, stopped by to pick up a friend of Nadia's who was coming with us, and off we went.

The resort, nestled at the side of a lake, was beautiful, had all the facilities of a resort complete with multiple swimming pools, tennis courts, all the various day and evening activities, water sports, paddle boat rides, and all sorts of entertainment. We'd rented a three-bedroom cottage quite close to the swimming pools, with a beautiful patio complete with braai that backed onto a large communal grassy area where the kids could play soccer and cricket.

It was a scorching hot day when we arrived so we unpacked our belongings and headed straight for the pools where we spent a good amount of time frolicking in the water, and for Chris and me, sunbathing on the sun loungers. Edgar and Denise chose to sit under sun umbrellas, laughing and not understanding at all why we would want to darken our skin.

What we were not aware of, until Edgar mentioned later when we were back at the cottage, was that we were very clearly the centre of poolside gossip. People whispered behind hand-covered mouths, and eyes were directed over to where we were sitting. Once Edgar pointed it out to us, we watched closely, and sure enough he was right.

One evening after dinner, the two teenage girls went off for a walk around the resort, and when they came back proceeded to tell us how they were stopped by a middle-aged white couple. They asked the girls what they were doing with the white people, which of course was us, to which Nadia replied that we were family from New Zealand and proceeded to walk away.

Stopping Nadia again, the woman asked her, "What do you mean they are family? They were very clearly white and you are very clearly coloured."

The girls shrugged and walk away.

Once we were aware of this, we definitely noticed that people were talking about us. Chris and I didn't think we would ever get used to the reactions of local people based purely on the colour of our skin.

During our stay, Edgar and I spent many precious hours poring over the family stories and our very own feelings of how we'd met, and how much it meant to be in each other's lives. For Edgar, it was a time of healing and coming to terms with everything in his past he had to deal with simply because of his skin colour. He constantly thanked me for coming into his life, and said that since we'd met, he learnt to feel perfectly comfortable walking into a packed room or hall and that it was very ok to have been blessed with coloured skin. There were many tears shed during our time spent talking and a sense of very deep connection between us.

We also had a lot of fun together. We got on fantastically well as an extended family, and slotted into each other's lives with total ease.

One day Chris and I decided to venture into town for a day, so Edgar dropped us off and instructed us to phone him when we were ready to go home and he would collect us. He also said that under no circumstances were we to leave the main CBD and wander off as we were inclined to do. We strolled around the gorgeous small town, and ventured down to the waterfront, but after a couple of hours we had had enough. There was a small shopping mall that we had previously visited, and I had seen a digital picture frame in a pharmacy there that I wanted to buy for Edgar and Denise as a gift. I hadn't seen them anywhere else, so we decided to make our way to this mall to buy the frame.

We asked locals for public transport directions and were instructed to catch a particular bus, which stopped on the main road opposite the entrance to the mall. We hopped off, and waited at the traffic lights for the green man signalling it was safe to cross the road, when all of a sudden we heard the loud honking of a car horn. Looking up, we saw Edgar in his car, stopped at the traffic lights, frantically wagging his finger at us, laughing, and shaking his head. We'd been snapped! The lights turned green and so he pulled over to the side of the pavement and proceeded to give us a lecture, in a humorous way, making us feel like naughty kids for disobeying the rules of keeping safe and not wandering off on our own. Edgar said he recognised my floral dress and couldn't believe his eyes as we were many miles away from where he had dropped us off. We often brought the story up when we were reminiscing about our time spent in South Africa with my beloved family.

Sadly our stay was over all too soon and we again found ourselves bidding a tearful farewell to Edgar and Denise at the same bus station that we now knew well, with bittersweet memories. We departed once more with a promise to return as soon as we could. My beautiful family was simply impossible to leave.

Chapter Thirty-Four

We arrived back to New Zealand to a flurry of people desperately wanting to hear the story of Koha School and how on earth we had stumbled head first into building a school and how were we going to fund it. At that stage we had no idea ourselves, on both counts. It had snowballed completely out of control.

Our children Craig and Hayley suggested we start up a sponsorship scheme and they promptly invited friends and family members to help by sponsoring a child, or donating to the school fund. The sponsorship fee was set at a very small $10 a month, and every bit helped.

People very quickly came on board and were signing up in droves, and the school fund grew very fast. Meanwhile the story started spreading at a great rate of knots, and very soon after arriving home I started receiving requests from clubs, schools, and other organisations asking me to tell my story. I suddenly found myself on the speaking circuit, and therefore further donations started to pour in. It was awesome, the school fund looked very healthy, and this enabled us to make choices with regards to buying resources.

About the same time, our niece Christine arrived back to New Zealand from the UK, via Kenya. She had visited the school and was able to update us with latest photos and news. She soon became part of the team and was invaluable to Chris, Mandy, and me with her energy and enthusiasm.

Keeping to our promise of holding a fundraiser to send back the funds to build more classrooms, we organised a movie night. We hired a local movie theatre, sold tickets with a mark-up to make a profit, organised a couple of raffles to be run on the night, and made over $1,000. It was simple!

Within six weeks of returning to New Zealand we'd built up enough funds to send to Ano, and one month later, the new three-classroom block was completed. The timing was perfect as school had closed for Christmas holidays, which meant Ano had time to outfit the classrooms, buy more textbooks, and get the classrooms ready for opening in the new school year. Now there were six classrooms at Koha School.

Back in Kenya, a lovely friend of mine Jane who I'd met at the orphanage where I volunteered the year before made contact with Ano, visited the school, and offered assistance and support where she could. She assisted with the new classroom block, and when school opened in January 2012 she said the school was going well, however she didn't have such a good feeling about Ano, and it wasn't long before she contacted me and said they'd had a falling out and she subsequently left Nairobi. I was puzzled about this, but dismissed it as a personal feud that had developed between them.

The school opened on 2 January 2012 with 165 students. This had not been the plan when we sent the funds back to build more classrooms. Our thought was that the new classrooms would enable the children to spread comfortably throughout the school so the classes wouldn't be so congested. How wrong could we have been? It simply opened the door to more children.

I couldn't wait to get back to Kenya, and Chris and I decided I would go back alone this time. He was more than happy to stay in New Zealand, so at the end of May that same year I flew out to Kenya for two months. We arranged to meet up in Melbourne in two months' time, to have a holiday with our children.

In the meantime I connected with Maureen in Australia through a friend, who was about to embark on six months of volunteering in several countries in Africa, Kenya being one of them. We arranged to meet up in Kenya where she would spend a month working at Koha School, co-ordinating her time with mine. I was really excited about this, it meant I would have someone to share my experience with, and we also arranged to live in the same guesthouse.

A couple of weeks before I was due to fly out to Kenya, I was enjoying a weekend away with a bunch of girlfriends and I received a text message from Ano.

"Hi Dee, I'm proud to announce our Masai guard stopped three robbers uplifting fence posts and stealing desks. Now one has chopped off ear."

I read the text over and over a couple of times because I didn't think I'd read it correctly, and I felt my heart miss a beat. I couldn't believe what I was reading. I sent a text back immediately explaining that we would phone Ano as soon as I got home on the Sunday evening, to find out what on earth had gone on. I worried for our guard and what repercussions may be incurred, and I also worried for the robber who was now minus one ear.

The following evening, we spoke with Ano and the story went like this:

One night the guard was disturbed from where he was asleep on the ground by a noise coming from the back of the school grounds. There was no power in this part of the village and the night was pitch black. Our guard was a Masai, and they were renowned for their remote living, hunting lions and other wild animals, and their senses were very finely tuned. The noise had woken him with a start, so he immediately grabbed his machete and very quietly and carefully made his way to where the noise was coming from. Masai, as part of their amazing hunting skills, walked so lightly on their feet that they could walk across a stack of twigs and you wouldn't hear a sound. He instinctively lashed out at whoever was there in the dark, consequently slicing one of the men's ears off. Next morning the police were called and traced the blood trail, which led them to the robbers, or would-be robbers, as they hadn't actually managed to break into the school. The village chief held a mock court hearing and they were charged with attempted robbery and sentenced to jail. In the meantime, our Masai guard was considered a hero.

I didn't know why, but I asked Ano what happened to the ear, and he said 'they'—meaning Ano and the guard—chopped it up and threw it in the stream behind the school. It was all too grizzly for us to comprehend from afar, and I hoped that we would never have another incident like that one again.

I left New Zealand bound for Kenya, again loaded up with the maximum luggage allowance—this time with all sorts of stationery and sports equipment for the school, board games, balls, and skipping ropes. I also had gifts for every one of our 165 students, and also the staff.

For some time I had pondered over ideas for small gifts I could take. Nothing too heavy or bulky. A friend came up with the idea of threading small pieces of polished paua shell onto thin leather cord that could be tied around their necks and worn as pendants. It sounded like such a great idea; not only would they be pretty, but they were lightweight, and took up minimal room in my luggage.

I gathered many fabulous pieces of paua shell from friends, the beach, and souvenir shops. Chris and I then spent hours in our lounge making our shell pendants; he would sit there drilling tiny holes into the paua, then pass them to me and I would thread narrow black cord into them. We made 200 pendants, more than we needed, but just to be on the safe side, I'd rather take too many than not enough. They looked gorgeous and I was very pleased to be able to take a small piece of New Zealand to all the children and staff at the school.

I was so excited as we touched down in Nairobi. By now, travelling on my own was a breeze, and I was well conversant with arriving in Kenya and the visa process involved.

As I stepped through the doors into the arrivals hall, I recognised a bunch of very familiar-looking uniforms and there was Ano standing with a dozen of our students, all proudly displaying immaculate looking Koha School uniforms. Joyce, Ano's niece, was also there with them.

There were shrieks of joy, hugs, and greetings all round, a few quick photo snaps outside the terminal, and then we piled onto a bus to take us to town, and then another one to Kawangemi. I was desperate to go directly to the school and see everyone, so that's where we headed before I checked into my pre-booked hotel.

We arrived at Kawangemi slum, and as we alighted, the driver took my luggage and placed it on the ground. Before I had a chance to argue, Joyce had hoisted my enormous twenty-three-kilogram suitcase on top of her head and started to walk off down the road to the school, heels and all. I was to this day in total awe of African women and their incredible strength.

The school was simply beautiful; I couldn't believe how much the garden had grown, thanks to 'Soldier' as we called our Masai guard, and the new classroom block looked fantastic. There wasn't a pupil to be seen, and I was a little disappointed, thinking we'd arrived too late in the afternoon and they had all left for the day. That was until we walked around the back of the school and there, filling up the entire back playground, was a sea of beautiful little faces, standing perfectly still and not uttering a sound. It was amazing and I would never forget the shock of seeing so many children and staff.

I asked Ano how many students there were, and he told me 300. I could not believe what I saw, or what I heard. There were also nine staff members that I didn't know about either, and my first thought was of how were they getting paid, as they certainly weren't on the payroll from our end.

Meanwhile while I was trying to process all this, Ano and the staff proceeded with a formal greeting to me, and in my honour a performance of various dance, singing, and drum items were put on by the kids. It was emotional, beautiful, surreal, and worrying all at the same time.

I was jet-lagged and tired, and so Ano called a taxi to collect me from the school and take me to the hotel where I'd arranged to stay the first two nights before moving on to the guesthouse I had booked from New Zealand.

Next morning, after a wonderful sleep in my amazing hotel bed, I headed straight for Koha School to see the children and to catch up with Ano. We had so much to discuss, and there was no time like the first day. I needed to know what we were going to do about all the kids, and how we would fund the teachers' salaries. I also wanted to have a quiet word with Soldier just to let him know that while it was a great thing to be defending Koha School, it would be much less of a drama if he kept his machete to himself. Not to mention the repercussions that could be imposed on him.

I discovered the teachers were working at Koha School for no wages. They were effectively volunteering with the hope that one day they might just be placed on the payroll; evidently this was quite common practice in Kenya. I wasn't at all happy with this arrangement, and promptly looked at making provisions in our monthly budget to pay them something small; it wouldn't be a lot to begin with but hopefully we would find some solution to assist them financially. I wanted to set Ano up with a proper accounting structure, and we also discussed the possibility of parents paying a very small school fee, when and if they could manage it, to top up the support we sent.

Meanwhile I moved into my guesthouse, the location of which I discovered on the first night wasn't ideal, directly behind a busy matatu stage, where the noise continued 24/7. It also rained that night and the roof above my room leaked, soaking my bedding and narrowly missed drowning my laptop that was lying on the floor next to the bed. I didn't sleep, and apart from one guy Silim who was really welcoming and kind to me, and who went on to become a new friend during my time in Kenya, the other housemates weren't friendly, and I was not happy there. The thought of spending the next two months in that place was ghastly.

Meanwhile Maureen had arrived into Nairobi and we made plans to meet up in town for coffee. We clicked immediately and our coffee meet turned into lunch, which then continued on in a bar with drinks.

She was due to move into the same guesthouse as me the following day but we soon discovered there had been a double-booking and Maureen was suddenly without anywhere to stay. The housekeeper who seemed to be running the place found her temporary accommodation at another guesthouse about two kilometres up the road and Maureen moved in there.

We kept in contact and she phoned me to say there was a spare room that I could move into. I packed up my stuff within a few minutes and without even informing the housekeeper, I simply left, dragging my luggage behind me.

Fortunately there was a taxi terminus quite close to the guesthouse so I walked over to a cab, asked the driver to open his boot, threw my suitcase in, slammed it shut, hopped in the back, and off we went. And I never went back.

Maureen met me at the gate to the compound and ushered me upstairs to the guesthouse. It was a nice, clean, and quiet place with five ensuite rooms and a shared kitchen. There were three other occupants at the time—a girl from Democratic Republic of the Congo, a young teenager from Ethiopia, and an Indian guy, who all seemed nice. I immediately felt comfortable with my new surroundings, and with Maureen the Aussie, and me the Kiwi, we called ourselves a small United Nations.

Maureen and I rapidly became friends and quite inseparable. We spent a lot of time together both at school, and on weekends; often visiting the markets and sightseeing local areas. Our after-work ritual was quickly established; gin and tonic for her, vodka and soda for me, a platter of nibbles thrown together, and a debrief of the day. What initially started as a 5:00 p.m. after-work wind-down however very quickly changed to 3:00 p.m..

Maureen was wonderful and a true asset to have on board while I was in Kenya. She made it her project to set up and implement simple recording and accounting systems into the school; easy enough for Ano and perhaps an office clerk to follow should Ano ever employ one. She put in a huge effort during her month at Koha School so that by the time she left, it was all up and running and in use. She also set up a petty cash allowance for Ano for buying day to day things such as soap, chalk, and morning tea for the staff.

When we were in Kenya the previous year, the focus was on establishing the school without any thought put into setting up systems for transparency of record keeping or monetary records. The new system was great, and meant Ano could now keep accurate records of everything, including what he was spending money on. We needed this and it was a high priority.

Maureen and I went over and over this with Ano, ensuring he understood how the system worked and how crucial it was to keep all records strictly up to date. I set up an email account for him with instructions to send through figures to me every month so there was accountability. I felt we were slowly but surely starting to make progress and I was pleased.

One of the first projects I decided to concentrate on when I first arrived in Kenya, and saw the lack of space in the school, was to build an office. Somewhere we could house all the school resources, textbooks, library books, as well as a place for the teachers to plan lessons, sit and have morning tea and lunch, as well as a meeting room for Ano and parents or visitors.

The school fund was very healthy and I knew we could afford to build an office.

Ano found a builder and they started construction right away. Within a week the office building was up and partitions installed to separate a small office area for Ano, with a strong, secure lockable door. We went to the village and bought a desk, chair, and steel cabinet so Ano could keep valuable documents and personal records etc. safe and secure.

Our small office immediately became a multi-purpose structure: used to secure all the school valuables; parent/teacher meeting room; Ano's office; staff room; library; administration office; kitchen; Soldier's sleeping quarters; and garden shed.

The topic that cropped up from time to time between Ano and I was the implementation of a feeding programme into the school. According to him many of our kids were arriving to school not having had breakfast, and without bringing lunch. We couldn't afford the feeding programme ourselves and I made that clear to Ano that if we went down the track of bringing the programme into the school that we would need funding from an outside source.

Ano produced a costings report and I decided to approach an NGO. I immediately thought of World Food Programme so I sat down and typed an email. My friend back home in New Zealand wrote a funding proposal request on my behalf. So I attached a copy and sent it off. A short time later I received a reply saying that within a few days they would be sending a Kenyan representative to interview Ano and myself and to take a look around at the facilities.

Sure enough a couple of days later I received a phone call from the Kenyan representative advising he would be visiting the school the following day. We were beside ourselves with excitement.

Next morning, a WFP vehicle pulled up outside the school, along with two other vehicles loaded with armed police. We had a very extensive interview and the WFP representative left armed with an abundance of paperwork and said he would be putting forward a recommendation to the head office in Geneva to provide assistance. Meanwhile as the weeks rolled on and we continued to wait for a response from Geneva, I started having mixed feelings about the feeding programme. I learned it wasn't going to be as clear-cut as just being provided with funding, it would be a lot more complex than that and I didn't feel we were ready. I decided to put it on hold. I felt too much was happening too fast at Koha School and we needed time for everything to settle. The school was not even twelve months old at this stage, and many changes were still happening.

Chapter Thirty-Five

A friend of mine, Jean Prime, who I'd met the previous year in a café in Nairobi when we were sitting next to each other, on our laptops, utilising the free wifi and casually started chatting, was doing an internship at a street boys' home situated on the outskirts of Nairobi. He invited Maureen and me to spend a day at the home; a centre for twelve- to twenty-year-old young men, most of whom have been living on the streets. The journey was a two-hour matatu ride, and a further ten-kilometre motorbike journey from Nairobi CBD.

The centre was set up and was run by Kiwi and Dutch missionaries as a working farm where the boys were taught farming skills, market gardening, and sustainability. The concept was fantastic, and we were so pleased to have been able to visit. We had a wonderful day, it was good to see how other projects were run and how they worked, and the boys took great pride in showing us around their farm, their self-made irrigation systems, animals, and flourishing crops.

It was Wednesday, and picnic day for the boys at the home, so after packing up lunch made for us by the wonderful kitchen staff, rugby balls, picnic rugs, and water bottles, we set out on a walk across paddocks, and set up our picnic under the shade of some trees. Zebra grazed in fields nearby. We spent the afternoon playing rugby and other games organised by the boys, casually sitting around, chatting, and enjoying the sun.

I had such a wonderful day that I sent a message to the home's Facebook page, explaining how much we had enjoyed ourselves, and following that we connected with the Kiwi couple Margaret and Robin and occasionally met up socially. They became invaluable to us with their expertise, knowledge and advice on running projects in Kenya and we often used them as a sounding board.

One day Ano announced that a new baby boy had been born in the village and his parents had named him Carnihan, after us. When I told Chris we initially thought it was quite hilarious, but Ano explained it was a huge honour. I was given an official invitation to go and meet him, so one morning I was escorted to the family home for a formal introduction. He was absolutely beautiful and it was a very special kind of feeling when I realised his parents clearly thought we were worthy of having our family name passed on to this baby boy. Before I had left New Zealand a very clever and generous, busy mum had kindly handmade and donated a beautiful baby quilt to me, and I had promised to keep it until I found someone very special to hand it on to. When I met baby Carnihan for the first time, I knew instantly he was that 'special someone' to receive this beautiful gift.

Maureen's month flew by and we achieved so much at the school; we were very pleased with what we had put in place in such a short time. However, all too soon Maureen was packing up, writing an abundance of notes and instructions for me on following through with her school administration set-up, and getting ready to move on to her next destination. It was a sad time; we had become good friends and looked out for each other, and when she left I missed her immensely.

One day out of the blue I received a phone call from Victor, a Kenyan friend. He explained that he had a boot-load of donated goods from a passenger on an overland trip he had just finished that week. Paul, the passenger, had instructed Victor to disperse of the goods where he saw fit, and he immediately thought of us at Koha School. Of course I was thrilled and invited him out to visit the school.

The following day Victor arrived with a friend, stopped outside the school, hopped out of the car, and opened the boot. It was exploding with the most incredible array of goodies. Brand new white polo shirts and Roman sandals, a variety of stationery, and soccer and rugby balls. We hauled it all into the office, and unloaded bag after bag until the entire office desk, chairs, and surrounding floor area was covered. It was amazing. The donor had left a letter and business card with his contact details requesting a handful of the children to write back to him. Ironically we noticed immediately on looking at his card that he was also from New Zealand, just three hours' drive from where we lived.

I knew that when I arrived back home, Chris and I would most definitely go and visit him. Meanwhile I emailed him, explaining where his donations ended up, with a promise to get in touch and meet up back in New Zealand.

One day our friend and former guesthouse mate from the previous year, Prosper from Rwanda, messaged me to say he was going to be in Nairobi attending a conference. I was very excited to hear from him again, and immediately made arrangements to go out to spend an evening at the conference centre where he was staying.

A couple of nights later I arranged my taxi driver Joseph to pick me up around 7:00 p.m. and drive me to the conference centre. It was dark and Joseph didn't know the area very well, but after many phone calls, we were apparently heading in the right direction. Then we got a puncture. It was a rural area, very dark because there was no power, and there was not a soul around.

Joseph told me to stay in the car and lock the doors while he sorted out the new tyre. I must say it felt a little unnerving to be in a car in the middle of nowhere, in the dark, with a taxi driver for protection. No sooner had he changed the tyre and we continued on our journey, than we arrived at our destination, approximately thirty metres on from where we had stopped.

Prosper was in the dining room with the other conference attendees when I walked in. Suddenly I heard a screech and commotion at one of the tables, as Prosper scrambled to get out of his seat and rushed to greet me. It was a wonderful reunion, we were both excited to see each other again. After taking me around all the dining tables and introducing me to everyone one by one, we settled down to catch up on our respective news of the last year since we had been living together in the guesthouse.

I didn't like to be out too late, so after a couple of hours of non-stop chat and a tour of the complex by Prosper, I phoned Joseph to come and collect me, whilst arranging with Prosper to meet up two days later before he was due to fly back home to Rwanda.

Again I got Joseph to drive me to the conference centre, this journey being very straight forward, no wrong turns, loss of direction, or punctures. Prosper and I spent the morning wandering around the expansive complex, taking all sorts of crazy pictures, and sitting by the pool, having chai and just enjoying each other's company. Prosper was a really awesome guy and it was one of the highlights of my trip to Kenya that year to be able to see him again.

One day I decided to take the afternoon off from the school and head to one of my favourite cafes in a large shopping mall near to where I was living. It was lunch time and the café was packed with people. There was one small two-seater round table vacant so I made a bee-line there, ordered my lunch, and brought out my laptop to make use of the free wifi. Shortly after, a middle-aged man approached me and asked if I minded him using the spare seat, to which I replied, "Of course not, go ahead."

He sat down and we started small talk, and he asked me what I was doing in Kenya. I told him as briefly as I could the story of the school and how we got involved. We chatted at length about the project and he also told me about a primary school he too was assisting in another large slum.

Then suddenly, out of the blue, he announced, "Today is your lucky day. I am going to build some classrooms for your school!"

He proceeded to say he owned his own construction company covering East Africa, so he wouldn't have time to come and see for himself, but that he would have one of his staff to contact me and he would assist with whatever we required.

"You just tell him what you want," he said.

With that he took out his phone and punched my phone number into it, then he stood up, and as he was about to leave he placed his business card on the table and added that if I didn't hear from a staff member within twenty-four hours to call him on his mobile number, pointing to his business card. With that, he wished me luck with the project, and then he left.

I couldn't quite believe what had just taken place. It was crazy. I immediately texted Chris back in New Zealand to relay the story, and although he was excited, he was dubious and told me to be careful and that it may be a scam. Likewise, I received similar reactions from many of our friends when I told them about the conversation I had with Al-Noor as well. It was just too good to be true. However, there was something very special and unique about Al-Noor, that I never once doubted him, not for a second.

Sure enough a couple of hours later I received a phone call from his foreman Jeff requesting we meet up so we could discuss the proposed new classrooms and also to arrange a site visit.

Next day we met in a mall, and after introductions and a brief chat about what we required to be built, we headed to Kawangemi, Jeff armed with a clipboard and tape measure.

He measured out a building, wrote a list of materials, instructed Ano to locate the builder, and then he left. The following morning a truck rattled its way down to the school and dumped a load of sand, rocks, and cement at the school gate, and building materials shortly after. That same day the construction of two classrooms and one library was underway.

It was yet another one of those incredibly special moments of fate that I seemed to constantly experience in Africa that I would never forget and got so much joy from sharing.

It was my last weekend in Kenya, so I decided to go back to one of my favourite out-of-town getaways, Lake Naivasha. I was starting to feel tired and drained from the two months and needed time out to escape the madness of the city and the very busy time at the school.

In my Kenya travel book I found what sounded like a cute little lakeside lodge and camping ground and booked two nights' accommodation. I packed a daypack with a good book and swimsuit and very little else, made my way into Nairobi, found the correct matatu to Lake Naivasha, and off I went. The idea I had in mind was to spend two days doing absolutely nothing but swimming and sunbathing.

After two matatu journeys, I finally arrived to the most peaceful, idyllic setting right on the lakefront complete with a beautiful pool and sun-lounging area. Perfect! That was going to be me for two days, I thought to myself. As well as the camping area, the lodge had various banda-type thatched huts dotted around lush green gardens and a manicured lawn. It was beautiful. I dropped my backpack in my room and headed out for a stroll down to the lakefront. There were signs up warning people to beware of hippos who had a tendency to roam up through the grounds at night time—a little scary, I thought to myself, considering more people were killed by hippos than any other animal in the world—but I knew I would be safely locked away in the confines of my little banda hut by evening, so there was nothing for me to worry about.

Generally the lake was renowned for its abundance of pink flamingo. It had something to do with the algae levels that attracted them, and there were sometimes more than half-a-million or more flamingo living on the lake. When driving north from Nairobi, which was elevated high above sea level, one could look far across the Great Rift Valley into the distance and see the lake with very large patches of what looked like bright pink carpet floating on the water. They were the pink flamingo.

My accommodation price included buffet meals. The first evening while having dinner in the dining room, I got chatting to a local who thought it helpful to highlight various points of interest in and around the lake vicinity. He told me about a bike ride through nearby Hell's Gate National Park, which combined stunning scenery, deep gorges, and an abundance of wildlife, and that I really shouldn't leave Lake Naivasha without experiencing it. Next minute I was arranging a bike ride for the following day.

I got up early and met my biking guide at the roadside, and after sorting out a suitably sized bike; adjusting the seat; ensuring the gears actually did work (I think three of the ten were fine); and grabbing some food and water from a kiosk nearby, off we cycled. I had not planned to be biking anywhere on this relaxing break so I was totally unprepared and had inappropriate clothing and footwear but it would have to do.

I hadn't asked too many questions about the actual day excursion but it didn't take me long to know that it was a good seven- to nine-hour return trip, the bike ride itself being seventeen kilometres of cycling through the national park to the gorge and of course back out again—so a total of around thirty-four kilometres. I couldn't remember the last time I had been on a bike either. Oh well, what was the worst that could happen, I thought to myself ... hmm ... probably a lot actually!

We set out on the bikes and by half-an-hour into the ride I had to stop at a roadside kiosk just before entering the park and adjust the seat of my clapped-out old bike, rearrange my daypack, and guzzle down some water. Even though it was early morning, the sun was beating down and it was going to be a hot day. I bought another two bottles of water, and then we were off.

We entered the national park and immediately the scenery took my breath away with its spectacular beauty. There were stunning backdrops of ancient rock formations; sheer cliffs that soared high into the sky; waterfalls and geysers; hot springs; and vast savannah with all kinds of wildlife grazing right at our feet. There was something very exhilarating about being at one with Africa's wildlife without the safe confines of a safari vehicle; to have zebra, giraffe, and warthog, to name a few, all right there beside us in the vast openness of the savannah was an experience I would never forget.

We cycled for about three-and-a-half hours before ditching our bikes under a tree. I frequently used the 'photo stop' card along the way, often just as an excuse to get off my bike for a minute or two because it was so uncomfortable. We sat and had a bite to eat and lots of water before embarking on the next stage of our journey, which involved clambering down steep ravines and rocks to the gorge floor some fifty metres below.

We were finally ready for our descent and when I peered over the edge of the cliff, I couldn't believe that we were actually going to climb so far down in amongst enormous boulders and rocks, so it was with great trepidation and concern at my totally inappropriate flip-flop footwear that I even thought about attempting it. My guide kindly offered to take my daypack for me; what that had to do with keeping me from slipping and falling fifty metres down a ravine, I didn't know, but off we went, and when we reached the gorge floor it was truly spectacular. We walked for about forty-five minutes, passing geysers and hot water springs and taking in the most awesome sights of the sheer cliff formations that encased us. When we came out into a clearing, we climbed a very steep embankment, at times forced back hard against the bank as herds of goats hurtled past us followed by their Masai herders. We reached the top of the cliff, to the most amazing, breathtaking view overlooking the savannah for as far as the eye could see. We found a good rock formation in which to sit and drink more water while admiring the spectacular scenery around us. I used this time to rest, ensuring I took my time eating and drinking to delay the journey back.

By the time we arrived back at the camp I was absolutely exhausted and headed straight for the swimming pool, and that's pretty much where I stayed for the remainder of my wee holiday, mainly because I could hardly move my tired and worn-out body; my muscles ached from head to toe.

It was, however, well worth enduring a couple of days of pain as my body recovered, as I was so thrilled to have had the experience, and equally rapt that I had coped with the whole biking adventure.

As luck would have it, when I went to check out of the lodge the following morning, I met a nice young Swedish couple who were keen to split costs to hire a taxi back to Nairobi as opposed to enduring the hell-raising, rattling, over-crowded matatu ride. Needless to say, I jumped at the chance.

I got back to Nairobi and headed straight to the school to see how far along the builders were with Al-Noor's new classrooms. The framing and some iron sheet cladding were nearly finished and it was starting to take shape. I knew it wasn't going to be finished before I left Kenya, but it felt very exciting to have another three rooms under construction just the same. Ano's plan was to bring in a further two class streams the following year, and I stuck firmly with my request that the third room be earmarked as a library.

I had still only met Al-Noor that one time, at the café when he offered to build the classrooms, and tried many times to make contact with him but without success. Jeff oversaw the project while Al-Noor just kept sending the funds through. I wanted to tell him how much his donation of the three new rooms meant to us and for the school and it was frustrating that I might leave Kenya without having the opportunity to tell him in person.

I was constantly amazed that it seemed every time I met someone in Kenya, something good came out of it. On one of my last afternoons before leaving, while waiting to meet our friend Ken at a popular outdoor bar in Nairobi, I unintentionally rescued a British guy from three prostitutes who had descended on him the moment he walked over to a vacant leaner to put his beer down. I had watched all this unfold, quite amused by the whole scene taking place, when suddenly the targeted guy picked up his beer, headed straight for me, plonked his glass down, and said, "Sorry about this, I don't know you, but today you are my wife, ok?" It worked, and the girls were gone in a flash.

So of course then we got chatting, and this guy Kevin, a psychologist working for the UN, had just finished a three-month stint at a refugee camp close to the Somalian border and had arranged to meet a tour guide at the bar to discuss his upcoming safari. We chatted about my reasons for being in Kenya and the school project, and he proceeded to explain that he was leaving the following week but offered to keep in touch with me and when he was next in Kenya, he would work for a week at Koha School voluntarily counselling and teaching the staff and students on psychological issues.

But that's not all that happened. Eventually my friend Ken arrived, and he had another friend with him. Chris and I met Ken on our trip back in 2009 and we had since become family friends. And then Kevin's safari guide arrived, and over a few drinks I sang Ken's praises as a fantastic cook, but he was often struggling to make ends meet, and desperately needed work. I thought that perhaps this safari guide may think about contracting him to cook on his trips. He said they were always looking for good cooks, so after discussing a few details, they exchanged phone numbers and promised to keep in touch. I felt happy about this connection and hoped it would work out.

There were so many Kenyans struggling and if I could help one or two out just by way of introduction, then I felt I was doing some good.

Meanwhile, also in that last week, another friend had been admitted for surgery to remove a tumour from her stomach. When I had arrived in Kenya and met up with Elizabeth I noticed her protruding stomach. She explained that before I arrived, she had been in enormous pain, and had gone to the doctor who had diagnosed a stomach ulcer and given her a prescription for antibiotics. They instructed her to take the full course and that should fix it. Well, it didn't fix it. By the time I arrived in Kenya, she was on her second course of antibiotics, and still not feeling any better. In fact, she was considerably worse, so at my insistence she sought a second opinion. This time she saw a different doctor who immediately diagnosed her as having a mass in her stomach, and it was by this time an emergency.

After a series of scans and x-rays, she was booked in for the operation the following week, and given a quote for the procedure, hospital stay, and post-care that she simply could never afford. In Kenya, the process was that you paid up-front, or no operation— simple as that. She said she had to fundraise for the amount needed, and quickly, but I couldn't help but think that this amount was beyond reach.

After rallying around family and friends, she still didn't have enough so she wasn't able to go ahead with the surgery, however the following week a friend suggested she try another smaller hospital where the fee was much less, but where the level of care and experience would also be much less. She had no choice but to agree to this option and underwent the surgery just two days before I left Kenya. I couldn't believe what I had heard when her husband said that he had been told he must wait outside the operating theatre during her surgery to receive the tumour, then deliver it by taxi into Nairobi pathology unit for testing.

As I was leaving Kenya, she was recouping in hospital and I was relieved that she had finally had the surgery.

However, I learnt that six months later she again went under the knife because some parts of the tumour had been left behind during the initial surgery, which had continued to grow and spread rapidly. At the time of the second operation, they removed a two-kilogram growth that had started strangling her kidneys. The operation that time was successful, and thank goodness she made a full recovery.

Chapter Thirty-Six

A nd so, once again, I departed Kenya with a heavy heart but already with plans going on in my head to return the following year with Chris. I didn't know how long I would keep feeling this way, but I knew I had to return. Africa was firmly cemented in my life, and that was just the way it was. I couldn't imagine anything else.

The children and staff conducted a beautiful but emotional farewell concert; parents and members of the community I had come to know well during my visits to Kawangemi all attended and it was a special time.

I felt comfortable that I had things in place as much as I could before leaving and happy with the knowledge that Ano and his team of staff and friends in the community were capable and would look after our beloved school until our return. My only disappointment was not being able to connect with Al-Noor, but I would continue trying when I returned to New Zealand.

After a lovely reunion with my family in Melbourne, I returned to New Zealand and settled back into normal life and routine, with thoughts of returning to Kenya never far from my mind. It didn't take long for me to convince Chris that if we really focused and saved extra hard, we could manage a trip the following year in 2013. This time we thought of renting our house out for the duration of our time away, which would bring in extra income.

Before the dust had time to settle on my laptop, I was again searching flight prices, routes, and dates, for maximum savings possible.

Meanwhile, reports from Ano were that everything was going well back in Kenya at Koha School. Despite repeatedly and sternly telling Ano not to take in more students, he seemed to take great delight in informing us that the school roll was increasing continuously. I often wondered and confronted him with, "What part do you not understand about capping the school roll?"

I worried constantly about the funding and became increasingly annoyed with him for not following our instruction. It seemed he just didn't understand the pressure we were under back in New Zealand to provide adequate funding. He clearly also couldn't see past the simple maths—more kids; more uniforms; more resources needed; more staff; more salaries, equalled more funding required.

Our sponsorship base by this time however had grown rapidly and we had 115 sponsors paying $10 a month, equating to over $1,000 a month coming into the school bank account in New Zealand to be dispersed to staff for wages, school resources, textbooks, stationery, etc. So, we were managing, but could have done without the work and pressure involved.

We also held occasional movie night fundraisers to raise money for extras such as outfitting the two new classrooms Al-Noor kindly built for us, school uniforms, and more textbooks. The movie nights were always highly successful and we could count on raising a good amount of money.

I was also fully immersed on the speaking circuit, raising extra funds by spreading the story of Koha School, and also my own personal African journey that ultimately led us to establish the school.

I spoke to various groups and private clubs and very soon it was school groups, and then private companies. I was even flown up to Auckland, a major New Zealand city, to speak to a couple of school groups there. Each time, I received donations; all of which went straight into the 'school pot'.

Then I realised I thrived on public speaking. And because I spoke straight from the heart, standing up in front of audiences of up to 300+ was a breeze. No notes and no rehearsals needed—I loved it.

I became completely absorbed in the school project and night after night I sat with my laptop, updating spreadsheets, sending emails and newsletter updates to sponsors, organising fundraising events, and chatting with other like-minded people about their charity projects, and it was rapidly consuming my life. But I didn't mind at all.

Shortly after arriving home, I received a text from Ano advising of another altercation between our Masai guard and a member of public. One afternoon one of our young five-year-old boys was knocked down and badly injured outside the school by a speeding motorcyclist. Our guard had witnessed this accident and immediately chased after the driver, lashing out with his machete, slashing his arms and hands. I realised our chats relating to physical violence had clearly fallen on deaf ears.

Chris and I started making plans for our trip back to Kenya for mid-2013, which had become a pattern mainly because it was generally the quiet time for his business. It also meant we escaped the harsh New Zealand winter.

We had a love of exploring developing countries, and I tended to book our route to Kenya via Asia mainly because it was always the cheapest option. However we decided that for the next trip we would go direct to Kenya; we knew we had a lot of donated items to take to the school, so it made sense to fly as direct as possible and do some travelling on the way back home. We chose India again. But this time we decided to explore the south. We also discovered that we would be less than a one-hour flight from Sri Lanka, so why not go there too.

So together with working, attending to all the school stuff, as well as public speaking, I was busy organising and booking flights and also researching Southern India and Sri Lanka for our impending visit. The time flew by and we were suddenly three months out from leaving New Zealand, again.

We took a punt and advertised our home for short-term rental of four months and we were inundated with calls and enquiries. We chose a middle-aged couple from Germany, who were coming back to New Zealand after living in Australia for a few years. We hadn't met them, but chose them based purely on a gut feeling; there was something we liked about them and so when they arrived back in New Zealand a few weeks before we were due to depart, we met up and immediately got on very well. We knew they would be perfect to look after our lovely home, and our beloved old cat Rosie.

Meanwhile, as with the previous years' trips to Africa, we again started receiving endless supplies of goods to be donated to the school from wonderful, generous, kind-hearted people. As the pile grew, we were happy with our decision to head directly to Kenya without going off backpacking with overloaded luggage.

Also, monetary donations were given freely, so they were stashed in the bank account, which was building up nicely. We had a good idea of projects we wanted to work on, including more toilets and a staff room, so the funds would be put to great use but I also had a notebook and I wrote down specific items if a donor had requested it.

Meanwhile Mandy was heading to Turkey for a holiday around the same time we would be in Kenya and so she decided to swing by Nairobi and stay with us for a month. We were also contacted by two Scottish girls Cheryl and Amy who had heard about the school and who wanted to come to Kenya and volunteer for a few weeks. We were very happy to have them come and I arranged accommodation at our guesthouse for them to stay with us.

We also had a request from a Wellington lawyer, Hanna, who was heading to Europe and wanted to spend a month volunteering with us first. Again, we were delighted to have her stay. There was always stuff to do at Koha School, and having experienced volunteer work myself, I understood how rewarding it was, and we were always happy to assist.

June arrived, and we prepared to vacate our house. In a mad flurry of extra cleaning and after a few minor repairs to the house, I also compiled a folder of handy tips; maps; rubbish days; local emergency contact phone numbers; the wifi password; and other relevant information for our tenants. We spent many hours going over everything to ensure that they would be as comfortable as possible in our home.

Finally the day arrived to depart our home. We had arranged for the tenants to meet us at 12:00 noon to hand over the keys. We were leaving all our own 'things' in our house so it felt a little weird, particularly as we were still in New Zealand for a further three days staying with both our daughter Hayley and also my mum.

What if we'd forgotten something really important? What if I really wanted to pack that extra top just in case? Too late. But it was our house ... too bad!

Finally we were checked in at Wellington International Airport, bound for Melbourne where we stayed a few nights with our son Craig and his now fiancé Tracey. I'd instigated an unspoken rule in our family that we didn't fly anywhere overseas without first visiting the kids.

We were soon on our way to Kenya, via brief stopovers in Kuala Lumpur, Chennai, and Abu Dhabi, arriving in Nairobi two days later. The flights were largely uneventful, except for a couple of horrible experiences while waiting for our connecting flight at Chennai airport. We arrived in the late evening, and had a ten-hour layover. We assumed we could kill time sleeping in the terminal while we waited, as we had done on many lengthy stopovers around the world. However we hadn't planned for the fact that all passengers in and out of Chennai had to clear customs and immigration, and exit the terminal completely.

Next minute we found ourselves outside sitting on the ground with our luggage strewn all around us, along with all the other hordes of transiting travellers. We had no local currency on us, nowhere to sit except on the broken concrete or our backpacks, and no food or drink. It was stiflingly hot and muggy and flies and other insects swarmed the air and us.

We soon discovered the only ATM working was inside the terminal; the same one we had just exited, and we had a ten-hour layover. The delicious aroma of glorious Indian cooking wafted through the air, and Chris and I could no longer stand it. I went and asked the customs officers and armed guards, of which there were many, if I could quickly go back inside the terminal and withdraw some cash from the ATM so we could eat and drink, with the promise to vacate the terminal immediately.

As I stood there trying very hard to explain my predicament of having no cash to a couple of guards, a fly flew straight into my mouth and became lodged in the back of my throat. I thought I would die. It was the most horrendous feeling and I was extremely agitated. I don't think the men quite understood my anguish but eventually, after a lot of pleading, they allowed me to go back into the terminal, all the while watching my every move.

I headed straight for the ATM and to my dismay there was a lengthy queue and the more I swallowed, the more I could feel the fly lodged in my throat and it was more than I could bear. Finally I got to the ATM to find it out of order. I was on the brink of tears, but then spotted a currency exchange bureau so I headed there and again joined a queue. The whole process seemed to take forever, but I finally had some cash, raced outside, and ran to where Chris was waiting in the cafe, hysterically trying to tell him of my fly incident. He ordered me three bottles of water, which I guzzled in seconds, and I felt utterly sick. I ate a couple of samosas and felt much better, but the thought of this fly floating around inside me was just ghastly.

I eventually calmed down and we went back outside and sat down on the ground making ourselves as comfortable as we could. But as time went on, we became increasingly sleep-deprived and went in search of an airport-hotel or somewhere where we could just put our heads down for a few hours. After all, we still had over eight hours to go before our flight to Abu Dhabi.

We were strolling along the pavement outside of the terminal and were stopped by an important-looking airport official asking if we would like a room to rent for a few hours. We jumped at the chance. He told us to wait while he hailed a taxi. It arrived, we threw our luggage into the boot, and off we went. The driver stopped outside a dingy-looking place and, beckoning to the stairs, told us to go up and the receptionist would look after us. Then off he roared.

I immediately felt uneasy but went along with the checking in process, paid a few rupee, we were shown to our room and we settled down for a few hours' sleep. But I felt frightened. And the more I thought about it, the more and more anxious I became and no more than half an hour after getting into bed, I was up, packing my stuff, explaining to Chris I wanted to leave. And so, we dragged ourselves and our luggage back to reception, asked the staff to call a cab, and we were soon on our way back to the airport. Nothing went wrong, but I followed my gut instinct and it didn't seem right. I felt relieved to be back to the safety of the airport, and suddenly the idea of spending hours and hours sitting on the ground outside the airport terminal with the flies and heat didn't seem too bad at all. And that's where we stayed and watched time go by for what seemed like an eternity, but I felt safe.

Chapter Thirty-Seven

We arrived into Jomo Kenyatta International Airport, cleared customs and immigration without a hitch, and entered the arrivals hall to a very excited bunch of children wearing all-too-familiar uniforms, a beaming Ano, his niece Joyce, and a couple of other adults all waving furiously at us.

There was the usual flurry and excited exchange of greetings and snapping of cameras before being escorted to a waiting matatu van where we all clambered in, kids piled high on top of each other in the back along with Ano and Joyce, while Chris and I sat in the front with the driver.

We headed straight for the school and were greeted by what looked like thousands of beautiful, beaming, cheerful children congregated around the school gate. It was extremely emotional. There were now 380+ students and twelve staff. We made our way to the back of the school buildings where a wonderful formal welcome was extended to Chris and me, combined with dance and song items. The children were then released from school for the day, so that was also our cue to leave, and we were exhausted. Ano organised a taxi to drop us at our guesthouse, the same one Maureen and I had stayed the year before, and we crashed.

We couldn't get back to the school the next morning fast enough. Koha School looked beautiful. Chris was absolutely amazed because he hadn't seen the school since we built that first wee building (for fifty children) nearly two years ago, and it was super exciting for him to see how much it had developed. He summed it up by saying Koha School felt and looked like a little village all of its own.

Classrooms were chockablock with many children, the gardens were flourishing, and there seemed to be a lovely feel about the school. Everything seemed settled, Ano seemed happy, and he had a fantastic team of staff, all young, energetic, fully trained teachers, seemingly really nice people doing a wonderful job of working with our kids. There was also an office clerk, a young girl Agnes who Ano had employed to take care of the admin duties. She seemed to take her job very seriously. And there was a head teacher, Tony, who we liked instantly; he was very efficient and always working, either marking, planning, or graphing students' grades. He seemed to have a lot of input into the day-to-day running of the school, and he was good at it. The staff respected him. There was a comforting feeling about this teacher; that his dedication and commitment were good to have at the school.

The children also seemed to be doing well and the teachers had the senior kids working their butts off. We discovered that not only did they come to school for a normal school day, but then they came back in the evenings for extra tuition, and then on Saturday mornings till 1:00 p.m.! Both pupils and teachers seemed to be fully focused on their national primary certificate exams the following year, knowing full well that the results of these exams could well have a huge impact on their future high school options.

And so the next day we began our daily routine of working at the school.

On our first morning visit to Kawangemi we were greeted by many welcoming locals who recognised us from our previous visits. The familiar hollers of "How are you, how are you!" from clusters of children amused us as we waved back at them, and the meet and greet of local passers-by and the familiar faces of local school neighbours as they came by to welcome us back to Kenya made us feel warm 'n' fuzzy.

We always felt quite safe in Kawangemi, and although it was a large slum village with an enormous population of extreme poverty, we walked through the village two to four times a day, back and forth from school to shops, or to the bank, café, or to meet visitors at the matatu junction, very comfortably.

Our first priority was to have a meeting with Ano, to define priorities for Koha School and what we hoped to achieve during our three-month visit.

By the end of that first day things were already on the move: the digging of the desperately needed four new toilet pits had begun; a desk supplier had been located and consequently an order of ten new desks placed, to be delivered the following week; book cabinets were in the process of being made and we had conducted the first meetings of the issues of both power supply and feeding programme.

Just as I expected, my library room was now filled with kids, which was initially disappointing so my thoughts turned to the possibility of building a small stand-alone library somewhere on the property.

Power supply was high on the agenda mainly because our seniors would need computer studies as part of the Class 8 curriculum the following year, so therefore power was essential. We initially discussed the possibility of installing solar panels, but Ano was reluctant; his view was that it would announce to the entire Kawangemi slum that Koha School was a school of wealth and therefore create further unwanted attention, and there might be not only the theft of the panels, but also whatever else might be of value inside the school buildings. Instead, he decided to investigate the cost of tapping into a power source already used in a couple of places near to the school. We also revisited the feeding programme issue, so I asked him to investigate it thoroughly first and then we would address it again. We would need a sponsor to fund the programme, but we were happy to help with the initial set up.

It was good to be on the move.

We settled easily; Kenya was by now our second home and the surroundings all too familiar. We had over the past few years formed many friendships there, so this visit was by no means going to be all work and no play.

We made contact with our local friends almost immediately, letting them know we were back, and organising to meet up. Paul, the guy who lived in NZ and had donated many fabulous items to the school the previous year, had planned a very short stop-over in Nairobi en route to New Zealand from Britain. He was due to arrive the first weekend we were in Kenya, as was Mandy, who was going to be with us for a month.

Paul arrived and we met up in a bar in Nairobi. We also invited another mutual Kenyan friend Ken to join us. We had a wonderful afternoon, which carried on into the evening, reconnecting and reminiscing.

We departed that evening with plans to go to watch the Kenya vs Uganda rugby match the following evening. Mandy arrived the next morning and had no sooner dropped her luggage than we piled into a matatu and headed into Nairobi to meet Paul, and then catch a local bus to the stadium to watch the rugby. It was a hilarious, fun night, the antics going on in the grandstand being the standout entertainment of the evening.

Of course we were the only mzungu surrounded by predominantly Kenyan supporters, however right next door were the Ugandan supporters and the behaviour between the two rival camps was outrageous. The dancing, chanting, singing, and constant banter kept us highly entertained and amused.

We couldn't wait till Monday to take both Mandy and Paul to Koha School. Mandy hadn't even seen the school operating as she had left Kenya before the school was opened, so this was a very special time for her, Ano, and for us. Paul also joined us for the day, making the most of his visit by playing with the kids, sitting in on lessons, and he also organised the purchase of much-needed cabinets, and other essentials for the school from the fantastic donation of money collected from his workplace back in New Zealand.

We found the staff were hard to connect with, particularly the female staff. We noticed this quite soon after we arrived in Kenya, so we held a staff lunch to break the ice. We called into a local butcher in Kawangemi one morning on the way to school, selected a nice large piece of goat and asked the butcher to roast it for us, along with a lump of ugali and some cooked green kale, and agreed to collect it all just before lunch time.

It went well, we wanted them to feel comfortable around us and interact as equals, but there was a distinct awkwardness from them that we couldn't work out. It bothered us.

Chapter Thirty-Eight

We settled well into our apartment; the same place my volunteer Maureen and I stayed in the previous year. They'd made some slight improvements, which might have had something to do with the list of requests I emailed before leaving New Zealand; remembering all the things that frustrated us the previous year—namely the lack of almost all kitchen crockery and utensils. According to our flatmates, an abundance of kitchen items and other things like a toaster and electric jug suddenly appeared the minute before we arrived.

This year there was also a lovely lady Purity working there. She was employed as the housekeeper, but incidentally who I had not requested! We struggled with the whole housemaid concept in Africa, something very foreign to us in New Zealand, however we often reminded ourselves that many jobs were created by employing domestic help. We also struggled with the manner in which they were often treated.

We had three flatmates in our guesthouse, all guys: Mehul, an Indian bloke from UK, John from Rwanda, and Julian from Nigeria. They were all very nice and we got on well, rapidly becoming good friends and often hanging out together. With our busy lives at Koha School it was also really important for us to have a life outside of the school. I'd read a flyer pinned up on a noticeboard in a local shopping mall about a Bizarre Bazaar to be held in Karura Forest, a location close to UN Headquarters, the following Saturday, so we decided to go and take a look.

We took our usual form of public transport, matatu into Nairobi CBD and then another one out to the forest. After alighting the matatu, we walked a good couple of kilometres into the forest following a dirt lane until we came to a large clearing where the Bazaar was being held. The convoy of Range Rovers, Mercedes-Benz, and BMW cars that hurtled past us on the road was reassuring that we were indeed heading in the right direction. It also alerted us to the fact that this Bazaar might well be an upmarket affair.

We noted quite surprisingly however that not one vehicle stopped to ask if we wanted a ride; very clearly we were heading to the same event.

We eventually arrived at this magnificent setting, in a clearing in a forest in Africa to find possibly fifty or so large, identical high-top marquees set up in an oval shape, brimming with local high quality crafts, art, and jewellery. Many tables, chairs, and umbrellas, combined with food stalls producing an abundance of delectable delights, were dotted throughout the centre of the oval.

The atmosphere instantly reminded me of *Out of Africa*—it was all very 'cashmere sweater, cream pants, and African safari hat'. We felt very out of place, having just arrived by matatu, traipsed through the forest wearing shorts, T-shirts, and sandals, and not at all in fitting with the ambience of this magical setting. However we had a wonderful time trawling the stalls, sampling the local fare, and listening to local music while enjoying a pleasant amount of people-watching and soaking up the peaceful atmosphere.

I never cease to be amused by the African way, and the pace at which the local people move; the only things moving faster than snail's-pace seem to be the matatu! I loved the laidback attitude and realised how much we could learn by not taking life quite so seriously as we tended to do in the western world.

One day Mandy and I decided to go into Nairobi CBD to look for a sports uniform for Koha School kids for when they represented the school in inter-sports games.

I'd seen a large uniform shop on one of my many shopping trips into town so we headed straight there. There were no other customers in the shop when we entered, but we counted twenty-one staff dotted all around the store; some were behind counters, others fussing with stock, and some were just standing around not doing much at all. They didn't have what we were looking for, so we carried on searching for other similar shops. We spotted a tiny kiosk set up on the side of the street, between some shops, where three staff members stood together behind the counter. We went up to them and I caught the young assistant's eye. She looked up at me with a look that seemed to ask, "Can I help you?" without her actually opening her mouth.

I asked if they had sports uniforms. She stared at me blankly for some seconds, then slowly proceeded to take an earphone out of one ear.

"Sorry, what?" she asked with an uninterested look about her.

Mandy and I looked at each other, shook our heads, started to laugh.

I muttered, "Don't worry," and we walked away, totally bemused.

My first matatu incident of that particular visit to Kenya happened one Saturday afternoon. I had been in town shopping, and got into a matatu to head home. We no sooner left the matatu stage, when the driver suddenly did a U-turn into a really busy street, and smacked straight into the back right corner of a very badly parked car. Hakuna matata, no worries—the driver simply slammed the van into reverse, prized it off the bumper, crunched into first gear, and off we roared. What I found so amusing was that not a single word was exchanged from the passengers, there was no expression of shock or horror—nothing at all. Just another normal day riding in the infamous matatu.

In another matatu ride, I sat beside a girl who sat next to a closed window. When we left the matatu stage, we pulled up into a traffic jam in a very busy main street in Nairobi CBD. The girl next to me was busy texting on her phone, when suddenly she let out a loud shriek and started screaming out the window while pointing to a man sprinting off down the middle of the road. Apparently this guy had snatched the phone right out of her hand as he casually walked past the window. The incredible thing was that the window was closed, but with precise timing, he managed to slide open the window and rip the phone right out of her hand before anybody saw a thing. No-one except the girl had any idea what had just happened, not even me, and I was sitting right next to her. I had a big wake-up call about being extra vigilant, especially when I thought of all the times I'd walked down busy streets in Kenya texting or talking on the phone.

One day I went out to visit my darling old friend Muli, the little old man who lived on the property and maintained the gardens of the volunteer house we stayed in, in 2010.

Muli was full of old African wisdom and it was he who had told me I should throw my toothbrush and toothpaste away and follow his teeth cleaning practises by using a twig plucked from a bush and dipping it in ash from his fire. However Muli was missing many teeth top and bottom, so I was very dubious about following his advice.

He was a truly delightful little man and every time I went to Kenya I made it a high priority to visit Muli and take him gifts, mainly of warm clothing. This particular time I took Mandy with me and we surprised him with our visit. He was wearing the merino wool sweater I took for him two years ago, looking like it had never been off his back!

He was really happy to see us, and despite the language barrier, with my small amount of Swahili and loads of hand gesturing, we were capable of having a fairly lengthy conversation, of sorts. Muli told me that the property had been sold and he had six weeks to move out. The owner of the property had since employed a younger gardener, and no longer required his services and that meant he would probably have to go back to his tribal area in rural Kenya.

I was really sad to hear that news and could not believe someone would kick this harmless old man out of his little home of over fifty years. The property was enormous and his tiny house took up a very small area on the property. I wondered and worried what would become of him.

I decided that next time I visited him I would take him a gift of roasted goat. That to Muli would be a huge treat. In Kawangemi where the school was situated, there were local butcher shops where you selected your meat and its size from the many carcasses strung up inside and outside the little kiosks. A couple of hours later the meat was ready to be collected, having been barbequed, cut into pieces, and wrapped up in newspaper.

When we were living in Kenya, we took up every opportunity presented to us to experience the local culture and accepted the invitations offered to us. One Sunday night while Mandy was still with us, we attended a fashion show charity event hosted by a worldwide charity organisation in India, featuring collections of saris and traditional Indian dress by two of India's most prestigious and famous designers. We had been invited by our flatmate Mehul, and of course didn't hesitate to accept.

The event was held at a beautiful safari resort situated just out of Nairobi. Set amongst a stunning combination of large, immaculately manicured gardens, waterfalls, little arched bridges, and pools with gorgeous grass-thatched huts dotted about the complex, it was a very prestigious event.

When Mehul invited us to attend, my first thought was, what will I wear? The selection of clothing and accessories I had brought with me from New Zealand was definitely not appropriate for such a posh event, so I spent that afternoon frantically looking for an outfit, as well as heels and a handbag of course. It was exciting to have an opportunity to get dressed up, far removed from the usual attire I was used to wearing in Kenya, and in particular the slum of Kawangemi, and by the time we were ready to go out I felt like Cinderella going to the ball.

The evening started with refreshments around the pool area of the complex. The 500+ guests were predominantly from the Kenyan-Indian community, however we were made very welcome and didn't feel at all out of place. After a couple of hours of mixing and mingling, we were ushered into the large auditorium and took our places alongside the runway. I found it difficult to describe the exquisite colour and vibrancy of the intricately sequinned and embroidered saris and traditional Indian dresses modelled that evening and we were in total awe of the workmanship that had gone into creating such beautiful garments.

Also during the evening were interludes that included other acts; two Indian singers and an African dance troupe entertained us, which only added another flavour to the event.

Just before the show ended one of the designers announced he would select guests from the audience to act as catwalk models on the runway. Much to our horror, Mehul and I were both chosen. We had to walk up on stage, and on cue sashay one by one down the runway, along with others he had also chosen, in front of this large crowd.

It was both embarrassing and nerve-wracking for a number of reasons. (1) Because I could feel Chris and Mandy's laughter penetrate right through me, (2) 500 other people were all watching, and (3) because the shoes I had bought earlier in the day to wear for the evening, were a fraction too big and I felt I would slip right out of them right there in front of the entire audience. However, I did get through the ordeal with heels still intact, and dignity holding on by a thread.

The evening was finished off dining al fresco with a beautiful banquet dinner under a perfect African night sky.

Chapter Thirty-Nine

One of the young security guards at our house was twenty-five years old and had four wives and three children. We liked Jimmy, he was a nice young guy and we had a lot of laughs with him. Chris tried for many weeks to make him understand that he'd lost his mind and that one wife was more than enough. It was legal in Kenya to have multiple wives, although you didn't really hear of women having multiple husbands. Much of it was different tribal beliefs where some practised polygamy, others strictly monogamy.

Tribes were fiercely staunch in Kenya, there were forty-two of them, and people generally greeted each other for the first time with a handshake and an exchange of the tribe they belonged to. In rural areas of Kenya, tribal clashes were still an everyday occurrence as many tribes just didn't get on, and perhaps never would. A lot of the tribal clashes occurred over the rustling of cattle, goats, and also land occupation. There were many tribes who led a nomadic existence and were always on the move, seeking fresh feed for their cattle and goats etc. They would often trespass to reach greener pastures, which inevitably led to violent clashes. This was part of Africa's ancient tradition that you just couldn't imagine ever dying.

When we started discussing the possibility of one day buying land for Koha School, Ano was adamant we would have nothing but trouble if we bought in Nairobi surrounds. Naturally he was pushing to move the school up-country to Western Kenya, his rural area and where his people were. We did think briefly that maybe we had no option, for a number of reasons, mainly cost, but after a lot of thought we realised that the school belonged in Kawangemi community and this was where it should remain.

Meanwhile there was a lot of activity going on at the school. The feeding programme was high on the agenda and we put a lot of thought into the pros and cons of implementing this into our school. However, after a lot of careful thought and taking on board advice from others who already owned schools, and also Kenyan friends who we knew and trusted, we again decided not to go ahead with the feeding programme at Koha School at that particular time, and were very comfortable and pleased with the decision.

A number of factors came into focus, and the main reason for the decision was that we knew our kids were being fed; they were bringing lunch to school, they were learning, and there were no obvious signs of starvation. However, we made the decision to revisit the issue the following year. But for time being we decided to concentrate on providing an education to 380+ children, rather than spreading ourselves thinly.

We had been donated funds to build the cookhouse and so after clearing it with the donor, we decided to turn it into a staff room/library. I had noticed there wasn't anywhere for the staff to go to have time out, mark books, set work plans etc., so the transformation of the cookhouse was absolutely perfect.

We also installed skylights in Al-Noor's three classrooms—and wow, what a difference! We were constantly amazed at how content everybody seemed to be at school—not a word was mentioned about the need for skylights until we arrived and saw that the kids in these classrooms were having lessons in semi-darkness.

One day we decided to go to Westlands and have lunch in our favourite café. We had no sooner sat down and I looked across the room and there was Al-Noor. We both spotted each other at the same time, and finally we had reconnected. Al-Noor immediately got up and came over to where we were sitting. I was with Chris and Mandy so I was also able to introduce them to Al-Noor, which was wonderful, as they had heard so much about him. I still hadn't seen or spoken with him since that one and only time we met in exactly the same cafe, at almost exactly the same table and time, when he offered to build us the classrooms. It was great to see him again, and we chatted for hours, arranging to go out for dinner the following week. He'd never visited Koha School so hadn't seen the three classrooms he so generously donated, and one of the first conversation topics I brought up was that he needed to see what he had built for us.

Mandy's visit was rapidly moving on and we knew her departure would arrive abruptly, so one Saturday we decided to spend a day on safari at Lake Nakuru approximately two hours' drive away. Unfortunately Chris had a touch of flu and was not well enough to join us, so we took Ano with us instead, and booked our safari with our friend Johnson who had just recently set up his own safari company.

We had a magical day game driving for hours, lucky enough to spot an abundance of wildlife in the most stunning surroundings of beautiful Lake Nakuru, and on a spur of the moment we threw in a rare touch of decadence by treating ourselves to lunch at a very posh safari lodge overlooking the lake. It was truly spectacular.

We all worked extremely hard in those first weeks in Kenya and completed a lot of projects. Within four weeks we had built, painted, and completed the four new toilets; organised a large cabinet to be purpose-built and installed thanks to Paul and his wonderful donors back home in New Zealand at Rose & Shamrock Hotel who had fundraised for months for us; we bought and had a large water tank installed; extended the playground by renting and clearing the plot next door to the school; built a fence; had ten new desks built and in place; two classroom dividers built and installed; four roof skylights installed; sponsored children's work completed and ready to be delivered to sponsors on our return

269

to New Zealand; new accounting and banking practices were in the process of being implemented; and a staff room was under construction.

It was exciting watching developments take place at such speed, but it was also a little draining mentally and physically when constantly working in the harsh slum conditions, mixing with a community of 500,000 people whose lives, culture, and language were so different to ours, meaning interpretations were often poles apart.

In Kenya life was hard, and in slum areas it was extremely tough. People such as us mzungu came along, and we were instantly thought of as their ticket to anywhere and anything. The community grasped at us like leaches, asking for assistance; money; food; education; jobs; sponsorship; medical assistance ... they were desperate and they asked constantly. This was very normal, and we became quite used to it, but it was also tiring.

It was Mandy's last week in Kenya and we needed a break from the school and environment. We also wanted some time-out to enjoy each other's company before she left us, so we decided to take the week off and essentially have a holiday. We thrived on leisurely mornings; trawled the craft markets; enjoyed long lunches; caught up with friends for BBQs, dinners, and drinks; went on safari game-drives; had more drinks; and did anything and everything we felt like doing.

We met another Kiwi family who were living in Kenya, who we had met through mutual acquaintances. They had extended family visiting from New Zealand at the time, and so one day they arranged to visit the school. They arrived armed with loads of pens, pencils, and other stationery, which was very exciting for everyone at Koha School.

When they arrived at school, our senior classes were heavily involved in an organised debate on monogamy versus polygamy, a topic very important here in Kenya.

We sat in on the debate and it was very interesting to hear the children's various views on having multiple wives. We also took part in a light-hearted way, which the kids found highly entertaining. Chris added his input by announcing through Mr Speaker that he was all in favour of monogamy because of his 'one wife = one headache' theory, which had them laughing hysterically, stomping their feet, and slapping desktops.

While we were in Kenya the weather was, as usual, beautiful, with endless sunny, calm, hot days and balmy nights. It was supposedly the cool season so the common sight of locals dressed in multiple layers of clothing and hats, with babies and toddlers sweating under layers and layers of blankets and full balaclavas, squashed firmly against their mother's backs in a kanga cloth draped and tied with just a peek of a wee face peering out, truly puzzled us.

Late one night we were woken by what sounded like a very large animal running across our ceiling. It was so loud and not the usual scuttle of a large rat we'd heard the week before; this sounded like the grand-daddy of all rats. I couldn't sleep for fear of this rat possibly finding a little hole and ending up inside our room. First thing in the morning, I alerted the landlord, who called in the exterminator. He arrived as usual looking very important in a doctor's coat, gloves, gumboots, and carrying several packages. He left soon after with a couple of dirty plastic bags that clearly contained the aftermath of his visit from the week before when he had laid some bait, informing us as he left that he would return in a couple of days to pick up the latest victims.

We didn't hear the rats run across the ceiling again for several weeks, and I had almost forgotten about them, until one morning while making breakfast, a large black 'thing' ran out from under the oven, scuttled across the floor, and disappeared behind the fridge. From that moment on, I avoided the kitchen as much as I could. The rats in the ceiling returned too, and it became quite a routine of contacting the exterminator, who would come one day to lay bait, and back a couple of days later to retrieve the bodies. I almost looked forward to his visits.

Chapter Forty

One day I was busy in the office, and decided to tidy up the stationery cupboard. As I hauled all the books; stationery; paper; exercise books; and other paraphernalia out I stumbled across a basket full of used receipt books sitting at the back of the shelf. Curious, I flicked through a couple of books and recognised immediately that they were school fee receipts. But our kids very rarely, if ever, paid school fees. Ano always insisted the families could not afford to pay, and when they did, it was in very small amounts. These receipts were written out for what I thought quite substantial amounts; certainly more than what I thought the parents could afford. My heart almost stopped beating as alarm bells rang loudly in my head. I grabbed a handful of books and stuffed them into my bag to take home where I could have a good look at them to find out exactly what was going on, and to establish how much money was being received.

Sure enough, that evening Mandy and I verified that yes, they were indeed school fees, and they added up to a large amount of money. The books were divided into months, and after checking off the names with the school register, it was very clear that the parents were paying school fees, and not just in small amounts every now and then, but every month the same amount. It wasn't necessary to have it spelt out to us, but very clearly parents were paying considerable fees ... but to where? The Kenyan school bank account was all but empty, there didn't seem to be any evidence of new equipment or resources at the school that could have been purchased with the money, so that left only one very clear picture—Ano had to be pocketing the money.

What to do, what to do? We pondered and deliberated for hours. It was absolutely heart-breaking. We had given this man possibly a once-in-a-lifetime chance of a better life, by not only picking him and his young family up out of their harsh and miserable life, but we had also given Ano a purpose—he was headmaster of a primary school. He had staff, he had an element of prestige in the community, and yet he chose to abuse that generosity. How dare he steal from the very people who struggled to survive just like he had? I immediately hated him and I wanted to confront him, but that wasn't the right thing to do. We had to come up with a strategy, and then stick to it.

For the time being we agreed not to mention it to anyone. The first thing we had to focus on was to stop this from continuing, and so we came up with a plan. We would go to school and casually drop into a conversation with Ano that we had been advised by many Kenyan friends to implement a school fee to be paid by the non-sponsored parents, to assist with the running of the school. We would tell him this would be in place at least until we had grown our sponsorship base large enough for all of our kids to be sponsored. Something small, that was manageable. For security reasons we would open a new bank account and have the parents pay directly into the account. This would be a safe-guard against robbery, and also provide transparency.

Our thoughts were that this would immediately stop any further cash being pocketed and would suffice until we decided what to do next. It was a dreadful time, and we were absolutely crushed to think that our trusted friend, headmaster of our school, and the person we had literally picked up out of the gutter and helped get on his feet, could so deviously pull the wool over our eyes. We didn't want to believe it.

And so, next morning when we arrived at school, we casually mentioned to Ano our new plan of implementing a small fee to be paid by the parents, and informed him we would open a bank account. The parents paying school fees was fine with Ano, but he disputed the bank account idea however, arguing that the parents were not educated and most would never have stepped foot inside a bank before—they wouldn't know how to deposit money, they worked long hours so wouldn't be able to get to a bank, etc. There were a million reasons why a bank account wouldn't work. However, we made it clear that we were going ahead with the plan, and that he had no choice but to go along with it.

Mandy was due to leave Kenya the following week so we enlisted Ano's help in co-ordinating a parent meeting the Saturday morning before her departure, to explain our new system of paying school fees directly into the bank account. We printed endless flyers for the staff to send home with the children explaining the new concept, and informing them we would hold a special meeting to explain the proposed system. We also organised with the bank to have a couple of staff members come down one day to assist the parents with completing a deposit slip. The idea was that we wanted to make it as easy as possible for the parents to understand the new process.

Saturday morning arrived, the day of the meeting, and we turned up to school to a flurry of activity. The classroom dividers were pushed back against the wall to form one large room, chairs were set out in rows, and four desks were placed across the front for Chris, Mandy, Ano, and me to address the parents. Students in full uniform were busy practising singing and dancing items out in the back playfield.

The parents started to arrive in dribs and drabs, and we recognised a few of whose children who were sponsored that we had met on many occasions previously among the relatively small audience, but didn't really think much about it. We waited a further hour-and-a-half and more parents arrived, but overall we were disappointed with the attendance.

The meeting opened with a small concert put on by the senior students, and then Mandy addressed the parents on our behalf while Ano translated. She started by acknowledging the school's success thus far, the commitment from staff, parents, and pupils of Koha School, and the overall care and support offered to us and the school from the community. She went on to inform the parents of our new plan of implementing the payment of school fees to be deposited directly into the new school bank account and clearly stated that bringing cash into the school was no longer accepted. She stressed that this was going to be strictly enforced, explaining the safety aspect, that the school was too vulnerable to robbers and would also safe-guard Ano, his staff, and pupils from any finger-pointing should money go missing.

At that point a heated discussion among the audience in native tongue ensued. We had no idea what had happened and assumed it was to do with the new fee structure and bank procedure, so Mandy reassured the parents again that bank staff would assist with this transition and offer help to those unfamiliar with banking processes. Meanwhile Ano continued to translate. And still the voices continued to rise, with a lot of stern looks and gestures directed at us.

Ano said they were angry about suddenly having to pay fees, which puzzled us quietly because we had seen the receipt books, the evidence that they were already paying fees. He suggested we excuse ourselves from the meeting, which we did do.

We left feeling puzzled with what had unfolded and we were angry and annoyed as to why they had reacted so ungratefully.

Little did we know, until it transpired much later on, that Ano had actually invited the sponsored parents to the meeting, because he didn't want the non-sponsored parents alerted to paying fees into the bank account, and not Ano's back pocket.

Ano informed us the next morning that the meeting had ended with the eruption into a fairly violent protest all to do with parents suddenly having to pay school fees, with some parents marching up and down the lane outside the school with placards. He said the police arrived and a handful of parents were arrested and spent the night in the village jail cell. We could not believe it—it was totally outrageous. Parents were already paying school fees. We knew that, we had clearly seen the evidence, but still we remained completely silent and said nothing to Ano.

It was very important to us that we stood firm on this bank account idea, and it was also very clear that something wasn't quite making sense, so we again wrote out a parent notice outlining the new bank account process. We photocopied hundreds of notices, and left them with Ano to be distributed to all children, ensuring they were taken home that same day.

Meanwhile our instruction to staff was very firm and very clear; that under no circumstances was any cash to be accepted from any parent, and that if a parent tried to give cash they were to be taken to the bank and shown how to deposit into the bank account. We were so insistent on this message getting across that we told staff they would be breaking a vital rule of the school if they didn't adhere to it. It was our way of ensuring as much as possible that Ano would not be taking any further money from parents and pocketing it.

As far as we knew, the letters went home to parents and we hoped this would be sorted.

Mandy left Kenya and for the following week it was just Chris and I. We decided to keep a low profile in Kawangemi community for a few days after the meeting to let the dust settle amongst hostile parents, but by the time we went back to school, everything seemed to be ok.

Meanwhile the girls from Scotland arrived the following week. Cheryl and Amy had arranged to be with us for a couple of weeks, overlapped by Hanna, the Kiwi girl from New Zealand who would be with us for a month. We rapidly became one big family: Chris, me, and the three girls.

Hanna immediately set about helping with Cheryl and Amy and their school programmes, and assisting anywhere she could. Ano reminded us often that Koha School kids and staff were very lucky to have mzungu at school and we agreed. We also felt very lucky to have them too.

The girls took Chris and me, and the school by storm with their enthusiasm and fabulous spirits, and everybody adored them. The timing couldn't have been better as a pleasant distraction from the ugly events that had taken place in the weeks beforehand.

Cheryl, a trained teacher, Amy who worked with kids in care, and Hanna, a lawyer, were a perfect balance of help at Koha School with both our pupils and teachers. As well as teaching curriculum lessons and taking structured PE, they also introduced fun activities for the children. One of the highlights for our kids was an el fresco painting session. The girls set up desks outside in the playground, mixed up bright, fun paint colours, gave the children blank sheets of paper, and asked them to paint feelings-related pictures. The results were fantastic and the kids had a ball letting their creative juices flow freely.

The girls also worked on a Positive Behavioural Management programme, holding teacher workshops and discussion groups on related topics. They were initially nervous and not entirely sure how receptive the teachers would be; we were always mindful about suggesting ideas that may seem wonderful to us, but not so for them. We were not Africans, and they had their own ways, which was completely understandable. Ano however, seemed to be open to most suggestions, and if he didn't think a particular idea would work, he said so, but generally he loved the input from mzungu.

One morning, I received a phone call from my young Kenyan friend Kalimbo who lived in Mombasa, informing me he was coming to Nairobi to spend a day with us. Kalimbo was an accounting student and so this trip entailed spending the day at university lectures, boarding a bus in Mombasa in the evening, travelling all through the night, arriving in Nairobi at 6:00 a.m. the following morning, spending the day with us, then boarding a bus back to Mombasa that evening, arriving the following morning and going straight to university for another day of lectures. Hakuna matata, no problem! Kalimbo oozed loveliness and had an infectious personality and had been wanting to visit Koha School since the previous year when we first connected. Chris and I met him off the bus in the early hours of the morning, and took him back to our apartment for breakfast before going to spend the day at school. Kalimbo had a wonderful time, playing and interacting with the kids and staff. He also managed to take a couple of senior maths classes, and relished in his new teaching role—his first ever, he informed us.

We were always very mindful of keeping the work/leisure balance while staying and working in Kenya, and so one Saturday shortly after the two Scottish girls arrived, we visited an elephant orphanage; a wonderful project focusing on the rescue of baby elephant and rhino orphans, located not far from Nairobi. There were twenty-six of the most adorable baby elephants in the orphanage at the time, all rescued from Kenyan savannah, but sadly there were very many more babies out there who hadn't yet been found. Poaching was still a huge problem in Kenya and even though enormous amounts of money was injected into the protection of the wildlife, particularly through the wonderful work of various conservation and wildlife trusts, it was still a very serious problem. We had a fabulous time and left having signed up to foster a baby elephant for our son Craig, until such time as the elephant was released into the wild. Arruba was just two months old.

Our Nigerian flatmate Julian was in Kenya for the purpose of filling a container of African crafts to stock up his shop in Uruguay where he lived with his family. It gave us the idea that we could also do the same; buy crafts and take them back to New Zealand to sell, with a portion of the profits going to the school fund. So we spent many hours with Julian trawling local craft markets buying handcrafts, beautiful artwork, jewellery, and hand-carved animals and figurines from local carver co-ops. It didn't take long before our purchases were rapidly taking over our room and we were not thinking for a moment how we would get it all home.

Meanwhile back at Koha School with one week till school holidays, the children were busy sitting national exams, with teachers working hard to ensure good results. Our senior teacher Tony had his class attending evening tuition, and then again on Saturday mornings, and the children never complained. Not once!

Finally exams were over and school wound down till closing day the following Friday. With the children away, this was a good opportunity to work at the school fixing and repairing everything in sight. We started work on the teachers' staff room, with the aim of having it ready for the return of school in one month's time. I was also busy building up the book supply for the new library.

It was around this time we started thinking about land, and ownership, and how much of a huge difference it would be for our school to have permanent premises and land.

Our friend Al-Noor suggested we approach a contact at City Hall to explain how important being allocated a plot of land would be to the future of the school. We were after all, providing an education to some less fortunate children of Kenya.

So the next day Ano and I took a matatu into town to City Hall and after being security checked, were directed to the offices. We entered the foyer and were immediately stopped by a clerk who wanted to know our intentions. I explained our situation and that we had opened a school that was literally bulging at the seams and we wanted to speak to someone regarding the allocation of land. The officer asked me to send an email outlining the purpose of our visit and he would pass it on to the appropriate department. I was quite excited by this response—it wasn't a straight out 'no'. We left town, and I hopped off the matatu, went home, and immediately drafted an email, read it back, and then re-wrote it a few more times until I thought it was perfect, and sent it off.

A couple of days later, I received a phone call requesting a meeting the following morning at 10:00 a.m. at a CBD cafe. We were suddenly very excited.

The following morning Chris and I headed off bright and early to ensure we were well ahead of time for our 10:00 a.m. meeting, having instructed Ano to do the same. We waited outside the cafe for almost an hour before Mr O, as we knew him, and a bodyguard arrived. Over morning tea I put to him our proposal, asking if he thought there was any possibility this may be something we could be assisted with. To our delight it was indicated to us that this was indeed something they could possibly help with, requesting we first search for a suitable plot and from there they would investigate ownership, title, etc. It was the best news.

The following evening I received a phone call from an over-excited Ano announcing he had found some government land just up the road from Koha School and that we needed to see it as soon as possible the following morning. At that point it all seemed to be too good to be true but nevertheless we couldn't wait to see for ourselves. The three girls were away at the time, on safari in Masai Mara, and we wished they were around to be involved in our excitement.

We viewed the prospective plot of land the following morning and left Ano with instructions to find out as much as possible about it and, more importantly, confirmation of who owned it.

Chapter Forty-One

Before we had time to blink, the Scottish girls' time was up in Kenya and they were on a plane homeward-bound, leaving Hanna and us behind. We had had a wonderful time with them, and Chris and I really enjoyed having the young ones live with us. We weren't ready for them to leave and likewise, they weren't ready to leave either, and after putting so much effort and work into their volunteering, it felt like unfinished business.

The day they left, we felt a little lost. The house was too quiet, so we decided to take a hike in Karura Forest, just a few kilometres from Nairobi CBD, the same forest where we had gone to the Bizarre Bazaar with Mandy a couple of months previous. It was a very pretty, peaceful forest with loads of walking tracks of varying lengths and degrees of required fitness. We chose a five-kilometre track, a walk of approximately one-and-a-half hours, and which encompassed waterfalls, the MauMau Caves, Butterfly Lake, and Lily Lake. It sounded gorgeous. So, two matatu rides later, we arrived at the entrance to the forest and made our way to the checkpoint desks where several guards and important people were seated behind desks. We told them of our selected walk, signed in, and off we set.

Then, we got lost. Of course we did—it goes without saying for Chris and I being the hopeless pathfinders that we are. Three hours later, and after directions from several people we met along the way, we finally arrived back to our starting point, and had to explain a little sheepishly to the guards who questioned the length of time it took, as opposed to the length of time we had written in the log book, that we had gotten ourselves a little lost. Nevertheless we'd had a really lovely day and the peace and tranquillity of the forest, especially for being situated so close to Nairobi CBD, was beautiful.

Meanwhile back at school, we worked hard to finish as much building work as possible before the pupils came back from holidays. We finished the staff room, it looked great and I was feeling very happy that finally the teachers had somewhere to plan lessons, have lunch, and chill out at break time, instead of having to either cram into Ano's office or sit outside on the narrow seat that consisted of three lengths of timber; two legs and one plank nailed across the top to form a seat.

Ano and I went up to the village one day and bought stacks of plastic chairs; the same ones you find in every country in the world, I noted. We asked the kiosk keeper if they could possibly be delivered to the school.

"No problem," he reassured us.

As we walked back to the school, a hilarious picture evolved as we watched as a small bike puttered past us with chairs piled high in all manner of angles, legs sticking out in all direction, the driver buried somewhere underneath it all.

We also bought three large tables and a couple of cabinets, which arrived by hand-driven cart, and the room was complete.

During this time, Chris took upon himself the responsibility of buying the huge supply of text books requested by each teacher for every subject; one for every child in every class. Until then, kids were forced to share books, some of which were out of date, and some subject textbooks were missing altogether. We had earmarked a lot of donated money to the supply of textbooks, and it was a great feeling to finally have enough funds to buy complete sets of curriculum books.

On the last weekend before school was due to open, which also happened to be Hanna's last few days before she was due to leave

Kenya, we decided to take a small break and head once again to what was now our favourite retreat, Lake Naivasha, to camp for the weekend. We didn't get off to a terribly great start, with our matatu driver stopped ten kilometres out of the CBD by police and the driver charged and slapped with a fine of ksh5,000/- , however there was much confusion over what the charge was actually for. To the best of our knowledge, he hadn't done anything wrong at all. The driver disputed the charge, while the police officer maintained he was illegally carrying too much cargo, and this was a passenger matatu, not a freight carrier. We thought too much cargo meant he was referring to us passengers, but he actually meant the cardboard cartons stacked up sky-high in the back. As a result, the police officer climbed into the front passenger seat, pushing the existing passenger into the back of the van, and accompanied us to the police station some ten minutes' drive away, where the driver was charged and ordered to appear in court the following Monday.

We were dropped off at a T-junction twenty kilometres from the lake, on the side of the desolate main highway, the connection point with matatu that serviced the lake area. We waited in the blazing heat until a familiar van came screeching to a halt, sending dust billowing into the air, and the touter leapt out of the moving matatu, grabbed us by the arms, and shoved us in before roaring off down the road.

We finally arrived at the camp three hours after setting off from Nairobi—twice the time it should have taken. We thought we'd hire a tent big enough for the three of us, however by the time we arrived there were none available, and the only options were an old converted VW Kombi van, which Hanna took, and an old zebra-striped painted bus that was converted into three bedrooms, of which Chris and I could rent one room.

Hanna slept ok in the Kombi van, but Chris and I got absolutely no sleep at all as every minute the little movements in the bus from any parties in any of the other two rooms caused the whole chassis to creak, groan, and shake us out of even the deepest doze. We also heard every tiny little sound—even the whispers of our next door neighbours.

Luckily for us the following morning a staff member came and offered us a newly vacated banda complete with thatched roof and comfy bed, so needless to say that night's sleep was blissful.

On the Saturday morning, Chris and Hanna set off on the biking safari, the same one I had done the previous year, into the canyon. I had loved it so much that I firmly suggested they should do it. A full-day safari pedalling old ten-speed bikes (with not necessarily ten speeds all working, however, as I had discovered the year before) riding through the stunning scenery of sheer cliffs, prolific wildlife, and a climb down into a fifty-metre-deep canyon into the gorge below. After seeing them off, I headed straight to the swimming pool and grabbed a sun lounger, and spent the entire day soaking up the glorious hot sun until Chris and Hanna arrived back. It was late in the afternoon when they appeared, shattered, but revelling in their safari experience of what they had seen and done.

The following morning we decided to go and see if there were many pink flamingo, which congregated on a neighbouring lake, so after breakfast we walked across the road from camp, and waited not more than one or two minutes before another overloaded matatu grinded to a halt. We piled in and headed for the smaller Lake Olo Dien, meaning 'Small Lake' where I had viewed thousands of flamingo the previous year. Workers at the camp had said the flamingo had moved to another lake as they did depending on water levels and alkaline levels, but we decided to go and take a look anyway, even just for a spot of sightseeing along the way if nothing else. I had forgotten the directions of where we were supposed to go, but knew we were heading in the general direction of the small lake. However, when the matatu came to an abrupt halt and everybody piled out in the middle of unfamiliar surroundings, I knew I'd most definitely forgotten the way.

We started walking down the country road, which we thought would hopefully lead us to a main road where we could hail another matatu, but we hadn't been walking very long before a guy on an old boda-boda came puttering along and coughed and spluttered to a stop beside us. We explained where we wanted to go, to which he promptly hauled out his mobile phone, dialled a number, and spoke to someone who immediately seemed to appear from nowhere. The three of us hopped onto the two little bikes and off we went to Lake Olo Dien. As soon as we came to a crossroads, I realised I had made just one mistake, and we should have gotten off the matatu at that location, but instead we had stayed on-board, thus leading us in the wrong direction.

The scenery while ambling along the road was simply stunning. As we climbed higher over a hilly pass, many wildlife grazed the side of the roads, sometimes just one metre away from us—animals including warthog running in the grass; zebra by the hundreds grazing in the fields; giraffe munching on tree tops; monkeys scuttling across the road in front of us; impala and Thomson's gazelle cautiously grazing while watching their backs at the same time; and also buffalo, the very reason why the gazelle and impala were watching their backs. Meanwhile, bald eagles soared above our heads, diving in a little too close at times.

We arrived at Lake Olo Dien and immediately spotted the very large familiar pink carpets scattered across the lake; pink flamingo. Not just a few, but tens of thousands.

A couple of men were leaning on the side of two old wooden motorboats offering hippo and flamingo viewing excursions out on the lake. After negotiating the price for a half-hour trip, we stepped into one rickety old boat and set off out into the lake. This half-hour ride turned out to be yet another of my most beautiful, breathtaking African experiences. Thousands upon thousands of pink flamingo resting in huge clusters on the lake were such an amazing sight, and as we got closer they flapped their wings, sprinted across the water, and soared up into the sky. One after another, and another … thousands of them, almost in a Mexican Wave type of effect. It was simply stunning. Suddenly large groups of hippo started popping their heads up from beneath the surface of the water, a mere three to five metres away from the boat, occasionally one letting out an enormous, deep, loud gruff.

There was one heart-pausing moment when the little old motor in the boat suddenly ran out of puff, and stopped. The driver very casually fiddled around with hoses, clearly not entirely sure what to do, so Chris clambered over to give him a hand. I sat silently hoping and praying that a hippo wouldn't decide at that moment to pop his head up right underneath our boat and fling us up into the sky, only to smack back down into his wide-open jaw. However with a huge sigh of relief, the old motor suddenly roared into life, and we were able to move on for further flamingo viewings before heading back to the safe confines of terra-firma.

We got back to camp really excited by what we had experienced and saw, and wondered where else in the world you could ride along on a rickety old motor-scooter, or cycle along the road on a bike and there were zebra; giraffe; warthog; impala; buffalo; and other animals literally one or two metres away from your bike, grazing on the side of the road in the grass, with bald eagles soaring above your head, and then five minutes later being out on the lake in a battered old boat amongst clusters of hippo popping up and down in the water, with pelicans and hundreds of thousands of pink flamingo right at arm's reach.

We arrived back in Nairobi later that afternoon to a very excited Ano who couldn't wait to tell us his news. He had managed to get hold of a land survey map of Kawangemi and had found someone knowledgeable to read it, and it appeared by all accounts that the land Koha School was built on was actually government land, and not private land belonging to landowners as we had been led to believe. So on Monday morning Ano, Hanna, and I headed to town to the government offices to discuss the possibility of obtaining the occupied land, however we spotted the officer handling our case Mr O, out on the street about to get into the back of a waiting car, so we ran over to him.

A discussion took place right there on the street with land maps splayed over the bonnet of the car, and he agreed to visit the school the following week to view, take photos, and compile a report. It all sounded exciting and promising, and we were feeling very confident.

So we waited and we waited for the school visit but every time I phoned his mobile, it was either switched off, or he answered abruptly that he was in a meeting and would phone back. He never phoned back. And still we waited.

Finally I'd had enough and one morning off I went to City Hall armed with laptop, photos of the school and surrounding area, plus a Kawangemi site-map on the off-chance I might catch Mr O in the office. Sure enough I did manage to see him, however he was rushing out the door, and so I able to coerce him into meeting the following morning. I was not giving up. 'Keep calm and breathe deeply' became my frequently recited mantra.

Next day, armed with the same paraphernalia, I arrived for our meeting well ahead of time. I waited for some forty-five minutes before an office clerk came in and ushered me into an office suite where Mr O was waiting. I laid everything out in front of him, so he had a complete full picture of the school, where we were at, and what we needed. And I was not going to stop until I was comfortable we had him on board helping us.

I left feeling pleased with the way the meeting went and was sure I had Mr O on-board. I was also fully aware that if it was something we could pursue, the acquisition of land ownership would take a lot of time, but if we could at least get the ball rolling before leaving Kenya, then it was a definite step in the right direction.

Meanwhile back in Kawangemi, I was running back and forth to the bank, becoming frustrated that our bank account was taking so long to be opened. I had arranged to have it set up so that only myself and either Chris or Mandy were signatories and the plan was that we could operate this account from New Zealand via internet banking. We didn't want Ano or anyone else to have access. However, this took way too much time and with school due to re-open and with our new rule of no cash coming to the office, I was getting a little frantic because I knew that school fees would start rolling in and if the bank account wasn't opened, then we would be forced into allowing parents to pay cash, meaning we would have to start all over again with our new rule. We were also mindful we didn't have a lot of time left in Kenya and I was going to need some basic training on the internet banking system before we left. I figured I'd rather have it in Kenya than try to figure it all out when we were back in New Zealand.

I felt we were rapidly running out of time to have everything in order before we left. The hold-up seemed to be red tape related, so after a lot of rushing around and delivering what was required of us, we finally received the official ok from the bank that everything was in order and that the account would be opened within the following few days. I was also notified that a training session would be booked as soon as the account was officially opened. This was all good news, and assured me that all this would be completed before we left Kenya.

Chapter Forty-Two

School re-opened for the term and from day one, with our bank account finally opened and operating, we diligently kept a very close eye on school fees, checking the account daily for deposits. It became the normal morning routine that when we arrived at school we walked into the classrooms to greet the children and teachers, and then we would find Mary, Ano's daughter, who was by now running the office and admin, asking if she had received any bank receipts from parents. And we received the same reply every time: "No, no receipts."

As each day passed, we became increasingly frustrated and suspicious that somehow Ano was still receiving cash and that our plan wasn't working. However, we steadfastly remained silent, but kept working behind the scenes.

We had new children enrol into school for the last term of the year, and for one little three-year-old boy, his first day at school sadly turned out disastrously. All started well for this wee boy wearing his brand new uniform with pride, and who seemed happy enough in his classroom, until he spotted Chris. One glimpse and he completely disintegrated into hysterical fear, screaming and running around in circles trying to escape this monster before finally running into Ano's office. His terror was devastating. I rushed in to comfort him and found him cowering in a corner, shaking and screaming at the top of his lungs. At that point his teacher Margaret came into the office and managed to calm him down slightly. Large blobs of tears poured from his big brown eyes as he fought to contain his breath. Finally between Ano and the teacher Margaret they got to the bottom of this hysteria, and it transpired that the little boy had never before seen a white person and on spotting Chris just dissolved into absolute terror.

We decided to stay away from school the following day, and then ease in slowly so he got used to us. It was a new experience for us also, being used to quite the reverse, where adults and children tended to go out of their way to come and speak to us, touch our skin, or wave furiously.

He never did warm to us during those last days and made a huge effort to avoid us at all times.

Meanwhile another drama unfolded. One day while at school, Eunice our landlady stormed into the school looking angry. She asked to have a word with me, however in her anger she spoke rapid Swahili of which I could make little sense, but in a roundabout way I gathered she was angry about the rent, or something to do with the rent.

On translation from Ano, it transpired she was asking for a further twelve months' rent in advance, because according to Ano, she had 'eaten' the rest of the advance rent we had given her. I explained that we couldn't possibly give yet another rent advancement at which she became hysterical, kicking at the iron sheets of the school buildings, smashing her fist into the fence, cursing and swearing and threatening to have us evicted from the premises before storming off in a huff.

This outburst highlighted that we needed to pursue the land issue and find out once and for all whether it was actually Eunice's land the school was built on, or whether it belonged to the government. Whichever way, we needed proof—a lot of proof. Ano was connected with a land surveyor so one morning, armed with the map, he headed to town to meet up with this man. We never heard a word from him until evening when I received a phone call from a distressed Ano, announcing that he had been arrested and was in a police cell. He had apparently aroused suspicion while sitting in the waiting room at the government offices, having sat there for over three hours in possession of a land survey map. They suspected he was part of a real estate brokering racket operating in the slums of Kenya whereby land was acquired illegally and sold off to unsuspecting buyers. He was approached by a couple of detectives, who after a brief exchange marched him into a waiting vehicle, where he was taken to the CID for further investigation before being driven to the school for evidence that Ano was in fact head of a school and that his land enquiry was indeed genuine. He was finally released but when we saw him the next day he was not a happy man.

Hanna's time in Kenya rapidly came to an end as she was about to embark on the next leg of her trip, Europe. We had loved having her stay with us, and she was a huge help with interpreting the legal stuff pertaining to the land issue. We realised just how important it was to the school and the children to have volunteers come in for a few weeks with their fresh energy, new ideas, and enthusiasm—they were a real asset to Koha School.

And so it was just Chris and I who remained in Kenya and we had unfinished business to concentrate on, but things were starting to feel dramatic and all-consuming. I was becoming increasingly tired of all the drama that seemed to constantly unfold around us and I felt I was running from one chaos to another in those final weeks, rapidly exhausting me of energy. I had just about had enough. We decided it was time for another little escape to Lake Naivasha, our last for this trip. This time we hired a tent, and completely relaxed at the camp, not bothering to do anything other than lie by the pool and swim. It was heaven on earth and exactly what we needed. We met up with a group of Red Cross workers, who had been on a mission to Burundi and Ethiopia. It didn't take long to cotton-on to the fact that there were a couple of Kiwis amongst the group who of course invited us to join them for a drink.

We arrived back to Nairobi on Sunday evening recharged and ready for the last week, which we had already decided to use to focus on the school fees and the land issue. We were happy everything else we had wanted to achieve on this visit, was ticked off the list.

At the same time, we started winding down from the work, and breaks away from the school became more frequent. We spent more time socialising with other ex-pats in Nairobi who we had met, or we meandered the gorgeous local craft markets, or we hung out with local Kenyan friends, went on day safaris, or lazed in sunny Uhuru Park. It all added to taking away the strain of life and drama in Kawangemi and at school, which was definitely starting to take its toll. Ano was starting to annoy us, especially with his non-commitment concerning the school fee issue. We suspected something was still not right, and that perhaps he was up to something, and it was very frustrating.

But then it would take just one simple comment about how it could only happen in Africa, to make us laugh and jolt me back to the reasons I was so in love with Africa.

One morning we were standing out on a very busy main road connecting Nairobi with the rest of Kenya, waiting on Ano, when a brightly painted, colourful bus hurtled past us at breakneck speed, loaded up with people inside. On the roof rack however, instead of the usual sky-high stacks of luggage and furniture, there were mountains of live chickens, feathers flapping furiously in the wind, loud squawks coming from atop the bus. We both simply laughed and laughed—only in Africa!

Chapter Forty-Three

Koha School's 2nd birthday was fast approaching and we had decided to celebrate with a special lunch for all the pupils and staff. We would organise ugali and kale for the children, and roasted goat and ugali for the staff. We knew they would really enjoy that, what a treat! I bought balloons to create a party atmosphere.

Before leaving for Kenya we were given a sum of money from a very kind donor who requested it be spent on food for needy families, which sounded great. However, Kawangemi had a population of over 500,000 people (nobody really knew for sure) and they were all needy, so for a start this was always going to be difficult. We discussed narrowing it down to families with children at Koha School, but then we decided to spend the money on our birthday lunch.

Al-Noor also said he would join us at school one day before we left the following week, and he would organise to bring a couple of friends along, including a highly respected chef in Kenya, and arrange for him to cook for the children and staff. This was going to be a separate occasion to our birthday lunch and more a leaving party for us as we were leaving Kenya just a few days later.

Quite suddenly a close relative to Ano died and he immediately dropped everything and travelled to his rural area to help with the funeral arrangements. This was Thursday and he would be back Sunday night, in readiness for our birthday celebrations the following Tuesday, and our impending departure from Kenya two days later.

The next morning on Friday Chris and I arrived at school and as usual, wandered around the school greeting the staff and children.

Mary was in the office, and Chris asked her if any parents had brought in bank receipts for school fees, to which we had come to expect the usual 'no' response. However, this time she said, "No, but I have some cash." With that, she pulled out a wad of notes from her skirt pocket. Chris, who by now had become really frustrated and angry with this whole cash situation, sternly snapped back, reciting the rule of no cash. He then told her she had broken a fundamental rule of the school and that this was just not acceptable. He then turned on his heels and stormed out of the school, and I closely followed. He was absolutely furious. We had to sort this out so close to leaving Kenya, and as time went on we were under enormous pressure to make this happen.

Just a few minutes later, my phone rang and it was Ano, who immediately bellowed down the phone that we had no right to be angry with his daughter, and that he was putting steps in place to ensure the parents followed the new procedure, but that it took time. On and on he went before finally hanging up on us.

We were by now so furious that I suggested to Chris as we were walking that we go to the chief and ask for his help in getting through to the parents and Ano and staff that we were not, under any circumstances, accepting cash. Clearly we needed assistance because we didn't know what else to do.

We headed straight to the chief's compound, and approached one of the guards, asking if we could see the chief. We were told the chief was out but would be back in half-an-hour, so we replied that we would wait for him. We sat on some steps and proceeded to wait. A few minutes went by and a woman, dressed in a military-type uniform, came out of an office.

"Can I help you," she asked.

"No thank you, we are waiting for the chief," I replied.

"But I am a deputy chief and I can help you," she insisted.

With that, she ushered us in, and we proceeded to explain the entire story of the school and that we needed help with our parents' school fees issue because we had found receipt books clearly pertaining to school fees that weren't listed on the school fee register. She was extremely attentive, listening to every word. Finally she said that the problem could easily be fixed. She would contact Ano immediately and summon him to her office on Sunday evening when he returned from the funeral, to arrange a meeting of school parents. She said she would be in attendance and would explain the new structure of fees. Easily solved, she reassured us. She took down our contact details and also Ano's details, advising that she would keep us updated.

We got up, thanked her most sincerely, and left, feeling much better.

Within a couple of minutes, my phone rang and it was Ano again screaming hysterically down the phone, abusing both Chris and I for approaching a deputy chief that was new to the area, that we should have gone to the chief because he understood Koha School and so on. On and on he went, and then hung up the phone.

That was the final straw for Chris and I, for we both knew right then and there that Ano was clearly still up to no good, and that bringing him to the attention of an 'outsider' was freaking him out, hence his behaviour.

We decided to have no further contact with Ano, even though there were dozens of missed calls and abusive text messages coming in on my phone. We also made up our mind to have him removed from the school, and sooner rather than later. We could not have him running our school when it was very clear he was misappropriating funds.

It was imperative that we maintain our silence so we stayed away from the school and community over the weekend. Meanwhile the deputy chief phoned to say Ano was being difficult and uncooperative and that she would have to consult the chief to have a summons issued to Ano to attend the meeting.

On Monday morning Chris and I decided to seek advice from Margaret, a welfare worker who was very familiar with Ano, Koha School, and its history. She was a good person and we often used her as a sounding board. Margaret was furious when we told her what we had uncovered and suspected was happening at Koha School. She told us it was a police matter and immediately phoned the police station. She said that many government agencies had been watching Ano for some time and that he was definitely up to something. Before we had time to think we were in the back of a taxi heading to the police station. We arrived and were taken to a room, and relayed all of our concerns, starting from finding the receipt books three months earlier. Everything was recorded, and we waited in the interview room for some time before being advised Ano had arrived after being summoned to appear. We were led into an office where Ano was sitting with the Inspector of Police.

The inspector asked me to explain our version of events. After telling the entire story right from when Ano and I had met, how we decided to establish a school, and all events leading up to that Friday the week before, he then asked Ano for his story, which for most part was the same as mine, except for a fundamental difference. He stated that the school was his. He also concocted a story that the school fees collected were all spent on providing resources for the school; but he could not provide evidence of this. Of course I argued straight back that no, the school was not his—he was running it and making decisions in conjunction with us back in New Zealand, but essentially the school ownership was ours.

An argument ensued and so the inspector called a halt to the meeting, and asked us to resume the following morning, Tuesday. He asked Ano to bring with him proof that the school was his, all the receipt books that I had found, and also the school registration certificate.

298

With that we left the station. Our taxi driver was still waiting for us, so we walked out and into our taxi and left. That was the last time we ever spoke to or saw Ano.

Driving off down the highway, I was suddenly overcome with anxiety and paranoia, and I felt scared. Scared of Ano, scared of his family, and scared of what they may be capable of doing, now that he might possibly be charged for misappropriation of funds, and subsequent further counts on other issues. I had experienced his anger, and I felt very fearful.

I announced to Chris we needed to move out of our apartment and spend the last three nights in a hotel in a secret location. Ano knew where we lived, he'd been there several times. Chris sensed my fear, and agreed. We pulled into our compound and with our taxi driver waiting for us, we raced upstairs to our apartment, and embarked on a rampage, stuffing everything in sight into suitcases and plastic rubbish bags, and leaving behind surplus clothes and shoes for our gorgeous housemaid Selina.

We threw everything into the boot of the taxi, said very quick goodbyes to Selina, asking her to tell our landlord we would be in touch to explain everything, and we were gone.

We headed straight for a hotel I had stayed in for a couple of nights the year before when I first arrived in Kenya. Fortunately they had a room available, so we paid the taxi driver off, and carried backpacks and bags up the stairs and dumped them in a big mound on the floor of our room. I was hit by a sigh of relief.

We had some lunch in the hotel restaurant before venturing out for a walk. We were in a very different part of Nairobi but I found myself constantly looking over my shoulder. I still felt anxious and paranoid. We told only two friends of our whereabouts, and I was very determined to keep it that way.

Mindful of our meeting scheduled for the following morning, I had a sudden panic attack and told Chris I wasn't going to the meeting. I was concerned that if the police did charge Ano then I would have to stay back in Kenya to appear in court, and that was never going to happen. No way.

I made a decision and phoned Margaret, and explained that we were not going to pursue police action, and that we just wanted to spend the last two days in Kenya in peace. She was bitterly disappointed and told me the police were ready to throw the charge book at Ano, but I said I couldn't do it and I'd made my decision and felt a sense of relief in doing so. I wanted to get as far away as possible from Ano, his family, and Kenya for the time being.

I asked for Margaret's help to act on our behalf in having Ano removed from the school, to which she agreed immediately. She asked me to type up a termination letter for Ano, his daughter Mary from the school, and also a trespass notice for them and any other family members, and that she would action it on our behalf. I asked if she could hold off presenting the letters until we had left Kenya, to which she agreed. I told her it was imperative that the parents and families of our children were fully informed of Ano's theft of their school fee money with the hope that perhaps the community might assist in driving him out.

Sadly, the scheduled birthday celebrations didn't go ahead. And sadly we never had a chance to say goodbye to the children, the staff, or friends in the community of Kawangemi. We also had a lot of unfinished business, including the land issue, but by now this had become the least of our worries.

We were still concerned about the future of Koha School however, and needed to have someone ready to move in and take over once Ano was tossed out. We both agreed immediately that Head Teacher Tony would be the perfect person—the only person. We trusted him, and yes, we had also trusted Ano, but there was something very uniquely different about Tony.

We managed to get a message to him and arranged to meet at a café in town, far from Kawangemi and the school. After explaining the entire situation and what we had uncovered, we asked him if he would consider taking over the running of the school. He said he would do anything and everything possible to save the school, but made it very clear that steps had to be in place to ensure transparency, even requesting we hire an auditor of our choosing to regularly audit the school records and funds. We liked that, it was what we'd wanted all along. We gave him Margaret's number and asked him to liaise with her and be ready to move in as soon as Ano was out.

Having clearly gained our trust, he too told us stories about Ano: his relationship with the staff, or more to the point, non-existent relationship with the staff; how he'd threatened each of them not to become too friendly and familiar with us because we were 'his' friends, not theirs; his bullying stand over tactics; and how he had spent less and less time at Koha School and more time drinking and didn't really care too much about the school.

The more we heard, the more everything seemed to make sense. We realised that if we became friends with staff, that they may disclose stuff that was going on at Koha School that Ano definitely wouldn't want us to know about.

We thanked Tony for his support, stated that we trusted him to take care of the school, and wished him good luck and goodbye.

Meanwhile I still hadn't had my training session with the bank, and this was vitally important before leaving Kenya because I knew that trying to learn a Kenyan banking system from New Zealand would be quite disastrous. I couldn't go back to Kawangemi, so I called into another branch of the bank, explained my situation and the importance of internet banking training to a bank clerk James, and asked if he could please help.

James went out of his way to help me, even taking a bus to Kawangemi to uplift the bank paperwork, security codes, etc. on my behalf. On the morning we were leaving Kenya, we spent an hour together learning the system. As added reassurance, he gave me his direct phone number and email address should I get into difficulty back in New Zealand and insisted I could rely on him. I felt comfortable.

We spent our last evening in Kenya with some friends at one of our regular favourite spots, a bar in Westgate shopping mall, before going on to a nightclub where we danced till the late hours of the morning. It was an awesome, fun night, a very late one at that, and I finally started to relax a little in the safety confines of the busy night club with big burly security guards on the entrance.

The next afternoon we were in a taxi bound for the airport but I was still paranoid that Ano would show his face just one last time. Getting out of the taxi at the airport, amongst airport officials, security guards, and police with AK47s slung over their shoulders, I was still fearful. Clearing customs and immigration checkpoints, I was convinced that we would be stopped and not allowed to leave, due to a pending court case at which I was required to be a witness. My mind was in overdrive and I didn't relax at all until we were taxiing down the runway, away from Kenya, and bound for India a million miles away.

I spent many, many hours on the plane thinking over the last few days. I was completely heart-broken that Ano had betrayed me and also let down the people who I had brought in to the project, to such an extent as to steal from the very people who could least afford to be stolen from. I hated him—I really hated him. I was immensely sad, and for a brief moment, Africa had left a sour taste in my mouth.

But then I started thinking about the funny, quirky incidents that we had experienced on this trip and I knew I would miss the simple things about Kenya: the beautiful people, the lovely simplicity of their life, and their ways that often kept us very entertained. I wondered if we would ever feel comfortable about going back, when suddenly, as if a light switched on, I snapped out of that negative mind set and felt an overwhelming determination to fight for what was rightfully ours and I refused to allow one person to ruin my great love of Africa, destroy our beautiful school, or to deny the many children of the right to an education. Koha School was not Ano's school to destroy and Africa was not going to be tainted, in my mind, by the senseless act of one person.

I started wondering about a few incidents that had happened during my time in Africa that were firmly etched in my memory and simply made me smile. Like the evening when Chris and I were out walking around our neighbourhood and heard what sounded like the distinct, deep hum of a Harley Davidson motorbike, which incidentally would be a rare sight in Kenya. It got louder and louder and suddenly this very badly painted, multi-coloured, clapped-out old Harley lookalike motorbike puttered past, the rider all decked out in the same matching multi-coloured riding gear as the paint job on his bike, complete with matching coloured helmet, sunglasses, and the added accessory of an un-lit cigarette drooping from his mouth, all the while making damned sure everybody noticed how cool he looked. It was priceless.

That same evening, soon after easy-rider rode past, a guy rode by on his old push bike, laden sky-high with big sacks of coal, and if that wasn't enough, lengths of steel rod were laid in between the coal, protruding either side of his bike by at least a metre if not more. Heaven help you if you were walking down the road and didn't make an effort to get out of his way.

I thought of the time we were walking along one of the main busy roads leading into Nairobi when we came across what looked like a matatu that had suddenly died, parked diagonally half on the road, half on the dirt path beside the road, with rocks piled up under the missing back right wheel. This was clearly an improvisation of a car wheel jack. The most amusing part was that the van was completely full of passengers who simply sat there patiently inside, and yet there was no sign of the driver or touter, so we wondered how long they would just sit there without making an attempt to get out and wait for another matatu to come screeching by.

On another evening walk around the neighbourhood an old badly converted Datsun ute, piled up with pieces of furniture, legs sticking out in all directions; chairs; tables; and other paraphernalia literally thrown haphazardly on top came spluttering and bunny-hopping past us, hazard lights flashing, tyres screeching horrifically, when suddenly it came to an abrupt stop right in the middle of the road. No worries, other vehicles simply drove around it. At home there would be horns blasting and irate drivers gesturing and mouthing obscenities through the window.

I loved the many women employed to clean the bathrooms in the shopping malls and the importance placed on their jobs. It astounded me that they could spend forty hours a week mopping floors, starting at one end of the bathroom, working their way to the other end, and then back again. And how they would rotate duties, with cleaning the toilets, and washing the hand basins to maintain pristine condition. For these women this was a job and they were grateful.

On reflection, it was hard to believe that just two years before we had established a school for fifty children, and we now had a roll in excess of 380. The whole thing was completely and utterly crazy. But we had done it, and in hindsight, it hadn't been that hard. Frustrating at times, for sure, but nothing we couldn't handle at that point.

Chapter Forty-Four

We arrived into Mumbai to be greeted with the devastating news broadcast all over the TV that our beloved Westgate Shopping Mall back in Nairobi that we had just spent our last nights at was attacked by terrorists and a hostage siege was underway. We were shocked and deeply saddened to watch with horror the terrible atrocities unfold right before our eyes. We had spent a lot of time at Westgate, particularly me, as it was one of my favourite places to head to, and over the course of years I'd got to know familiar faces of some of the staff; whether it be the ladies cleaning the bathrooms, the security guards on the entrance, or the café staff. I couldn't comprehend that these people's lives could potentially have been senselessly destroyed.

By the time we had settled into our guesthouse, two emails were waiting: one from Margaret and the other from Tony.

Margaret informed us that she had delivered the termination letter to Ano, his reaction being to rip it up in front of her and throw it on the ground, claiming the school was his and nobody was going to kick him out. She advised she was about to issue a second letter, and had decided to enlist the help of the local police to accompany her to deliver it and that this would happen over the next few days.

Meanwhile Tony's email enlightened us as to recent information he had discovered on the inappropriate actions Ano had been involved in while at Koha School that had come to light during new recent dealings with Margaret. A lot of it started to make sense to him, and the other staff.

In my reply to both emails, I reiterated the importance and urgency for the community to be made aware of Ano's actions so they could get behind the removal of both him and Mary from the school. And so began a very long string of emails that followed, over some months, between Tony, Margaret, and myself. Every day I received not one, but many emails either directly to me or copied into others, and before I knew it I was right slap-bang in the middle of what I can only describe as an all-out war. Ano steadfastly refused to budge from the school, threatening violence of all description, whilst Tony, Margaret, and various district agencies and police battled to have him removed.

Somewhere in all this email bombardment was an underlying message: that they were having extreme difficulty removing Ano, which we couldn't fathom. Why was it so difficult when we, being the owners, had the right to kick him out? It not only frustrated us, but puzzled us deeply. Three months passed and no real progress had been made.

Finally we were told the reason why kicking Ano out had been so difficult was because as soon as we left Kenya, he and the chief at the time schemed to have the ownership of the school transferred into Ano's name; clearly cash was at the centre of his attention. It all started to make sense, and it was then we understood why Ano was so adamant we deal only with the chief, because dealing with an outsider had the potential to unravel their scheming very easily—which was in a sense what had happened.

We were advised by some of our Kenyan friends to walk away from Koha School and rebuild somewhere else, but at that stage we weren't happy about that at all, and the issue became about what was rightfully ours. What gave Ano the right to simply fraudulently obtain ownership of our school that we had worked so hard to establish, without us having any legal comeback?

Meanwhile differing opinions and viewpoints were emerging between Chris, Mandy, Christine and me, and also dilemmas about when was the right time to walk away. I personally wasn't prepared to give up without exhausting all possible efforts, so as a last, final attempt, we hired a Kenyan lawyer, a man who was recommended to us to fight on our behalf. He handled a lot of child welfare cases in Nairobi and we contracted him to have the court bring the legal ownership back to us.

Meanwhile we notified all our sponsors to cease their sponsorship payment to our New Zealand school bank account pending further notice. We were no longer financially supporting the school and wouldn't do so until Ano was out, and the new headmaster in place. Then we would resume our funding.

The so-called great lawyer didn't appear to do very much for us at all, and it was really only with Tony's insistence and stand-over tactics when he stormed into his office in Nairobi and forced him into taking action to file court papers, that we saw much input from him at all.

After five months of roller-coaster riding, with positive vibes coming one day, only to be dashed the next, we had all had enough. We weren't really making any headway and so the time came when we had to make a decision to walk away from our beloved Koha School. Stress levels were high between us all, and the constant drama was very rapidly taking over my life. It was heart-breaking and I was devastated.

Meanwhile, however, I couldn't help but think of the children, and the bitterness I felt towards Ano that he dared have the power to take away the rights of those children to have an education. They didn't deserve it. And so behind the scenes, Tony and I began plotting and planning a new school. With a lot of persuasion I managed to convince Chris, Mandy, and Christine, and we all agreed that the structure of the new school had to be different. Owning and trying to run a Kenyan school from New Zealand was just too hard.

Once we decided that we would establish a new school I asked Tony to find suitable land on which we could build a set of classrooms, or better still, find an existing set of rooms that we could turn into a new beautiful school.

Tony worked in a very different way to Ano. He took his time, ensuring everything was exactly in order; he liked everything meticulously planned out and once I learned this about Tony I knew the new school would take some time to develop, but I also knew this was a good thing and that he was the best person we could possibly find to lead the school and take it into the future. We discussed many times the rapid rise of Koha School and agreed that was not going to happen again, that with careful planning, the success of the new school would largely be attributed to its slow development and growth.

His plans were to start the school with the three baby classes only, and that over the next two or three years we would gradually bring in the other class streams to eventually make up a full primary school.

He searched all over Kawangemi for land or buildings but to no avail, so he moved to the outer regions. Six months later, I received an email announcing he had found the perfect plot of land, with nine derelict rooms that could easily be turned into classrooms.

Tony immediately swung into negotiation with the landowner who couldn't commit to a long-term lease until his wife had returned from Saudi Arabia, which was to be three weeks later, and they would all sit down and draft out a mutually agreeable contract.

Meanwhile, shortly before his wife was due to arrive back in Kenya, the landowner died suddenly so understandably this put a temporary halt on negotiations until after the burial and mourning period. The new widow took an instant liking to Tony; she found him to be very astute, smart, and sensible, and he suddenly found himself in the midst of assisting with the family funeral arrangements.

Once everybody returned to Nairobi from the burial, they all sat down and mutually agreed on a lease. Tony, being the smart man that he was, negotiated the occupancy of just four rooms to begin with, refusing to pay rent for rooms he wasn't initially going to be using.

And so, as we had done just three years before, we were suddenly supporting the establishment stage of a brand new primary school, though this time the structure was set up differently. We didn't want to be the owners, more along the lines of sponsors/supporters only.

Tony set about putting everything formally in place. He went through the correct channels, he liaised with the correct agencies in Kenya pertaining to education, he had the school registration set up properly—everything was done the correct way, which ironically dragged up a whole new set of alarm bells relating to Koha School that when Ano and I were going through the legal aspects of setting up the school, much of what Tony was doing was not done for Koha School. Was the school set up illegally? Who could really know.

With a touch of irony, suddenly the chief dropped dead, and Ano was very much on his own.

And so the all-too-familiar task of setting up a brand new school began in earnest once again. Brand new toilets were dug; roof repairs carried out; rooms painted; holes in the floors patched; desks purchased; water tanks installed; fences erected; curriculum textbooks bought; and two teachers and one security guard/caretaker hired. It was exciting, and once again I became completely immersed in the whole project, the difference being that I watched from a distance.

On 29 September 2014, Tamariki Learning Centre opened its doors for the very first time with twenty-one tiny foundation pupils proudly wearing their school uniforms and bursting with enthusiasm and a zest for learning.

As for me, personally? This was simply the beginning of another chapter of my African journey.

Acknowledgements

This is my beautiful African story, and I want to share it. It would not have been at all possible, however, without the very many people who have all contributed in some way to the whole amazing story, and I am deeply grateful to each and every one of you for your part in this fateful journey of the last few years.

There are a few whose contribution to the story I simply must acknowledge—because without you, there would be no story!

To my son Craig, who at the age of twelve years completed a school project on family trees. My boy, you have no idea how much that project on your great-grandfather changed my life.

To both my children, Craig and Hayley, for your amazing all-round support during the entire African journey. Thank you for your wonderful initiative in establishing the school sponsorship scheme, without which we simply could not have financially supported the schools. Also, a big thanks for your encouragement, support, and loyalty during this book writing journey. I love the way you inspired me to keep writing and get my book finished and published, and how you encouraged me to keep it up when my enthusiasm waned.

To my mum Shirley, thank you for eventually sharing this part of your life with us. Gosh, I'm so very glad you did.

Gregory—oh wow! There would be no story without your help and input into finding my beloved South African family. I am eternally grateful to you.

Edgar, what can I say? Firstly, you welcomed me so warmly and generously into your heart, and the extended Hermanus family. Then you did the same thing for my family also. For that I am truly grateful. I love the strong bond that we share Edgar—what a crazy, amazing journey this has been for both of us.

To the very many friends I have made during my frequent trips back to Africa, some who are mentioned in the story, and some who are not, and who have become a large part of my story and life: your resilience to the harsh environment in which you live never ceases to astound me, and plays a big part in what essentially led me to building schools in Kenya. You have also taught me that when the going gets tough, never give up! I have nothing but the utmost respect for you.

Mandy, an enormous thanks to you for your continuing support of our schools. We're so very grateful to have you on board.

Christine, a big thanks to you for your awesome support of the school. We sincerely appreciate what you have done for us.

Al-Noor, you are a truly wonderful, generous man. Thank you for your very kind donation of three classrooms for our school, particularly when you didn't even know me or the project.

Volunteers to date—Maureen, Amy, Cheryl, and Hanna. A huge thanks for giving your time to volunteer at our school. We appreciate the long distances you travelled from your home countries and also the financial commitment you made to come to work at the school. We understand the huge importance volunteers make to our projects and you all made large contributions, which we so very much appreciate. You were all simply fantastic.

Tony Ngotho Muthoni … you are a godsend! You encouraged me not to give up on the kids of Kenya. I admire the great lengths you went to, to gain our trust and lead us to believe that not everyone is a 'bad egg'. I am eternally grateful for the enormous effort, passion, and drive you have for the success and growth of Tamariki Learning Centre and the huge respect for education and its importance. Asante Sana.

To every person who is or has supported us in any way at all in our school projects over the last 4 years, you are truly wonderful people and the schools would most certainly have not survived without you all. An enormous 'thank you' or 'asante sana' from us and the children of Kenya. You are changing lives.

There are so many people who have directly contributed in some way or another to the eventual publishing of this book. I wish to acknowledge you, because you have all been truly amazing in so many ways.

To the fabulous friends and family members in my life who convinced me that my story was worth writing and that someone would want to read it. I'm so glad you did!

Heather, thanks heaps for the countless hours you must have spent compiling all my emails I wrote while travelling through Africa over the past few years, and which essentially became a research tool for writing this book. You have no idea how helpful that's been.

And to Ocean and your team at In-House Publishing for your fantastic professionalism and expertise in assisting me to bring my story to life. I can never thank you enough.—yay for you! Thank you for believing I could write a story good enough to be published. I am so very grateful and happy to have been connected with you.

And finally to my wonderful husband Chris: there are many things I need to thank you for. Thank you for not getting too annoyed when I spent hours and hours researching family genealogy websites, or for spending pots of money travelling back and forth to Africa to meet and visit family and take part in volunteering projects. Thank you for listening to and supporting my whacky idea to build a school in the middle of Africa. An enormous thanks for encouraging me to write my story, your support has been truly appreciated. I loved your subtle input ... and only when I asked for it! You recognised when I needed solitude to write, and stayed away and let me get on with it. I loved how you erected an umbrella on the grass in our backyard so I could sit in my comfy beanbag outdoors and write in peace, and loved the way you seemed to know exactly the right time when a cup of tea was just what I needed.

You are all amazing xxx

For further information on Tamariki Learning Centre, Kenya, the website address is: www.tamarikischoolkenya.com